AMERICA, THE WEST, AND LIBERAL EDUCATION

AMERICA, THE WEST, AND LIBERAL EDUCATION

Edited by Ralph C. Hancock

ROWMAN & LITTLEFIELD PUBLISHERS, INC.
Lanham • Boulder • New York • Oxford

ROWMAN & LITTLEFIELD PUBLISHERS, INC.

Published in the United States of America
by Rowman & Littlefield Publishers, Inc.
4720 Boston Way, Lanham, Maryland 20706

12 Hid's Copse Road
Cumnor Hill, Oxford OX2 9JJ, England

British Library Cataloguing in Publication Information Available

Library of Congress Cataloging-in-Publication Data

America, the West, and liberal education / [edited by] Ralph C.
    Hancock.
        p.   cm.
    Includes bibliographical references and index.
    ISBN 0-8476-9230-2 (cloth : alk. paper).—ISBN 0-8476-9231-0
(paper : alk. paper)
        1. Education, Humanistic—United States.   2. Education, Higher—United
States—Philosophy.   3. Culture conflict—United States.
4. United States—Intellectual life—20th century.   5. Civilization,
Western.   I. Hancock, Ralph C., 1951–   .
LC1023.A44   1999
370.11'2—dc21   98-38237
                                                                CIP

Printed in the United States of America

∞ ™ The paper used in this publication meets the minimum requirements of
American National Standard for Information Sciences—Permanence of Paper
for Printed Library Materials, ANSI Z39.48–1984.

Contents

Introduction

America, the West, and Liberal Education

Ralph C. Hancock

More than a decade ago Allan Bloom's frank and intellectually challenging defense of "the good old Great Books approach" (in *The Closing of the American Mind*) renewed and deepened a perennial discussion of the essential purposes of higher education in America. In particular, this book raised the philosophical stakes surrounding the question of the importance and proper role of the study of the most highly esteemed authors of the Western tradition, from Plato to Marx and Nietzsche. Bloom's argument for the Great Books employed both the rhetoric of knowledge "for its own sake" and that of the broadly political uses of education. He seemed to argue that liberal education is as essential to the health of liberal society—and of the United States of America, in particular—as it is to the fulfillment of the thinking individual. But the question of the precise relationship between the intellectual and the moral-political ends of liberal education was not Bloom's theme; though he clearly opposed the political radicalization of the curriculum espoused by many who styled themselves "postmodernists," he may not have adequately addressed their contention that all education is deeply political. The essays in this volume attempt to advance our understanding of the proper purposes of liberal education in America by exploring the relationship between the free pursuit of truth and the practical ends embedded in a particular tradition or political community.

In the first chapter, "Liberal Education and the Idea of the West," Michael Gillespie, of Duke University, argues that the question of our relationship to the tradition of Western civilization is at the center of the crisis in contemporary American culture (and thus in the American university). This question takes the form of a debate between those who

1

see a positive value in our connection to this tradition and those who see it as a source of repression that we must overcome—between the supporters of Western tradition, the traditionalists, and their critics, the postmodernists. To understand what is at stake in this debate it is necessary, Gillespie believes, to come to terms with the origin of the idea of Western civilization, to show why it has become questionable, and to determine the consequences for American culture of the victory of one side or the other.

Such an inquiry reveals the inadequacy of the alternative postmodernists/traditionalists. Both sides of this debate fall within a late modern horizon that excludes multiple human possibilities; such a perspective may illuminate certain aspects of our lives, but it obscures more profound sources of our humanity. Postmodern anti-Westernism is thus, in a sense, a sham, although no more a sham than the traditionalist notion that the "West" is something real and definitive of our being. In order to come to terms more profoundly with existence, Gillespie argues, it may thus be necessary to go beyond both modernity and postmodernity, beyond both the West and the non-West.

According to Timothy Fuller, dean of Colorado College, in a chapter entitled "Liberal Education in the Confines of the Liberal Tradition," most academics today assume that liberal education and modern liberalism are inseparable. This is a mistake, since the former long antedates the latter, and to confuse the two meanings of "liberal" is to risk narrowing the possibilities of contemporary higher education. Liberal learning and liberalism can be friends, but never identical.

He argues that recognizing the distinction between the specifically educational and political meanings of "liberal" becomes all the more important as the dilemmas of the late twentieth century identified by Peter Berger (abstraction, futurity, individuation, liberation, secularization) press upon our academic institutions, threatening a domination of technical, managerial, and narrowly professional perspectives over a sense of learning as a vocation or way of life. Against or in the midst of this pressure, our duty is not to presume to set ourselves apart from the human condition, but to "embrace it with critical intellectual and moral habits," speaking to our time, but not only to that.

In "Diversity, Canons, and Cultures," the late Professor Allan Bloom, of the University of Chicago, renews his defense of an education based on the classics and invites the reader to consider him "the first victim of political correctness." He believes he earned the status of heretic, and even enemy of mankind, above all by defending the Great Books as the core of a truly liberal education. In suggesting that we might learn something by actually approaching Aristotle or Shakespeare in the belief that they might have something to teach us, Bloom seems to have touched a nerve connected with the deepest prejudices of modern scholarship: the confidence that we already know enough to put an Aristotle or a Shakespeare in his place, his "context," and in particular that we already know what it means to be just or fair. The effectual truth of this latter confidence, this complacent moral passion, is that we know the majority's "truth" to be false and whatever bolsters an official minority's self-esteem to be true.

According to Bloom, the contemporary rhetoric of "diversity" represents a subversion of the liberal ethic of toleration and masks a passion for homogenization: if all "cultures" are equally respected a priori, then none are taken seriously on their own terms. We want the benefits of "culture"—in truth, the benefits of religion, namely commitment, meaning—without the cost, which is exclusion, orthodoxy, and hierarchy. Our "multiculturalism" thus makes impossible the true study of cultures, a study made possible by the philosophical tradition of the West. Bloom's prescription would be to use liberal education, especially the Great Books, to study culture before acting on it.

In my chapter, "Tocqueville on Liberal Education and American Democracy," I note that although Bloom makes the university the core of a polity founded on the principles of the Enlightenment, he seems to see the Enlightenment at once as the root of America's problems and as the basis of a solution or response to these problems. This reading of America as the stage on which the internal logic of the Enlightenment is played out seems in one sense to ask too much of the university, and in another sense too little: Bloom seems to look to higher education to form and sustain the moral or spiritual core of American society, but he does not accept the obligation to explain the connection between the university's pursuit of knowledge and society's pursuit of not only prosperity but also happiness.

Tocqueville's *Democracy in America* can contribute much to a reflection on just this connection. Precisely because Tocqueville understands and takes account of the blind spots of the Enlightenment, he provides a rich reflection on the relationship between the life of the mind and the political health of democracy. In effect, he praises Americans for being enlightened, but in the right way—and, one might almost say, not too much. In fact, he regards it as good news that Americans are not guided by the theory of enlightened self-interest as much as they like to claim, that the relative health of American institutions and of the American soul derives from religious and traditional sources beyond the scope of Enlightened theory. If Tocqueville is right, the implications for the role of liberal education in relation to the moral and spiritual health of America and Americans would be significant.

Stanley Rosen, of Boston University, in "Conservatism, Liberalism, and the Curriculum: Notes on an American Dilemma," takes contemporary curricular debates to be a kind of replay of the "battle of the books" between ancients and moderns, and at bottom a natural response to the inherently revolutionary nature of modernity. He deplores, however, the quality of this replay, in which both parties seem to have lost their bearings and fail to represent seriously the real stakes of the argument: The conservative assertion of the prerogatives of the superior few and their defense of old ways is adulterated by a thoughtless populism, and the liberal cause of freedom and confidence in human nature is spoiled by relativism. Both sides forget that the ends of education are prior to and higher than political ends, and in their partisan zeal both ignore the deep connection between openness to eternal truth and creativity.

This deep connection will never admit of a final, stable articulation, since "man is a disrupted harmony," a being whose freedom is constituted by the necessary but never realized attempt to unify theory and practice. To address more adequately this freedom in our higher education would mean to put aside sterile debates between relativism and adulation of the classics and to turn to radical philosophical thought. In today's world, "moderation can be made palatable only when it is adorned with the habiliments of extremism."

Michael Platt, Shakespeare scholar and author of a fine and substantial review of Bloom's *Closing* (*Interpretation* 18, no. 3 [1991]), offers wide-ranging reflections in "The Young, the Good, and the West." Platt observes that the West is both what we are and what we have failed to be. We are the product of the mingling of reason, especially as the Greeks first practiced it, and of revelation, as the Jews first received it. Thus we are especially the products of that special mingling of these accomplished by Christianity. The tension between the two elements in this mingling eventually issued into the modern resolution, of which we Americans are again the product: the mastery of fortune, through lowered sights and grand designs, through a decrease in aspiration and an increase in active conquest of nature, and through a policy of freedom and toleration. As this modern resolution exhausts itself, appearing as the home of Nietzsche's "Last Man," we must ask to what degree America is implicated in this exhaustion. Does America rest on the foundation of modernity, and will such a foundation now suffice?

Reading the best minds of the West, we are aware that they not only made the West but are in a sense superior to it or to anything it might have been or might become. Thus the sources of the West are also the powerful critics of the West, and liberal education in the West must be simultaneously an experience of the comparative good of the West and of its comparative imperfection. Socrates and Christ made the West, but this does not mean that the West would not repeat the crimes of Athens against Socrates and those of Jerusalem against Jesus.

Like the West itself, liberal education in America, at the college level, tries to combine moral virtue and intellectual virtue. It seeks the true, without losing the good; it holds to the good without ignoring the beautiful. Considering the present orphaned condition of the young souls arriving at college, so well described by Allan Bloom, liberal education must not only have the fire of inquiry that the great philosophic books encourage and require, but also the habituation in the good that families, villages, and parishes used to inculcate. Some acquaintance with good taste, good manners, and good morals, such as the *good* books of the West do provide, is needed for this generation, before and along with the *great* books of the West. Such a good book is Owen Wister's *The Virginian,* which gives an elevated account of the American regime, an account in which equality is understood not only as fairness and as proportion, but as responsibility as well. It thus illuminates the distinctly American modification of the Enlightenment.

James Nuechterlein, editor of the journal *First Things,* observes in "The Religious University and Liberal Education" that in the religious university faith and learning inevitably meet. What do they have to say to each other? A look at the history of higher education in the United States suggests to Nuechterlein that learning ends up doing most of the talking; as Richard Hofstadter noted almost forty years ago, this history is marked by a "sustained . . . drift toward secularism." Indeed the very nature of the religious university is such that the balance of forces in the Athens/Jerusalem tension always pulls in the direction of Athens.

And yet the resolution of this tension in favor of secular learning would be a pity, Nuechterlein thinks, not only for faith but for learning itself. Religious universities can place learning within the context of a coherent frame of values in a way that secular institutions find almost impossible. Religious universities are unique in their ability, not necessarily to answer but at least to ask ultimate questions, questions of the Good and of God. If these universities are to retain this ability, they will have to remain continuously and actively self-conscious of their identities as religious institutions.

Finally, in the concluding essay ("Of Liberty and Liberal Education"), I return to the question of the relationship between the freedom of learning and the freedoms proclaimed in more immediately practical discourse, reviewing certain implications of the earlier chapters and exploring whether the American Founders' "liberty" is in any way relevant to liberal education.

Acknowledgments

A number of these essays originated in papers presented at a pair of symposia on "America, the West, and the Liberal Arts," hosted by Brigham Young University. Thanks are due to the Colleges of Humanities and of Family, Home, and Social Sciences; to the Departments of Political Science, English, History, and Philosophy; to the David M. Kennedy Center for International Studies; and, especially, to the College of Honors and General Education and to then Dean Harold Miller for their support.

Chapter 4 was previously published in *Tocqueville's Defense of Human Liberty,* edited by Peter Lawler and Joseph Alulis (New York: Garland, 1993), 121–33, and is reprinted here by permission.

1

Liberal Education and the Idea of the West

Michael Allen Gillespie

At the center of the crisis in contemporary American culture is the question of our relationship to the tradition of Western civilization. This question takes the form of a heated and at times even vitriolic debate between those who see a positive value in our connection to this tradition and those who see it as a source of oppression that must be overcome. The vehemence of this debate, however, has all too often blinded us to the relatively novel and idiosyncratic character of the object of our investigation. In this essay I will try to come to terms with the origin of the concept of Western civilization, to show why it has become questionable, and to explain what is at stake for American culture in the current debate.

The Concept of Western Civilization

We speak of the West and Western civilization as something self-evident and long-standing, but the idea of the West as we use it today has a relatively recent origin. While the distinction of the East and West can be documented in English as early as 1205 and in Latin much earlier, it is doubtful that the term was used in its current sense much before the 1840s and it is unlikely that it was widely understood in this sense before the twentieth century. The term "Westernize," for example, was apparently not used before 1842; "Westerner" only in 1880; and "Western man" not until 1909.[1]

While "the West" was originally a geographical concept, today it is a predominantly cultural and historical category. This transformation occurred over a long period of time. In English the concept first came to have something more than a geographic meaning in the distinction of the Western and Eastern Church in 1533 and the Western and Eastern Roman Empire in 1577. This usage, of course, was much older in Latin. The related term "occident" occurs sporadically as early as 1390 in English, but the distinction of occident and orient can be documented no earlier than 1689. The story of the concept in other European languages is much the same. In German, for example, the term *Abendland* (occident), as opposed to *Morgenland* (orient), can be documented no earlier than 1780. This distinction solidified in the early part of the nineteenth century with the increased interest in the East among German Romantics. Goethe's *West-östliche Divan* is only one of many examples of this fascination. As a term describing the totality of European culture, however, *Abendland* first appears only in 1886 and it was not widely used in this sense until after the 1918 publication of Spengler's *Decline of the West.*

The development of the concept of the West would have been impossible without a number of important changes in the way in which human beings understood themselves and their world. Perhaps the most important of these was the decline of the idea of Christendom as the overarching cultural category that united the individual European peoples. The rise of the idea of the West thus presupposes the decline of Christianity, or what was later called the death of God.

The decline of Christianity, however, cannot explain the selection of the concept of the West as the general term for European and American civilization. The rise of the idea of the West depends on Westerners coming to distinguish themselves as a group from Easterners. In fact the concept of the East is older than the concept of the West. In coming to understand themselves as Westerners, Europeans began to think of themselves in the same undifferentiated way as they had long regarded the various peoples of the East. The Enlightenment clearly played an important role in this change by helping to create a more homogeneous European culture, but it was imperialism that was probably the decisive factor in establishing the distinction of Western and Eastern culture. This distinction is already clear in Kipling's famous declaration that "East is East and West is West and never the twain shall meet."[2] Appearances to the contrary notwithstanding, Kipling does not mean that the distinction of East and West is unbridgeable. The concluding lines of the same stanza read, "But there is neither East nor West, Border, Breed nor Birth, when two strong men stand face to face tho' they come from the ends of the Earth." Kipling was convinced that men could meet as men regardless of their origins, but it is clear from the poem that he considers this a rare exception rather than the rule. While such humanism was probably more widespread during the imperialist period than we generally assume, the imperialistic stereotypes do help to explain the rapid and broad dissemination of the distinction of East and West. Westerners from this point of view are free, enlightened, industrious, and Christian, while non-Westerners are slavish, benighted, lazy, and pagan. It is thus the duty of Westerners to liberate, enlighten, industrialize, and Christianize their black, brown, and yellow brethren. This "white man's burden" propels Western man into an attempt to remake the world in his own image. At its inception the idea of the West is thus not a conservative principle but a dynamic and revolutionary impulse for world conquest and world transformation.

The importance of Spengler in popularizing the idea of the West was considerable. Indeed, his magnum opus was the principal event in the formation and propagation of the concept of the West not merely in Germany but in other Western countries as well. Spengler sees the idea of the West as an important innovation in historical studies. He argues that it should replace the outmoded division of history into ancient, medieval, and modern, which privileges Europe and thus distorts our understanding of human civilization.[3] His West, however, is limited to Western European and American civilization from 900 A.D. to the present. It does not include the Greeks and Romans who, he argues, may be more alien to us than "Mexican gods and Indian architecture," nor does it include, for example, Russia.[4] The West, like all other spiritual epochs, begins in his view as a culture, becomes a civilization, and ends in imperialism, which he argues is "civilization unadulterated."[5] Led by great entrepreneurs such as Cecil Rhodes, Western civilization seeks to establish itself in all corners of the earth.[6] It thereby becomes a world-historical force.

While Spengler may have popularized the concept of the West, he did not give it its determinative meaning. Philosophically most important in this respect was perhaps Heidegger, who adopted Spengler's terminology to describe what he called the tradition of Western metaphysics that began with Plato and came to its conclusion in Nietzsche. Heidegger employs the concept of the West to describe the sequence of ancient, medieval, and modern epochs as a whole, reversing the idea as it appears in Spengler and extending it in a way fundamentally at odds with his thought. While both of these views remain salient, Heidegger's more extensive definition has become more widely accepted.

While the West only comes into being in opposition to the East or the non-West, this distinction depends upon the antecedent interpretation of human life as essentially historical, that is, as the product of human will and activity. Our idea of history, however, is also of relatively recent origin.[7] As a science or way of knowing, history is at least as old as

Herodotus, but it was not until the end of the eighteenth century that it was regarded as a mode of being. Since that time it has come to be understood as the human reality and has superseded nature, God, and reason as the basis for moral and political judgment. The idea of the West only makes sense when we view culture as a historical artifact that is created by human effort and unified by a common principle. From this perspective, Western culture is the product of willful human activity rather than the totality of practices that arise out of devotion to a particular god and his laws, as was the case in Christian and Islamic culture.

As a historical category, the idea of the West is intimately bound up with the idea of the modern. Modernity is the culmination of the West, the working out of its original premises. The idea of the modern and the whole distinction between the ancients and moderns derives from the scholastic distinction between the *via antiqua* and the *via moderna,* which differentiated two twelfth-century schools of philosophy: realism and nominalism. Those who followed the *via moderna* rejected Aristotelian ontology and syllogistic logic and asserted the preeminence of will and the radical individuality of all things. At the end of this long and twisted philosophic path lay a new epoch, the so-called modern age. However, the term "modern" is first used in English to distinguish modern times as opposed to antiquity only in 1585, and the term "modernity" first occurs only in 1627. This distinction of ancient and modern ages took on a new meaning when a third age, the so-called medieval period or Middle Ages, was inserted between them. This occurred as early as 1667, but the concept does not appear in English until 1753.[8] The idea of the Middle Ages is already implicit in Raphael's early-sixteenth-century notion of a Gothic period separating his times from antiquity. While he and his contemporaries distinguished themselves from the Gothic barbarism of their predecessors, however, they did not think of themselves as charting a new, modern path but rather as reviving an ancient way of being. It is really only with the Enlightenment that the idea of modernity as a distinctive epoch arises, and with it the so-called quarrel of the ancients and moderns. In contrast to the Renaissance, the Enlightenment thus distinguishes itself not merely from the medieval world, which it recognizes as dominated by superstition, but also from antiquity, which it sees as unsystematic. Bacon, for example, argues that the ancients never advanced beyond a rudimentary level because their efforts were not coordinated by a universal science. The early moderns believed that such a coordination would make possible not merely the understanding of nature but its actual conquest and mastery. Science thereby establishes modern man as superior to all of his precedessors. Voltaire, for example, asserted that the *lycée* graduate of his day had a more profound understanding of the world than the greatest philosophers of antiquity. While Rousseau and others disputed this conclusion, it has remained a principal element in modernity's self-understanding.

The turn to the idea of the West reflects an important transformation in this self-understanding, for it represents an attempt to understand modernity *not* as a rejection of and alternative to antiquity and the Middle Ages but as their result and conclusion, as the culmination of an original cultural impulse that began with the Greeks. In this way the deep differences of the ancients and moderns are reinterpreted as stages of a unified historical process. The revival of antiquity or ancient virtue that filled the imagination of Rousseau, for example, thus becomes an absurdity. For Hegel and his contemporaries, there is no longer a choice between the ancients and the moderns, for the ancients, their magnificence and heroism notwithstanding, are only the imperfect predecessors of the moderns.

The question of our relationship to the Western tradition is nearly as old as the idea of the West itself. Indeed, the idea of the West in its fullest sense arises as the idea of the end of the West, as the retrospective recognition of a horizon that we have now transcended. It is the cry of the owl of Minerva as it takes wing at dusk. In this sense, the rise of the idea of the West is concomitant with the rise of nihilism.

Explicit nihilism has a long history dating back to the end of the eighteenth century, but it comes to popular consciousness through the thought of Nietzsche. Nihilism, as Nietzsche predicted and the first half of our century made clear, is a cataclysmic event. For some, however, it is also a great opportunity. There are two quite different views about the character of this cataclysm and opportunity, and the differences between these two views lie at the heart of the contemporary debate about Western culture and civilization. These two positions are postmodernism and traditionalism.

Tragic Postmodernism

Postmodernist thinking sees nihilism and all of our contemporary social and political problems as the consequence of the defective character of the Western tradition itself, stretching back at least to Plato. This interpretation leads to the conclusion that we must deconstruct the West in order to overcome nihilism. Postmodernism, however, is not a unified movement or school of thought. It includes a variety of positions that stretch between two extremes. I will discuss the two most important: tragic postmodernism and deconstructionist postmodernism.

Tragic postmodernism accepts the contradictions of the West as necessary and unavoidable and recognizes that any postmodern world will also be shot through with contradiction. The father of this view was Friedrich Nietzsche, who proclaimed the advent of explicit nihilism with his assertion that "God is dead." For Nietzsche, this meant not merely that the Christian God was dead but that all of the absolutes that had hitherto given direction to European life and thought since Plato were no longer tenable. The death of God signals the end of the European culture that Socrates and Plato established and that Christianity universalized. No one can fathom, Nietzsche argues,

> how much must collapse now that this faith has been undermined because it was built on this faith, propped up by it, grown into it; for example the whole of our European morality. This plentitude and sequence of breakdown, destruction, ruin, cataclysm that is now impending—who could guess enough of it today to be compelled to play the teacher and advance proclaimer of this monstrous logic of terror, the prophet of a gloom and eclipse of the sun whose like has probably never yet occurred on earth.[9]

The language of this passage notwithstanding, Nietzsche was not altogether unhappy with this great collapse. From his earliest days, he detested much of European culture and dreamed of founding a tragic culture in its stead. European culture in Nietzsche's view has degraded man. It culminates in bourgeois society, which undermines all greatness and creates only the last man, the man who is unable to appreciate or be moved by beauty or nobility and who is ultimately only the pawn of his own petty desires. This world of bourgeois freedom lacks the discipline and order necessary to produce anything great and lasting. The attraction of nihilism for Nietzsche is that it brings this European world, and with it the last man, to an end. Thus, it is not a dismal or terrifying event but an entrancing possibility. In the conclusion of the passage cited above, he asserts that

> we philosophers and "free spirits" feel, when we hear the news that "the old God is dead," as if a new dawn shone upon us; our heart overflows with gratitude, amazement, premonitions, expectation. At long last, the horizon appears free to us again, even if it should not be bright; at long last, our ships may venture out again, venture out to face any danger; all the daring of the lover of knowledge is permitted again; the sea, *our* sea lies open again; perhaps there has never yet been such an "open sea."[10]

The advent of nihilism opens up for the first time since the pre-Socratics the possibility of a heroic culture. The destruction of all standards undermines all previous philosophy and morality and reveals at the heart of the world not a universal reason but a will to power that courses through all things and determines all human actions. All forms of life and culture in this sense are hierarchies of power, the creation of those who have the will to be master. European culture is also a manifestation of such a will to power. It is a culture, however, that has grown old and weary. Its institutions are no longer vital. Indeed, in Kant and Schopenhauer, the highest values devalue themselves. Reason, which since the dawn of European culture has been the highest goal, concludes in a demonstration of its own impossibility. Western rationalism ends in nihilism. This nihilism, however, also makes possible a higher and more vital human freedom and creativity. Bound by no rules, beyond good and evil, true human greatness again becomes possible. But there is also great danger, for a further descent into decadence is also possible. A watered-down Christian morality, a morality of universal pity, may also triumph. Such a morality, in Nietzsche's view, would serve to universalize the despicable last man. Nietzsche hopes that the great wars of nihilism that he foresees will cleanse us of pity and clear the ground for new commanders, for new philosophers, poets, and statesmen who will impose a new discipline on humanity. These "overmen," as Nietzsche's Zarathustra calls them, are distinguished by a higher strength and freedom. Freed from the spirit of revenge that arises from the immutability of the past by the acceptance of the doctrine of the eternal recurrence of all things, they are capable of a true innocence and spontaneity. The figure that Nietzsche uses to describe them in his notes is Caesar with the soul of Christ.

It is this overman, in Nietzsche's view, who will create the tragic culture of the future. This culture will be tragic not because it is founded on violence but because it recognizes its own transience. It thus will not flee from the actuality of universal becoming into the dreamworld of being, but will inhere in the actual world, where all values are relative and all order ephemeral.

Nietzsche's most important heir was Heidegger. Like Nietzsche, Heidegger saw the advent of explicit nihilism as the end of Western culture. However, Heidegger disagreed with Nietzsche about the origin and character of nihilism. Nihilism for Nietzsche begins with Socrates' ideal of reason. Unable to bear the inconsistent world that tragedy revealed, Socrates found a solution to the suffering it engendered in the notion of universal reason. This flight from suffering, in Nietzsche's view, was the basis for Platonism, and Platonism was at the heart of Christianity and thus at the heart of the entire European tradition. For Heidegger, the blame lies not with Socrates or Plato but with Being itself, not with man but with "the gods." The history of the West since Plato has been determined by what Heidegger calls the withdrawal and

forgetfulness of Being. Being, as Heidegger understands it, is the fundamental mystery or question at the heart of human existence. It strikes
man and evokes wonder, and out of this wonder arises thinking, and out
of thinking all of the structures of the world in which we live. The
central and guiding question of human life is thus the question of Being.
The pre-Socratics were the last Westerners, in Heidegger's opinion, to
experience this question as a question. The rest of Western history is
nothing other than a series of answers to this question. Insofar as the
question of Being directs us to seek answers, it directs us away from
itself as a question. It thus withdraws and conceals itself within its answers. It ceases to appear as Being itself and appears only as the Being
of beings, as the essence that lies behind actuality.

The initial withdrawal of Being established the post-Socratic Greek
world, and the further successive withdrawals established the Christian
and modern worlds. For the Greeks, the Being of beings is *physis,* or
nature, for Christianity it is God, and for modernity, subjectivity. This
history is a history not of progress but of decline. Part of the lesson that
Heidegger teaches is that the supposed superiority of modernity to the
preceding ages is a distortion of the truth. Indeed, it is precisely modernity's claim to dispense with God and to establish the world on the
basis of man alone that places it at the furthest remove from the truth
of Being.

The advent of explicit nihilism in the thought of Nietzsche marks for
Heidegger the completion of modernity and of the West itself. Nihilism
is the complete forgetfulness of Being as a question and the establishment of the universal hegemony of Being in the form of the will to
power of world technology. Man who attains his humanity only in and
through the experience of the question of Being is reduced at the end of
the West to just another raw material that can be formed and reformed
according to the dictates of economic and technological necessity.

Heidegger recognizes the great danger implicit in nihilism but, like
Nietzsche, also sees it as a great possibility. Indeed, it is the abyss
opened up by nihilism that may be the source of our salvation. Nihilism
is the recognition that the distinction between Being and being is unten-
able, that Being, as Nietzsche put it, is nothing. Heidegger sees this
nothing, however, as no-thing or no being. Being in this light appears
as the no-thing that is radically different from ordinary, everyday beings
like tables and chairs. The advent of nihilism thus opens up the possibility for the experience of Being as radically different from beings, and
thus as a question. For the first time since the pre-Socratics, it is possible for Western man to experience the question of Being and thereby
become human Being or *Dasein* as the place, the *Da,* of the advent or
revelation of Being, of *Sein.*

In contradistinction to Nietzsche, this is not a possibility that can be willed. Being is not in the service of man, man is the servant or shepherd of Being. Whether Being will reveal itself is thus unknowable. Our task is to prepare for its arrival. Such a preparation requires what Heidegger calls the destruction of Western metaphysics. This destruction involves the demonstration of the insufficiency of all of the answers of Western metaphysics to come to terms with Being. The result of this destruction is the completion of nihilism and the universal revelation of nothingness as no-thingness. This recognition marks the end of the West and may even prepare, in Heidegger's view, for a *rapprochement* with the East.

The dangers of this destruction are evident to Heidegger. Indeed, he himself characterizes the course of action that he recommends as the path of Oedipus. It leads beyond good and evil, beyond the political realm, beyond all morality to the abyss out of which both politics and morality spring. The man who follows this path becomes apolitical, stateless. It is in this sense a fundamentally tragic path that leads one into the most heinous crimes. Such crimes, however, may not even be recognizable as crimes. For example, Heidegger argues that from the perspective of the history of Being, there are no essential differences between America, Stalin's Soviet Union, and Nazi Germany. Similarly, he argues that the production of corpses at Auschwitz was in principle no different from the production of fertilizer in a modern chemical plant. Both are products of the revelation of Being at the end of modernity as world technology. From a moral perspective, we may be aghast at such conclusions and wonder at the blindness of such a way of thinking. These conclusions, however, are not the result of blindness. In an early lecture, Heidegger remarks that we "must call before ourselves that which causes terror," because "only where there is the danger of horror, is there the blessedness of wonder."[11] Viewed in this light, his own attachment to Nazism seems to be deeply rooted in his thought, and his example in this respect casts a long shadow on contemporary postmodernism.

Deconstructionist Postmodernism

Contemporary French and American postmodernism is deeply indebted to Nietzsche and Heidegger. The depth of postmodernism's self-understanding, however, varies considerably. The more philosophic postmodernists like Derrida see their thought as a rejection not merely of modernity but also of the West, as such, which has its origin in the "logocentric" notion of truth established by Greek philosophy. Post-

modernism as a strain of literary theory, by contrast, seldom comprehends its own philosophical foundations and often understands itself
only as the rejection of the literary modernism of such writers as Joyce.
The more philosophic postmodernists see Western civilization stretching back to the Greeks, the more literary see only the culmination of
this tradition in the present. While the former feel compelled to confront
the whole of the Western tradition, the latter are drawn, often following
critical theorists such as Adorno or Horkheimer, to a radical critique of
contemporary culture.

For contemporary postmodernism, the Western tradition, especially
in its liberal conclusion, is based upon a lie. Liberalism claims to promote human freedom, dignity, and diversity but in fact it only produces
a particular and quite limited kind of self and world. Moreover, it maintains this self and world through a rigid, if largely invisible, structure
of discipline and repression. Modernity assumes that human beings are
autonomous individual selves or subjects. Following Heidegger, contemporary postmodernism thus characterizes modernity as the realm of
subjectivity. Central to the delusion of modernity is the notion that these
subjective selves are autonomous, that is, that men are the lords and
masters of an objectified nature. In fact, they are objectified and mastered in their turn.

These selves, for postmodernism, are not naturally given but rather
determined by the relations of power that prevail in modern society.
Here postmodernism draws heavily upon Nietzsche's notion of the will
to power and Marx's notion of the means and relations of production.
These power relations manifest themselves not only in the institutions
of social and economic life but also, and indeed preeminently, in the
categories in which we think and act. Following Nietzsche, postmodernism declares that grammar is destiny. Western civilization maintains its
established power hierarchy by privileging the rational over the irrational, white over black, male over female, history over myth, literacy over
illiteracy, sanity over madness. Foucault's work, for example, is in large
measure dedicated to revealing these hierarchies of oppression.

Insofar as postmodernists turn away from the autonomous subject,
they also turn away from humanism. In this respect they follow the later
Heidegger who rejects all previous modern thinking as anthropocentric
and attempts to develop a way of thinking that is ontocentric, centered
on Being.[12] Derrida and other explicitly antihumanist deconstructionists
follow this path but replace Heidegger's Being with "difference" or
"otherness," understood in a Nietzschean sense as continual becoming
and self-overcoming. They argue that we are prevented from recognizing this "other" by the oppressive categories of language, which produce the illusion of endurance or self-identity. In reality, there are no

enduring things, and words at best only point in often contradictory ways toward slices of becoming. The postmodernist rejection of the modern notion of the self, and thus of humanism, is consequently an affirmation of what they see as the immense productive vitality of difference.

In the practical realm, this turn away from identity to the other is a turn toward all of those elements in existence that Western culture devalues and rejects. The liberation of this other, however, requires the deconstruction of the language, social mores, and political institutions that characterize Western civilization. This liberation, which in theory aims at maximizing diversity, in practice becomes the liberation of the oppressed.

This process begins with a reversal of all the recognized dichotomies in order to establish the legitimacy of the other. Thus, for example, unreason is elevated above reason, sickness above health, black above white, female above male, and homosexual above heterosexual. There is little or no philosophical basis for this move in postmodernism itself. The pursuit of maximum diversity, which is intrinsic to the idea of difference, provides no grounds for privileging one side of the dichotomy over the other. The reversal of the dichotomy thus reveals an ideological motive at work in the postmodern enterprise. Deconstructionist postmodernism in this way often tips over into a kind of class, race, or gender warfare that is driven not by the love of the other but by the hatred of the same, not by creative imagination but by resentment. In contradistinction to tragic postmodernism, deconstructionist postmodernism sees the contradictions in the Western tradition not as inevitable but as the result of oppression. It sets off in search of enemies and finds them in the famous Dead White European Males who, it argues, have produced and sustained the Western tradition as a hierarchy of power at odds with the greater good of the majority, be they blacks, women, gays, or the peoples of the non-Western world.

Deconstructionist postmodernism rejects the hierarchy and oppression of modernity and aims at a new social order based upon difference and diversity, a rainbow coalition of humanity. It seeks to recover, for example, the repressed other, concealed in the history of gays, women, and minorities as well as in non-Western cultures. This form of postmodernism rejects the hierarchical projects of tragic postmodernism and sees every culture as a form of discipline and repression, arguing that there are no enduring values, that everything is relative, and that we may therefore simply do, to paraphrase Stanley Fish, "what comes naturally." In practice, this maxim leads at best to an anarchic egalitarianism. At worst, it ends up inscribing a new tyranny of thought and action. Nietzsche recognized the inherently inegalitarian character of the insight that the world is the will to power and nothing besides. The initial premises of postmodernism in this respect seem as compatible with oppression as with liberation, with the same as with the other. The postmodernist privileging of diversity is thus either the result of a theoretical confusion or camouflage for a new form of the will to power.

While tragic postmodernism remains an important philosophic force, its political significance has waned. By contrast, deconstructionist postmodernism has proven to be much more appealing to the egalitarian sentiments of many Americans, and especially to the aging New Left, which settled into it as its Marxist home crumbled around it. Given its emphasis on the liberation of the oppressed, it has played a central role in feminist activism as well as in movements for black and gay liberation.

Traditionalism

There is a liberal and a humanistic form of traditionalism. In its liberal form traditionalism sees Western culture, and especially its greatest philosophic and literary works, as the basis for the formation of individual personality. Through the study of these works one becomes cultured. The more elitist version of this view is that the study of Western culture helps one to become a gentleman or gentlewoman. While this view was predominant in the nineteenth and early twentieth centuries and appears in our time in the notion of culture as an ornament of personality, it has for the most part been replaced by the republican view that the study of the great works of Western civilization prepares one for citizenship in liberal democracy. Liberal traditionalism in this sense focuses only on modernity and assumes that this modern bourgeois world is the necessary consequence of historical development. It is thus oblivious to the contradictions within the West itself, between, for example, Athens and Jerusalem and all that they represent. At its best, liberal traditionalism tries to explain such differences as the result of historical progress. In this respect, however, it only reveals its fundamental attachment to the present. Liberal traditionalism for the most part does not recognize the problem that nihilism poses for the idea of Western culture and civilization.

By contrast, humanistic traditionalism is intensely concerned with nihilism. In this respect it resembles postmodernism. In contrast to postmodernism, however, it discovers the origin of this nihilism not in the defective character of the West but in the defective character of modernity. This view leads not to a rejection of the West as a whole but to a reappropriation of what these traditionalists see as the authentic Western tradition that modernity subverted, the tradition of classical antiquity.

This form of traditionalism is the product of the discovery and experience of totalitarianism. While many humanistic traditionalists were deeply influenced by tragic postmodernism, they rejected and attacked it because of its connection to fascism. Leo Strauss and Eric Voegelin in the United States and George Grant in Canada, for example, sought in the deeper history of the Western tradition an alternative to tragic postmodernism that was also an alternative to the modern problems that tragic postmodernism had revealed. Their West is thus a different West than that of the postmodernists. This West is also different from the imperialistic West of the late nineteenth and early twentieth centuries. Western culture in their view is not a unitary tradition but an amalgamation of competing possibilities. We are living out one of these possibilities but it is not the only one available to us nor is it undeniably the best. Their defense of the West, like the postmodernist attack on the West, is in fact highly critical of modernity. In contrast to the liberal traditionalists, their position is thus much closer to Renaissance humanism and classicism than to liberalism.

In contradistinction to the tragic postmodernists, the humanistic traditionalists advocate a return to Greek philosophy and particularly to Greek political philosophy. They maintain that the postmodernists, and especially Heidegger and Nietzsche, do not understand the Greeks. The return to the Greeks in their view can provide us with the means to rise above the bourgeois life of liberalism because it teaches us that we can rise above our times and our subservience to our times. For the humanistic traditionalist, our historical circumstances are not inescapable. They are rather the dark cave of Plato's *Republic,* and the study of Western philosophy and literature is the upward path to freedom and nobility. Humanistic traditionalism does not aim, as is often supposed, at a return to the Greek political actuality. It is not the *political* model of antiquity but the study of ancient philosophy that is crucial and that can inform our political life in important ways. In particular, ancient thought teaches us that political differences, for example, in the structure of the regime, are not epiphenomenal expressions of social or economic forces beyond our control, but rather independent factors of decisive importance to our lives that human wisdom can make better or worse. Ancient thought also teaches us that it is dangerous to give the city over to the philosophers because their idealism too readily turns into a fanaticism that will brook no compromises with political actuality. In this sense ancient thought alerts us to the totalitarian dangers of all idealism and provides a needed support for liberalism against its enemies. It thus demonstrates that while liberalism may not be the best regime, it is perhaps the best practicable regime. Finally, the study of ancient thought, for the humanist traditionalist, teaches us that there are certain qualities of character that are necessary in every regime to ensure decent government. In this way, ancient thought helps remedy what the humanistic traditionalist sees as liberalism's mistaken notion that all of the problems of political life are susceptible to technical or organizational solutions.

Postmodernism versus Traditionalism

The differences between the postmodernists and the traditionalists are multitudinous. For the postmodernist, the world is only in and through language. It is thus something purely conventional. For the traditionalist, it is an intelligible, if obscure, natural reality. For the postmodernist, there is no such thing as logic, there is only rhetoric; language is a vehicle of power not of truth. For the traditionalist, language reflects an independent reality and gives us access to this reality so that we can rise above the merely conventional. For the postmodernist, God, a symbol of white male hegemony, is dead. For the traditionalist, God remains a question, a Jerusalem opposed to Athens. For the postmodernist, human beings are self-constructing selves who can make themselves into whatever they can imagine and enforce, independent of all natural characteristics; for the traditionalist, human beings have a soul with determinate capacities and limitations. For the postmodernist, morality and ethics are neither natural nor God-given but rather instruments of repression established by ruling elites; for the traditionalist, they are forms of human excellence that allow men to rise above lives that are nasty, poor, brutish, and short. For the postmodernist, politics is an instrument of repression that must be seized and turned to the end of human emancipation; for the traditionalist, politics is either a necessary evil that protects human beings from the wanton violence of their fellows or a stage for the expression of human virtue and excellence.

The different consequences of these two positions for social and political life can be summed up as the distinction between diversity and pluralism. Postmodernism supports a politics of diversity that is in practice a radical particularism. From this perspective, all values are created equal. There is no objective truth but only your truth and my truth. In practice, this pushes postmodernists to support, for example, different laws, different standards of excellence, and different types of education for groups depending upon their race, ethnicity, gender, and sexual preference. Traditionalism is pluralistic and encourages the free exchange of ideas in an effort to reach objective truths. It recognizes that there are many important differences between groups and does not actively seek to abolish them. It does, however, believe that there may be an objectively best human possibility, and that even if this possibility cannot be realized or understood, political stability and social peace depend upon the establishment of universal standards and a common core of experience and learning.

These differences become all too apparent when we examine the postmodernist and traditionalist notions of education. The traditionalists believe in the possibility of an objective and universal truth, or at least in the existence of universal or eternal questions that arise out of the way in which human beings are articulated into the natural world. Postmodernism rejects such a notion of logic and objectivity. "Truth" is only what one can convince others is the case. For Derrida, the world in a sense is created anew each time we utter a word. Nature is merely a mythic or poetic construct that was developed to secure a particular hierarchy of power. It is a common postmodernist assumption, for example, that if women or blacks had developed science, the laws of nature would have been different. Social science as well is thoroughly subjective and biased. The focus on power, for example, is merely a reflection of male sexuality that distorts political practice and thinking about practice. What is needed is a paradigm shift that takes its bearings from the oppression of women and minorities.

The natural sciences and the more scientific social sciences have been relatively immune to the postmodernist impulse. Postmodernism has enjoyed by far its greatest success in history and the humanities. History long ago abandoned politics to become social history; now under the tutelage of postmodernism it has become the new historicism that is largely devoted to the study of oppression and the recovery of the lost voices of oppressed peoples and minorities. In the humanities, the postmodernist project is canon revision, which attacks the traditionalist notion of Great Books that constitute the core of Western civilization. For the postmodernists, there are no Great Books as distinguished from non-Great Books because ultimately there are no books; there are only interpretations. What is crucial is not the author and his intention, but the reader and his historical circumstances. Seen in this light, *The Valley of the Dolls* may be more important than the *Iliad,* the study of mass culture more important than the study of high culture. The so-called canon, from this perspective, is only an instrument of repression, by which the ruling elite establishes its image of the rational human being and the good society. The society and the social roles these books portray are merely a fatuous rationalization of the elite's hegemony. Thus, the Great Books do not point us toward truth, or even the most important questions of human existence, but instead promote racism, sexism, and homophobia. Therefore, the canon must be revised by reinterpreting the books that constitute it in liberating ways or by replacing them with other works from previously suppressed (minority or female) Western and postcolonialist Third World authors.

For the humanistic traditionalist, the Great Books are not a unified tradition but a great conversation in which disagreement on fundamental issues is more evident than agreement. The study of the Great Books thus does not produce a particular kind of character nor is it conducive to a particular politics. Rather it reveals to a greater or lesser extent the vast array of human possibilities. For the humanistic traditionalist, the Great Books make possible the real encounter with otherness, with other cultures, other religions, other sexual mores, and so on. This encounter is in part the traditionalist justification for the rejection of merely popular books. Whatever their entertainment value, these books in their view only point human beings back into the world of their everyday experience and do nothing to lift them above the narrow horizon of their historical circumstances. Finally, the humanistic traditionalists believe that the Great Books, at their best, engage the abiding questions of human existence and bring human beings in some way into the conversation of great minds. They believe that such an encounter is particularly necessary in our times because, for the most part, thinking has been reduced to technical rationality and historical reflection. The study of mass culture only exacerbates this problem. The Great Books, by contrast, enable us to conceive of other ways of being and thus, in a rudimentary way, to begin to philosophize.

Conclusion

The debate between the postmodernists and the traditionalists about the nature and value of Western civilization seems to be of momentous importance. Both sides believe that the future of our civilization hangs in the balance. I want to suggest that we should not be so ready to accept this claim. The idea of the West is not nearly as broad or all encompassing as each side would have us believe, and their own alternatives are subject to a variety of constraints that they do not perceive or understand. Postmodernism, for example, defines itself at least in part by what it rejects. In rejecting the West, postmodernism thus in a sense also establishes it. This dialectical connection to the West is especially evident in postmodern practice. The postmodernist consideration of non-Western literature, for example, by and large aims not at the discovery of the exotic other but at the critique of the West. Postmodernists focus on the themes of anticolonialism and anticapitalism, but pay little attention, for example, to the praise of non-Western religions or to the biting criticism of Third World culture in much of Third World literature, or to the often racist, sexist, and homophobic aspects of this literature itself. This problem, however, is not fatal to the postmodern enterprise. Indeed, the tragic postmodernists come much closer to dealing with the other in a way that frees them from the tradition they seek to negate. The tragic postmodernists, however, face related problems of their own. For example, the other that Heidegger discovers in his concept of Being is so radically other that it seems to lose all touch with actuality. This vast gulf between the everyday world and the other poses real dangers when this thinking turns to politics, as Heidegger's association with Nazism suggests.

Not only is postmodernism unable to dissociate itself from the West, it cannot finally dissociate itself from modernity. Postmodernism in all of its forms rests upon a notion of man's relation to the world that is intrinsically modern. The world is not something in its own right but only exists in and through man. Indeed, the world is a human artifact. In this respect, postmodernism does not represent an alternative to the Western tradition or to modernity but the completion of the modern project of making man the master and possessor of nature.[13]

Finally, postmodernism, its protestations to the contrary notwithstanding, may not even reject the Great Books. It is rather an argument for a few Great Books against other Great Books. Thinkers of the stature of Derrida continue to press their case by confronting and wrestling with Plato, Rousseau, Husserl, and Heidegger; lesser postmodernist thinkers often prefer simply to castigate and censor what they cannot understand. It is, however, a faulty strategy. The Great Books cannot be effectively censored. Censorship only increases their attraction and, if they are truly great, they attract and capture even the censors themselves. We do not choose the Great Books, they thrust themselves upon us. It is thus not they but we who in a sense are defenseless.

Traditionalism is itself not immune to criticism. Liberal traditionalism simply does not come to terms with the challenge presented by nihilism and the advent of global technology. The Great Books do not necessarily inculcate virtue, nor do they necessarily provide a bulwark for liberalism. There are many Great Books that subvert virtue and many that are supremely antiliberal.

Humanistic traditionalism has problems as well, many of which grow out of its common origin with postmodernism in the thought of Nietzsche and Heidegger.[14] Despite its trenchant critique of historicism, for example, there is a powerful historical element in humanistic traditionalism itself. It often seems only to turn the history of Western thought into a moral drama whose protagonists are the great philosophers and poets. These men are imagined to be immensely wise and powerful beings, supermen who do battle with one another across the centuries to determine the course of history and the structure of social and political reality. Some fight for good, others for evil. Humanistic traditionalism in this respect has a gnostic element and true believers of its own. Moreover, whatever its salutary motivation, the deification of past philosophers and poets that humanistic traditionalism undertakes often stifles philosophical thinking. Fidelity to the text, which should be the beginning of thinking, all too often becomes its end. The traditionalists often forget that Socrates did not spend his time reading or writing the Great Books.

I would like to suggest that the real problem may not be the question of our connection to Western civilization, which the great debate between postmodernism and traditionalism addresses, but the fact that both sides so readily accept the fact that there is such a thing as the West or Western civilization. This concealed agreement reveals the relatively narrow limits of our contemporary ways of thinking. On the most fundamental level, postmodernism and traditionalism are both moments of the two-hundred-year-old attempt to understand the world historically. To think historically, however, is to exclude all other ways of knowing. There are many important questions that such thinking never encounters, let alone answers. We continue to think in historical ways not because it is intrinsically satisfying but because we find it difficult to do otherwise. Yet nothing is more needful. The danger in the present debate about the nature and value of Western civilization is that it engrosses our vision and prevents our exploration of alternative ways of seeing and thinking. If we always look at the world through the lens of history, we will never be historians in the original Greek sense of the term, for we will never truly be *witnesses* and will never experience the wonder that entrances the eyewitness. Without this experience, all talk of the other or of eternal questions will remain only talk. To transcend our current way of thinking, we must thus first learn to hear the questions that our own existence thrusts upon us.

Notes

1. William James's use of the term "Westerner" in 1880 is highly illuminating: "*Not* to fall back on the gods, where a proximate principle may be found, has with us Westerners long since become the sign of an efficient . . . intellect." "Great Men, Great Thoughts, and the Environment," *Atlantic Monthly* 46 (October 1880), 449.

2. Rudyard Kipling, *Departmental Ditties and Ballads and Barracks Room Ballads* (New York: Doubleday, 1911), 3.

3. Oswald Spengler, *The Decline of the West,* trans. Charles Atkinson, 2 vols. (New York: Knopf, 1976), 1:13–23.

4. Spengler, *Decline,* 27.

5. Spengler, *Decline,* 36.

6. Spengler, *Decline,* 37.

7. For a fuller discussion of this point see my *Hegel, Heidegger, and the Ground of History* (Chicago: University of Chicago Press, 1984), 1–23.

8. Spengler, *Decline,* 22.

9. *Gay Science, Werke: Kritische Gesamtausgabe,* ed. G. Colli and M. Montinari, 18 vols. in three parts and one supplement (Berlin: de Grutyer, 1967–), 2: 255.

10. *Gay Science,* 256.

11. Martin Heidegger, *Die Grundbegriffe der Metaphysik: Welt, Endlichkeit, Einsamkeit* (Frankfurt am Main: Klostermann, 1983), 255, 531.

12. On the antihumanism of French deconstructionist thinking, see Luc Ferry and Alain Renaut, *French Philosophy of the Sixties: An Essay on Antihumanism,* trans. Mary Cattani (Amherst: University of Massachusetts Press, 1989).

13. On this point see Robert Pippin, *Modernism as a Philosophical Problem* (Cambridge: Blackwell, 1991).

14. On this point, see Catherine Zuckert's excellent *Postmodern Platos: Nietzsche, Heidegger, Gadamer, Strauss, Derrida* (Chicago: University of Chicago Press, 1996).

2

Liberal Education in the Confines of the Liberal Tradition

Timothy Fuller

We often take it for granted that liberal education and the modern liberal political tradition are congruent. This is not so. The idea of liberal learning long antedated the advent of the modern liberal political tradition and could, in principle, survive if the modern liberal tradition were to alter drastically or pass away, even though, of course, there is no guarantee that liberal learning would then flourish. There has, it is true, been a cordial relationship between the two. For the majority of academics today any separation still seems almost unthinkable.

At the same time, there is increasing intellectual unrest about the liberal tradition, and also about the current practices of liberal education. The thesis here is that liberal learning cannot simply identify itself with any political tradition, even though it can recognize and should prefer those traditions that are receptive, and not hostile, to liberal learning.

From the time of Socrates and Plato, we have understood that the best regime altogether cannot be equated simply with any actually existing earthly regime. This is a discovery philosophers made when they examined the earthly regimes philosophically. This does not preclude practical judgments of better and worse under prevailing conditions of given times and places. Practical judgments of this sort are unavoidable; in fact, the Platonic Socrates' encounter with the best regime, disclosed in philosophic reflection, allowed him to see the earthly regimes more clearly in their advantages and disadvantages.

Liberal education has certain distinctive characteristics dependent on this insight of philosophy. For example, the search for wisdom cannot finally be satisfied (if it can be satisfied at all) within the structure of

27

any regime. Philosophy may make its appearance within the tensions of the city, but in responding to those tensions it opens to us a dimension of reality that is suprapolitical. So also does the liberal political tradition, in that part of it emphasizes individual liberty and responsibility, opposes coercion of opinion, and is skeptical about the concentration of power in governments. But the liberal political tradition also has a utopian, progressive, immanentizing dimension that is prone to abandon skepticism about human claims to wisdom, and to search for (and sometimes to claim it has found) an earthly regime that is either unqualifiedly best or leading to the best.

In our time, liberal learning frequently adopts the practical aspirations of modern liberal politics, looking there for its own inspiration and sense of purpose. But the defining characteristics of liberal learning do not have their source in the aspirations of modern liberal politics, and we cannot gain full clarity about them through politicizing the academic community, even for liberal purposes. On this point there may be a modest convergence among traditionalists and postmodernists, though they cannot remain together in the long run. Liberal learning and the liberal political tradition can be friendly, but they cannot simply identify with each other. What follows is a reflection on what this situation portends.

To begin, let us consider the current state of academic institutions. In no small measure, their condition today reflects a set of dilemmas imposed upon us more generally in our late-twentieth-century situation. The following list I adapt from Peter Berger's provocative book, *Facing Up to Modernity.*[1] There he describes five features of modernity:

1. *Abstraction.* This is rooted in institutional practices such as markets, bureaucracies, technological systems, and mass media, as well as in the process of urbanization. These structures, Berger argues, entail "the progressive weakening, if not destruction, of the concrete and relatively cohesive communities in which human beings have found solidarity and meaning throughout most of history . . . a quantifying and atomizing style," which "has invaded other areas from the theory of political ethics to the praxis of the bedroom" (72). The experience of abstraction confronts us with this question: "To what extent is the cognitive style of abstraction adequate to an understanding of ordinary human experience?" (72). Practically, what commitments or loyalties can be legitimated when all such commitments and loyalties are constantly under assault from the abstractive process?

2. *Futurity.* This is "a transformation in the experience of time . . . modernization everywhere . . . means a powerful shift in attention from past and present to the future. What is more, the temporality within which this future is conceived is of a very peculiar kind—it is precise,

measurable, and, at least in principle, subject to human control. In short, it is time to be mastered" (73). Clock time dominates, lives become "careers," and societies become raw material for designs and plans. Is it right for us to "become engineers and functionaries even in the most intimate aspects of our lives"? "Futurity means endless striving, restlessness, and a mounting incapacity for repose."

3. *Individuation.* As "concrete communities have been replaced by the abstract megastructures of modern society, the individual self has come to be experienced as both distinct and greatly complicated—and, by that very fact, in greater need of the personal belonging which is difficult in abstract situations" (75). We oscillate between protecting our autonomy and longing for identification in communal existence.

4. *Liberation.* In "large areas of human life, previously considered to be dominated by fate," we now see "occasions for choice" (76). We are Promethean in multiplying options for choice. As Berger sees it, the weakening of tradition is so far advanced that even those inclined to enjoy their inherited resources are not afforded the opportunity to do so. We are haunted by the felt need to distinguish what is and is not in our power to change. We seek to reduce the number of insurmountables. Yet we become more uncertain as to how to sustain social stability in the midst of social turbulence. The anguish of choice prompts some, at least, to seek escape from freedom. Thus the paradox of liberation: On the one hand, the "liberation of the individual from fate of any kind (social, political, even biological), and liberation of the individual from the *anomie* of a condition without fate . . . the ideal of liberation *as* choice and the ideal of liberation *from* choice" (78).

5. *Secularization.* Berger defines this as antagonism "to the dimension of transcendence in the human condition" (79). This is to be traced not only to science and technology but also to pluralizing and relativizing pressures. Whether one is or is not persuaded of the reality of the transcendent, "secularization frustrates deeply grounded human aspirations—most important among these, the aspiration to exist in a meaningful and ultimately hopeful cosmos" (79).

A common feature of all these symptoms of modernity is the uncertainty, or lack of conviction, about any particular interpretation of the world's meaning, engendered by the pressure of innumerable competing alternatives, coupled with incessant activism, as if meaning were either no longer crucial or else equated with participation in processes. There is no obvious symbolic program, no guideposts—the world is opaque.

I proceed now on the assumption that what I have described manifests itself in places of learning as well as elsewhere. Undoubtedly there will always be some who come to universities to escape from or, better, to transcend the anxieties of the age. But many come searching for a more exact understanding of the age in order to succeed within its terms.

These attitudes are not restricted to students; they affect us all, at the least in tempting teachers to interpret their vocation to mean serving these demands, which increasingly are reinforced by the power of government officials and large foundations who think they know what education needs. Liberal education is losing independent reasons to exist. It begins to appeal to its potential adherents in familiar and conventionally accepted, easy to assimilate, terms.

Let us separate the term "liberal" from the term "modern," looking for the meaning it has independent of modernity. If we look back, for example, to the medieval and Renaissance background of our universities, we see that then there began to be available to us a wealth of invitations to explore and to understand languages recognized as investments in thought; epic, dramatic, lyric, historical, and scientific literatures that gave new dimensions to human relationships, emotions, aspirations, and conduct. Learning began to be

> identified with coming to understand the intimations of human life displayed in an historic culture of remarkable splendor and lucidity and with the invitation to recognize oneself in terms of this culture. This was an education which promised and afforded liberation from the here and now of current engagements, from the muddle, the crudity, the sentimentality, the intellectual poverty and the emotional morass of ordinary life.[2]

I do not believe this understanding has been entirely snuffed out, but the elements of this educational venture are imperfectly remembered and no longer seem natural to us. There is strong pressure to resist remembering them; there is willful forgetting among us. We see this in curricula divided between distribution requirements and increasingly preprofessional, technique-oriented courses. We see it in "general education" requirements that lack concern with specific learning.

We see it in the increasing reliance on the term "excellence," which is used abstractly to stand in for all substantive questions, and which, as a result, more and more takes on the connotation of corporate efficiency and managerial skill. Committees and workshops spend vast amounts of time compiling lists of useful skills, attributes of good socialization, options for globalizing experiences, and the like. The content of what is taught and learned declines in prominence and significance.

A culture, however,

> is not an abstract set of aptitudes; it is composed of substantive expressions of thought, emotion, belief, opinion, approval and disapproval, of moral

and intellectual discriminations, of enquiries and investigations, and learning is coming to understand and respond to these substantive expressions of thought as invitations to think and to believe.[3]

Education as skills acquisition and recognition—or "cultural literacy"—are incomplete encounters.

I do not want to indulge in pessimism. These recent efforts, however inadequately imaginative, may have within them a residual lingering desire to restore the original adventure to understand, and not only to understand, but to understand from a high vantage point, to seek not liberation from culture but the freedom to explore endlessly within the culture, to renew its possibilities by the imaginative use of them. But the matter is open to serious question.

At its best, perhaps, liberal modernity has been an attempt to actualize what was to be discovered in liberal learning. Liberal learning, however, is not merely modernity intellectualized; it is the continual recalling of the human spirit to know what a truly human life might be, and a conversational engagement respecting the way in which we might live it. Liberal learning thus understood is not a technique or a set of skills—it is an education in imagination. What we need to do in order to restore to sight a clearer vision of our work is not an easy matter. The burgeoning of "higher" education cannot be equated with the preservation and enhancement of "liberal" education. The recent emergence of something called "K-16 education" is a chilling erosion of our ability to distinguish between "school" and "university," in favor of generalized categories of skills that are, presumably, thought to be the same at all levels, varying only in sophistication. There results categorical uniformity coupled with variability in standards, expectations, and requirements.

Among the consequences is the emergent domination of the university, not necessarily by administrators or managers as such, but by an administrative and managerial perspective that, implicitly or explicitly, supersedes the traditional self-understanding of the academic community as a distinguishable and historic place. There is much tension between the requirements for professional and graduate training and the historically nonvocational pursuits of liberal learning. There is much tension between the vocation to teach and the conditions for professional advancement.

Needless to say, professional work is not to be dispensed with, but it is not an end in itself, and it presents us with some perils: first, it often ignores, or only superficially deals with, the distinguishing assumptions of disciplines. Max Weber said that to choose a method is to choose a way of life, thus dramatizing the significance of the academic engagement, and retaining the sense of vocation inherited from an earlier time. To sustain this attitude is an arduous and often unrewarded task under the described conditions.

Conversationality admits that we cannot speak in a single voice or rely on a single method of knowing. But an academic institution has been, above all, a congregation of teachers and their students in which the teachers are learners no less than those whom they teach. It is a set of human beings collegially undertaking to participate in and to extend their intellectual inheritance conversationally. Education is an

> initiation into the skill and partnership of this conversation in which we learn to recognize the voices, to distinguish the proper occasions of utterance, and in which we acquire the intellectual and moral habits appropriate to conversation. . . . Each voice is the reflection of a human activity, begun without premonition of where it would lead[4]

but gradually becoming sufficiently self-conscious to try to specify its character and ground rules and, finally perhaps, to apply for acceptance as what we call a discipline, involving representative texts and a distinctive mode of investigating and knowing.

The emphasis is not on formulas and propositions but on understanding what lies behind them. This is the greatest and least dogmatic learning. Conclusions are seen to be momentary accomplishments—transitory releases—in the effort of each of us to understand ourselves in relation to what we have learned, and in relation to our conversational partners, without whom we are diminished.

Among the most urgent threats to this understanding today is the claim that the technological revolution of the electronic age has deprivileged universities, which no longer can monopolize access to information, and thus the collegial bodies we have known in various but recognizable forms for 2,400 years must lose—have already begun to lose—their sacral qualities, to be robbed of locational importance. And the preoccupation with understanding all human institutions according to corporate, commercial, and market standards powerfully affects the rhetoric and ultimately the understanding we have of what we are doing. These are complex topics. For the moment I only wish to point out that here liberal learning is being reduced to information access and vocationalism. I do not deny that these have always threatened the pursuit of wisdom. But we are confronted with an especially powerful and global form of this threat in our time. This is a transformation that will not disappear, and we shall have to respond imaginatively to it. It is, moreover, a much more powerful and long-term issue than the immediate issues of political correctness that we currently face. It is true that something like conversations proliferate electronically. What these are and could be requires careful reflection to be understood. It is not clear that the dilemmas of modernity Peter Berger describes will be alleviated electronically. Perhaps the electronic age will aggravate them. The differences of opinion on these matters are catalysts for the deeper thinking we must do.

In places of learning, as traditionally understood, disciplines are not abstract, futurity can without guilt be set aside, individuation serves face-to-face conversation and diversity within a common whole, liberation is of the imagination, and the aspiration to hope and meaning is neither rendered formulaic nor ruled out, itself becoming a matter to be clarified in partnership. Is this worth defending and restoring because it is an absolute insight? I think so.

If so, it is then our duty to act with confidence in the midst of continuous, but often unchosen, self-examination, and against considerable odds. The point is not that we are set apart from the human condition, but that we embrace it with critical intellectual and moral habits. So that future generations will know that we have not allowed this insight to pass away as in a dream, we must remember, and act in accord with the remembrance, that we engage not in truancy but in renewing the place where learning and teaching occur, in a place that speaks to its time, but not only that, without ceasing to be a place of liberal learning.

Notes

1. Peter Berger, *Facing Up to Modernity* (New York: Basic Books, 1977).

2. Michael Oakeshott, "A Place of Learning," in *The Voice of Liberal Learning,* ed. Timothy Fuller (New Haven: Yale University Press, 1989), 30.

3. Oakeshott, "A Place of Learning," 32.

4. Michael Oakeshott, "The Voice of Poetry in the Conversation of Mankind," in *Rationalism in Politics,* new and expanded edition, ed. Timothy Fuller (Indianapolis: Liberty Fund Press, 1991), 491.

3

Diversity, Canons, and Cultures

Allan Bloom

Call me the first victim of political correctness. I wrote a book that, counter to every expectation, became a number one best-seller, and thereupon became the target of very intense hatred. I discovered that there are passions afoot in our land, akin in their ferocity to those of the religious wars of the seventeenth century, which seek to transform education and to transform our souls. In me they found the perfect enemy and, in their concentration on me, revealed what they are. Very simply, according to them, one is not allowed to speak about race or gender dispassionately. One is not allowed to ask questions rather than repeat the correct answers proposed by today's activists. Those who would dare speak out would be forced to wear scarlet letters advertising themselves as racists or sexists. Sensitivity is more important than love of truth. I remember a young woman who, during the question period after a lecture I gave at Oberlin College, shaking with rage, and with tears flowing from her eyes, said, "I am offended by your calling on three men before you called on a woman. This shows that you are condescending to women." When a victim, and in this theology all women are victims, says she is offended, the one who offended her is prima facie guilty of insensitivity. Therefore, he must adapt himself to his accuser so that she will not feel *excluded*. Excluding persons from the community is the great crime. The community itself has systematically excluded, and therefore it must be transformed root and branch. In this atmosphere, there are three possible reactions to such assaults. The majority identify with their accusers and eagerly try to "clean up their act." Others avoid hot issues because they do not want to ruin their careers by wearing the scarlet letter. A third group continues to tilt with windmills, saying what they believe, and reaping pariahdom as their reward.

In my book, I identified this phenomenon under the ironic rubric "openness." I meant by this a dogma that everyone must believe there is no truth in order to guarantee respect for the diverse views of the truth present in the world. Translated into political practice, this means the majority's "truths" are untrue and the minority's "truths" are true. The very activity, proper to philosophy and so admirably represented in Aristotle's *Politics,* of trying to sort out and judge various claims of truth about justice, becomes suspect, or even itself an injustice. This is an absolutist relativism driven by the political intention to overcome liberal democracy's claims to justice.

The inevitable consequence of this position is gross intolerance, an unreasoning hatred of "Western Civilization," which has excluded and made unhappy all minorities. From this "openness" emerges the closing of the American mind or, I might amend this to say, the closing of any mind. A mind is closed in the most important respect when it can no longer rationally address the question "What is happiness?" or "What is the good life?" The light of the mind is dimmed or extinguished when this first and foremost of questions is suppressed. That question is the whole source of liberal education. Students are told today that they cannot and must not address it. They cannot address it because there is no truth to be found, and they should not because any truth they think they may have found might perpetuate the system of exclusion. This position has the wonderful effect of unmanning the beliefs of the majority and permitting the minorities to be thoughtless and passionate. Thus we produce intolerant tolerance. It is possible that relativism is theoretically true, but relativism can give no guidance, moral or political. When it is adopted as a political doctrine, it becomes self-contradictory, although it can be used as a blunt instrument to bludgeon opponents in a society whose insistence on rational discourse has weakened.

Finally, this ugly partisan spirit has been publicly identified, and Americans who take the First Amendment, with its protection of free speech, as the core of our regime have become concerned. The worm is turning, if ever so slightly. This New Left made a critical blunder when it identified its doctrine as political correctness. The liberalism of the silent majority was shocked by this and has begun to recognize a threat. However, this salutary political awareness remains superficial because political correctness is understood to be just another fanaticism in a society that, while granting free expression to its fanatics, is designed to prevent their easy victory. But this particular sect is not merely bullying. It brings with it a whole metaphysic, one that is actually shared

implicitly by many of the less thoughtful opponents of the new orthodoxy. Political correctness is possible only against the background of
theoretical decay, and its principles must be confronted. Arthur Schle-
singer attacked me for my criticism of relativism. He insisted that the
American tradition is relativist and that the Declaration of Independence's "self-evident truths" are a proof of that relativism. But when
he became aware that perspectivism, one of the new terms used by the
movement, carried with it an attack on his discipline, history, he started
shrieking that we must stop this attack on objectivity. Did he think
that relativism concerned preference for flavors of ice cream, chocolate
versus vanilla? Relativism in its contemporary form means precisely
that there can be no objectivity. There are an almost infinite number of
souls, connected to the almost infinite number of cultures, which interpret the world in different ways. There is no higher authority, no possible arbitration between or among their various views. Each folk or culture mind is its own judge and interprets an essentially chaotic world in
ways that are congenial to it. It does no good to scream at these dogmatic relativists if one is unwilling and unable, as is Professor Schle-
singer, to meet relativistic arguments.

I made this clear in my analysis of the almost universal use of the
word "value" for what used to be called good and bad. Value means a
belief, not a truth. It means that man gives himself views about good
and bad that have no ground other than his will to believe them. This in
turn means that will and passion are more important than reason. Diversity of values is the ground for war, although it is trumpeted today as
the means to peace. Only when we are willing to come to grips with the
arguments for this interpretation of good and evil as values will we have
grounds for resisting what is going on. The value interpretation or,
under one of its other names, historicism, has reigned supreme for two
generations in the humanities. The radicals are now just drawing the
conclusions. My insistence on this made academic conservatives (who
think they are liberals) suspicious of me. They want to remain in their
dogmatic slumber and call my radical arguments conservative. Let me
say simply that, for me, true openness is the willingness to doubt one's
own most cherished opinions in order to replace them by truer ones.
Openness in its current form is a license to stick by one's prejudices
without the necessity or possibility of criticizing them.

My most fatal error in the eyes of my politically correct critics was
to praise the reading of good books as the core of a liberal education.
This is an important part of what made my book so popular with the
public at large. Ordinary Americans sensed the absence of a worthwhile
leisure in their lives and an incapacity to address the big questions. In
addition, they were troubled by their children's lack of interest in books

and their inability to communicate such an interest to them. I gave a qualified and highly nuanced praise to the Great Books curriculum promoted by the former president of the University of Chicago, Robert Hutchins, and continued most notably in institutions like St. John's College. I have great reserves about the program that produced me, but I believe that it was the only game in town when it came to promoting the interests of liberal education. I am persuaded that it is much more important to read one or two books of quality seriously, and digest them so as to become part of one's flesh and blood, than to swallow a whole list of books. I won't detail here my doubts. They are in my book.

The Great Books idea has always been controversial. Modern scholars insisted that they were the only ones who could competently read old books, and therefore, that a direct reading by amateurs without the assistance of the scholarly apparatus is impossible. And these scholars were, almost to a man, historicists. You cannot read old books as though they might contain the truth. You can't pick up Aristotle and treat him as a contemporary and a friend. He is a child of his times, and you must let the historicists tell you what those times were really like and the essential limits on the thoughts of Aristotle that made it inferior to the thought of the historicists. The Great Books idea defied the premises of most modern scholarship. We Great Bookies were always in the minority, but there was nonetheless some kind of widespread unexamined and implicit assumption that it is useful to read the books of the tradition.

But my very modest intention to get people to read good books for the sake of the richness of their souls turned out to be the primary cause of the violent attacks on me. And now it is books themselves that have become bad. This violent assertion is implausible to most people and to common sense. But it is today the majority opinion among professors of humanities, supported by the moral pathos of exclusion and the money of foundations. Its respectable (respectable at least to television talk show hosts) expression is "multiculturalism" and "non-Western content." They say: "It's only fair that non-white, non-Western, non-male persons should have equal representation with their opposites who have dominated the curriculum." That seems only reasonable if you start looking at it in this way. Nobody ever thought of looking at it like this before, but that can be corrected by raising consciousness. In the past, Plato and Kant were read to get information about the nature of things and how to go about understanding it. We did not know that everybody was just telling tales or myths in order to establish himself at the top of the social heap. But now we know that and we can see that they are enemies that need to be deconstructed in order for the oppressed to replace them as kings of the hill.

Unarticulated in this, of course, is the fact that the disadvantaged want to become oppressors in their turn. This newly enlightened age has recognized that false consciousness is the cause of our moral flaws and that books are the cause of that consciousness. These half-Marxists turn Marx on his head. It is not the control of the means of production that causes thought, but the reverse. The washed out, tired and discredited, irrelevant professors of the humanities are reborn as the primary agents of revolution, the liberators from Eurocentric poison of the inmates of their discipline. They are no longer passive conveyor belts of the tradition, but the destroyers of it. My gentle advocacy of Great Books made me the enemy of mankind. I was even accused in the prestigious *Times Literary Supplement* of having blood on my hands in Nicaragua. All of this makes for an interesting psychological study.

As part of this movement, the books that people have perennially read for the sake of inspiration and liberation have been baptized anew and emerged as "the canon." And in popular newspapers and on television talk shows there is continuous talk about reforming the canon, which is treated as though it were a golf club that excludes blacks and women. Cast in this light, these great sources of independent thought and social criticism seem to be a part of the domain of thoughtless reactionaries, a doomed remnant of the past, as was segregation in the South. The revolutionaries say, "You exclude me," and the conservatives say, "This is the way we have always done things." They taunt each other across the barricades, the one group yelling "Western Civilization," the other "Non-Western Civilization." The reactionaries are somewhat hampered when they are qualified as white Western males, because in this day and age, no one is permitted to use the opposites as unflattering epithets. When the issue is framed thus, it is clear who is going to win. "You've got your canon, why can't we have ours? We need memories of our roots; we need role models; we need pride in ourselves and to show others, as well as ourselves, what we have accomplished. You are robbing us of our heritage and our self-respect." All this is very plausible to those who have no experience with the real meaning and purpose of books, particularly professors of the humanities. This rhetoric, although it is as superficial and noxious as the rhetoric of communist and fascist parties, is worth analysis, an analysis that requires a liberal education, to understand the longings that it expresses and the deep thought that lies behind it and that it trivializes. In this half-educated country, there is now neither charming natural common sense nor the presence of real philosophy. Words like "value," "culture," and "canon" are part of our sorry, impoverished slang. Behind each of these words is a whole, interesting but questionable, interpretation of the world of which those who use its language are unaware and of which they are hence prisoners.

In a preliminary way I would argue that books such as those of Aristotle and Machiavelli were read and can still be read because they tell us so much about ourselves, things one cannot find elsewhere, things on which almost all other thinkers are dependent. Aristotle tells us what courage is, and courage is of interest to all men and women, everywhere and at all times. The challenge is to find a better account. You won't find it easily, but there should be no attempt to prevent such alternative accounts from having their day in court.

Most people and even most scholars don't care to think very much, and classic books deteriorate into a mere tradition with them. But that tradition is useful insofar as it has preserved the memory of the existence of these books with a fair degree of accuracy as to their relative merit. When I was young I read histories of political philosophy by MacIlwain and Sabine, who had no real interest in Locke and were preoccupied with the latest, now dead, contemporary liberal teachings. But they somehow knew that Locke was essential and pointed it out to me. One had to go back and read him all over again, after which their books were almost useless. But without them, it would have been very difficult to discover him. We are now in a situation where, according to the great authority of Stanford University, we no longer need Locke. The tradition of scholarship is not able to argue adequately why we do need him, but it preserved him for a while from the barbarian invasions that, with their fancy intellectual terminology, are about to overwhelm us. Maybe Aristotle (who was from Asia Minor) was some kind of a Westerner, but this is not the reason why we read him. If there is someone, to quote Plato, "in some barbaric place," climbing the peaks of philosophy, there is no reason why he should not come to join the conversation. There is no good reason to accept the notion that there is an exclusionary rule against non-Westerners and that the statistical evidence proves discrimination. In the midst of all this demagogy, one must remember that most of mankind never learned to write. This incapacity is compensated for by anthropologists, who are more than willing to tell us what the unlettered think; but, until proof of the contrary, these interpretations must be understood as imperial attempts on the part of the anthropologists to empower themselves and must be accounted as part of modern Western thought. Then we are told that Islam, the thought of which has both Greek and biblical roots, is non-Western. And even more extreme is the edict that Latin America is non-Western, when the only real difference is that it was colonized by Spaniards and Portuguese while North America was colonized primarily by the English and the French. All are equally Europeans. When it comes down to it, practically the only non-Westerners who wrote books are the Indians, the Chinese, and the Japanese, and no one is saying their books should not be read. Of course, one can, and some do, take another step—in the name of antilogocentrism—and denigrate books altogether.

However stupid it may sound, a book should be read in the same way we read the instruction manual that comes with our computer or our stereo system to find out how it works. We don't ask about the race or sex of the person who wrote it, unless perhaps its writer doesn't know how to make the machine work. A long experience with and temptation by these sophisticated theories that emphasize the race, class, and sex of authors has proved to me that there is almost nothing to them, and that the deep and interesting thing is instead to try to figure out what an author like Aristotle meant. For example, he was the founder of women's liberation when he defined a barbarian not as someone who lives in this or that country but as someone who treats a woman like a slave. He meant that reason, observing nature, proves that this is a violation of the nature of things. But if there is no nature and no capacity to observe it dispassionately, then only custom and passion rule, and these, always and everywhere, have enslaved women. The attacks on philosophy always assume that its fundamental premises will still be maintained when nobody believes in them or even knows about them anymore.

Every educational system is, of course, a mass of stupidities and incoherences. I say stupidities, rather than calculations and intentions of the ruling class. Educational systems are always ripe for reform, but unfortunately, most of the reformers are the ones with the exploitative political intentions. The American universities are mixtures of responses to practical demands by the various groups that make up the country, half-hearted attempts to teach something about the political regime we live under, and a tiny bit of concern for eternity. With the unerring instinct of fanatical obscurantism, our new movements have zeroed in on that one little bit of concern for eternity and are succeeding in suffocating its already wasted vitality.

The word "canon" appeals to our taste for abstraction from real experience. It tells us all we need to know, without really knowing anything. The books we read are simply the expression of the will to power of dead white Western males, whose lifeless hand is upon us. As it is stated, this is so grotesque an interpretation that it could not be considered seriously by any serious person if it were not a part of current madness. How did this happen? That is the interesting question. Why do such people never ask themselves how it is that Greece, which was very weak, conquered by the Romans, managed to conquer them intellectually? But I need not go on, for all evidence confutes the theories of our revolutionaries.

It has been suggested that *The Closing of the American Mind*[1] did
not adequately address the radicals' claim that all education is deeply
political. Let me clarify my views on this issue. Throughout my career,
following my great teacher, Leo Strauss, I have argued that the humanities were withering away because they systematically neglected the political content, and even intentions, of the great writers in favor of a
concentration on intimate psychological details or their metaphysical
teachings. I am a follower of Aristotle in believing that man is a political animal and that his first concern is the quest for justice and the good
regime, which will incorporate it. This I argue is also the first concern
of the greatest writers. For example, most of the plays of Shakespeare
concern this quest, and the neglect of it diminishes their interest and
leads to misinterpretations of them. Moreover, I think it not unlikely
that Shakespeare wished to influence not only the political regime of
his own country, but those of all countries. I am persuaded that students
who do not have a healthy political passion, a love of justice that in-
quires about the best regime, are maimed in their pursuit of knowledge.
If they lack such a passion, or do not bring it to their studies, they are
likely to be either boors or triflers. I am all for political passion and
make every attempt to liberate young people from all the constraints
that forbid its expression.

What I deny is that there is no possibility of pure love of the truth
with respect to the quest for justice. And that is the crucial assertion of
deconstructionism, postmodernism, and all that jazz. Universities are
dedicated particularly to disinterested pursuit of the knowledge of justice, and these people deny from the outset that such knowledge is possible. Shakespeare must be, in a ukase published by the American
Council of Learned Societies, interpreted as an ideologist of early colonialism. I do believe that Shakespeare reflected on most of the great
questions of modernity as well as those of antiquity. But, until proof of
the contrary—and there is so far no proof, only assertion—I insist that
Shakespeare thought those questions through on his own and presents
independent views from which we can still learn. He was, I am morally
certain, independent of the prejudices of his own age as well as our
own. If indeed the relationship between Prospero and Caliban in *The
Tempest* treats of the confrontation between a higher civilization and a
lower one, it does so not in terms of the brute spirit of British conquest,
but in terms of Shakespeare's own and independent knowledge of justice from which we could learn so much if we could for a moment set
aside our furious spirit of party. Similarly, Aristotle says that he does
not belong to the party of the democrats, or the oligarchs, or any party
except that of the truth. He listens to the claims of all the parties and
helps us to distinguish between those that have merit and those that do

not. His is the still voice of reason that attempts to moderate the passions that lead men to believe that partial views of justice are whole ones. His is an austere and lonely discipline.

What the deconstructionists contend is that there is no such discipline, that everyone is a partisan of one of these partial and self-interested sects. We had become so used to hearing that Aristotle was a representative of the slave-holding oligarchs, as Marxists of one sort or another believed, or that his unresolved Oedipal struggle made him prey to systems of domination, as Freudians would have it, that we had very little with which to resist this somewhat more radical onslaught of the same. I believe that those who make these arguments, however intellectual they may be, have no experience of the philosophic spirit. They look within themselves and generalize that no one could really love the truth. But the possibility of this love is what is at stake, and what deserves our deepest meditation. If the love of truth is impossible, we must close up the universities and leave things to the real struggle for power.

These academics are followers of Nietzsche, who teaches that the love of truth is an affect of the will to power. Nietzsche was a serious thinker and deserves our careful attention. But we cannot begin by assuming that he is right and without thinking of the consequences of his assertions. My objection to the radicals is not to their contentions about politics, but to their being closed to any kind of thought about their contentions. I have been understood to say that there is nothing to these arguments about power. That is not correct. I was studying Nietzsche and Heidegger when they were either unknown or despised in this country, before they became fashionable and a means for getting attention. I insist that the study of Nietzsche and Heidegger is essential for us. What nauseates me is the philistinism and ignorance of these persons who think that a metaphysical argument ad hominem can take the place of discussion. Nietzsche teaches not only that we must apply our theories to others, which makes it easy to prove their truth, but that we must above all apply them to ourselves and see whether the shoe pinches. We need not so much a Freudian interpretation of some hysterical woman as a Freudian interpretation of Freud. Do his theories about dreams emerge from his desire to sleep with us or to dominate us, or are they intended to be truths? A Marxist interpretation of Marx might teach us about Marx's own ideological class interests. I do not think that this is easy to do in such relatively high cases, but it is quite easy to do with this new breed of academics, who use their theories to get control of universities and are succeeding quite well at it. They certainly are looking for and getting power. They have such shriveled souls as to want to dominate universities where, as Henry Kissinger put it, the struggles are so nasty because the stakes are so small. The only reason for a serious human being to be in a university is for love of the truth, and if that doesn't exist, a person with greatness of soul would inevitably go into politics. Only a pygmy would think a university worthy of conquest, but jobs there do feed bellies and the petty vanities of the vainglorious.

I want now to discuss two of the buzz words of our Newspeak: "diversity" and "culture." The two terms are related in that by diversity we mean diversity of cultures. Diversity is now taken to be something sacred; not something one can think about, but a kind of trump card. The accusation that someone is not favoring diversity is enough to send him scampering with his tail between his legs. The good thing about America, if there is still said to be any good thing about it, is its wonderful diversity of cultures, rather than, as an older way of looking at it would say, its miraculous forming of unity out of great diversity. It is alleged that we are now much more diverse than we ever were and therefore must transform our educations so as to encourage and fertilize our present diversity. Unity—how you get it out of heterogeneity of human types and principles—has disappeared as a theme.

Personally, I am very doubtful whether America today is any more diverse than it was in 1900, when it was teeming with immigrant Irish, Italians, Poles, and so on, as well as the despised WASPs, and the blacks. And there were even, so far as I can determine, women here. One might argue that the Asians today do indeed represent something different from the others, who were all raised, one way or the other, in the biblical tradition. But in general, the proposition about our new diversity requires examination, and in this, as in so many other things, one should not roll over and let such claims go unexamined when so much depends upon it. I would suggest that the change is much more in the status of diversity and in the stridency of the voices that promote it. In the past, right up through the civil rights movement, but prior to the emergence of the black power movement in the late sixties, the various groups strove to become Americans. Now they are told by intellectuals and their leaders that they should be inspired by what they once were and what separates them from the American public as a whole. Nothing could be further from Martin Luther King's insistence that blacks are the true Americans than the assertion that blacks are distinguished by forming a separate culture, one that is irreducibly opposed to Eurocentrism. It is argued that no education can be a good one without the presence of diversity in the student population. The conclusion of this line of reasoning is that Athens, Rome, Britain, France, and Germany did not have a serious system of education or high intellectual life. The political success of Rome and England was clearly founded on the homogeneity of their ruling classes. The decline and fall of Rome has usually been attributed to the bewildering diversity of nations and religions incorporated into it by the empire. There was no common ground left for political action. The American Founders wanted, and this is what is new in their understanding, to form a true nation or people despite the diversity of the elements that were to compose it. They concentrated on what men simply are, as in "all men are created equal. . . ." They planned a nation capable of common purpose and political determination without the harshness of the ancient legislators, who imposed a unity of belief and action on their citizens. It was not known whether this would be possible. They took it to be a great gamble, combining nation building with gentle tolerance. They would not interfere with diverse ways of life or religion, except within the very narrow limits imposed by absolute political necessity. But they would never encourage the extremes of diversity or regard them, as such, as a good thing. They would have expected that gradually, the differences brought here from elsewhere, or fostered by the terrible fact of slavery, would be attenuated by the common experience of the nation's life. This democracy was understood to be future oriented rather than past oriented. Its inhabitants, again with the notable exception of the blacks, immigrated here because they wanted to get away from the horrors of the lands from which they came. The nostalgia for the culture of their distant fatherlands is an indulgence of the third and fourth generations in this country, and the intellectuals want to impose this diversity on populations that frequently have little taste for it.

The changed status of diversity is a very interesting phenomenon, and we could set up a number of interesting courses to understand how it came to pass, how the charm of diversity replaced the striving for the unity of perfection. But the current insistence in America today on diversity, or the latching onto the idea of diversity celebrated by certain European thinkers, is fairly easily explicable. It is founded on the conviction that liberal democracy has failed in its project of treating individuals as individuals and offering them equal opportunity along with a relatively high degree of tolerance for the diversity of the groups that persist within it. The new project attempts to replace the old one with a scheme for treating this land as a mosaic of groups and forcing what are alleged to be the previously dominant groups to abandon their spurious sense of superiority. For whatever it is worth, this is the idea.

Insofar as we are talking about universities, the real and permanent attractiveness of this theme of diversity consists in the view that a serious intellectual life requires a diversity of well-thought-out opinions about the fundamental questions if there is to be any hope of achieving the unity of the truth. The truth is our goal, no matter how much the demagogues try to suppress our love of the truth in the name of sensitivity, but since we do not have full access to the truth, this high-level diversity in thought is very desirable for us. Political correctness undertakes to stifle the profound diversity in thought that existed in the past, the dangerous and attractive diversity that opposed believers to nonbelievers, materialists to idealists, democrats to aristocrats. I believe that we are in this decisive respect, to our great loss, much less diverse than men and women of the past were, and that the range of respectable alternatives of serious thought has been narrowed.

Milton Friedman may be opposed to the socialism of John Kenneth Galbraith, but only on the basis of a profound agreement, that the purpose of society is to provide material well-being to the population at large. The difference consists in a disagreement about the means to the actualization of their shared good. No one in this country is conservative in the sense of being able to believe or to speak publicly, as conservatives did in the past, about limiting the franchise to a small aristocracy or, as theologians once did, about dedicating society to the renunciation of worldly goods for the sake of salvation. Our diversity of groups is, as Harvey Mansfield has said, more like the Coca-Cola ad, where people of different races, nations, and sexes sing the same song "in perfect harmony." Such harmony is achieved by a reasoning akin to this: "If the beautiful think they are beautiful, they will try to dominate the not beautiful and make them have low self-esteem. Therefore, we must abandon the idea of the beautiful and suppress our longing for it for the sake of tolerance and everyone's feeling good about themselves." Aristophanes wrote a comedy about this, *Assembly of Women,* and I recommend it highly. The question is whether this maiming of our best instincts is really required for a reasonably tolerant society and whether this fragmentation is actually the royal road to our all getting along together.

Diversity as we understand it is connected with the idea of "culture"—a nebulous and elusive word that we use so easily without being aware of how difficult and fateful it is. Culture emerged as a category in the early nineteenth century and was a word used by conservatives to denote an opposition to the triumphant march of the Rights of Man throughout all nations, a march signaled by the American and French revolutions. Natural rights or the rights of man are cosmopolitan and are insisted on in every country, destroying the ancestral modes of organizing politics and everyday life. The self-determination of women destroys almost all traditional societies and is almost unstoppable when reason is taken as the highest authority. The strategy for defeating revolutionary cosmopolitanism was to argue that the great nations were a result not of reason but of a mysterious web of particular circumstances that produced Englishmen, Frenchmen, Germans, or Russians rather than human beings. This would justify their "peculiar institutions," such as the exclusion of the greater part of the population from political participation, an established church, the acceptance of its dogmas, even slavery, and put them above criticism. Superficial reason, it was alleged, could not reach the profound depths of culture. The argument was adopted largely to protect national ways of life and to prevent the homogenization of mankind that liberalism threatened. What a culture is, how it comes to be, and what authority it has over us remains murky, but as long as the cultures were identical to certain well-known political entities like England or France, much of the difficulty of the term remained masked. French culture meant the distinctive French way of life, and it was clearly distinctive. Why it should remain distinctive was answered by the assertion, "That is too deep a thing for analysis by superficial rationalist reformers." The nation is a mystic unity. In practice, the idea of culture was a kind of ideology of nationalism, and one can see why its first successes in the United States were among white Southerners.

The notion of culture was radicalized by Nietzsche who, in the light of the continuing decay of the European nations, was led to think about the origins or the foundings of cultures in the hope of founding a new European culture. Here is where the word "value" comes into existence as the crucial term for understanding human things. Man needs values in order to live, and no great or profound values can come out of Enlightenment or liberal rationalism. Cultures are essentially producers of values, beliefs about good and bad, tables of the law. They emerge from the creative unconscious of nations, a thing far deeper than the conscious reason of political men and legislators. Inasmuch as values cannot be the same for all men if there is to be a true culture, the diverse value systems are at war, beyond conflict resolution, because some values say that empire is good and others that national self-determination is good; some say that aristocracy is good and others that monarchy is good; and so on, endlessly. Great values, according to which peoples can live, are the products of great men and of victorious conflict. This means that the formation of man by culture is a harsh business, like the sculptor's hammering the stone in order to produce the statue. A lot of the stone is smashed, and the rest takes a terrific beating. There is no nature of man; man exists only in the peculiar vision of the artist culture-maker.

This teaching of Nietzsche's about culture is obviously much farther to the right in its profound rejection of equality than is its predecessor, and it provided whatever core of serious thought there was present in fascism. This assertion has earned me some of the nastiest criticism, but I can only reiterate that at the roots of much current leftist thought in the United States is fascist thought. My contention is supported by the fact that the profound philosophical source of it, Martin Heidegger, and Paul de Man, who popularized deconstruction in the United States, were both sympathizers with Hitler. The notion of culture, in its turn, is revolutionary, but revolutionary in the name of suppressing the spirit of the American and French revolutions, which did not respect culture. Whereas the identification of culture with Europe and Europe's mission to rule the world kept it within the limits of the comprehensible, now what a culture is and how to act in relation to it becomes even vaguer. What is interesting about our situation is that this dangerous, antiliberal notion has become sacred for the left in the United States today. Does it not really force us into war when we are speaking about peace? A thinker like Michel Foucault is very good at identifying the harsh bonds that culture imposes on us. He longs for liberation from them, but he too is a culture-thinker and does not realize that if there are no such harsh bonds of culture, man will not exist. He no longer has the option of resting his case with Enlightenment universality and the nature of man. He wants culture and doesn't want it. Like all such thinkers, he hates liberal democracy, that is, bourgeois society as one finds it in Europe and the United States, but he is unable to understand Nietzsche's clear-sighted vision of what it takes to make an alternative to that bourgeois society. All this is very far away from Marx's Enlightenment view that there should be a universal homogeneous society where man is only man.

The link of culture to the left was partly made by cultural anthropologists who examined and fell in love with various primitive peoples they were pleased to call cultures. They are aware that modern science would destroy those cultures, and therefore oppose the advance of science among them. They are, of course, wholly inconsistent when they want modern medicine to help save lives among these primitive people in times of plague or famine. They are even more inconsistent when they regret the presence in these peoples of such colorful practices as the circumcision of women. But in their inconsistency, they practice a halfway Nietzscheanism, and they insist that the distinction between high and low culture, which Nietzsche at all costs wished to establish, be suppressed. "Thus far and no further," to paraphrase Kant, "proud culture." This critique of pure culture insists reason cannot judge; reason cannot establish rights. But these same anthropologists are, without any grounds to stand on, great believers in human rights even though there are no human beings; there are only cultures.

Now I must confess my perplexity as to how this notion of culture can guide us in our national problems. What do you do, when so many "cultures" are co-present, to preserve them in any vital way? The culture proponents' real objection to modern liberal society was that it has no culture because it is too weak to impose its values. It is producing a decayed, brutish type of last man—last because the cultural conditions for humanity have disappeared. The highest unifying value of a culture was God, and a nation whose political regime is founded on the separation of church and state is already doomed. A national way of life separated from the way of life imposed by a serious religion is debilitated, according to the cultural understanding. Most of the anthropologists are atheists, but they tip their hand when they give such a high place to the publicly sacred in the primitive tribes they study. Culture becomes, in the American context, a kind of all-purpose category in which one includes all kinds of claims on the polity without having to argue for them.

Culture is taken to be a very high thing, but can one reasonably say, "I will die for my culture," as men used to say that they would die for their god or their country? Culture is, at least partly, a timid way for half-believers to have the advantages of religion without religion. So much of the talk about roots and community emerges from this murky source, this incapacity to speak decisively about this most important issue. Thus, the discussion of culture degenerates into things like musical styles, language, and tastes in food. The importance or the necessity of preserving these things is lost because their relation to the highest beliefs and principles is lost. Every year in Chicago there is a festival called Taste of Chicago, where the different nationalities have booths where you can eat their food. This is pleasant and charming, but nobody is willing to sacrifice anything to preserve the habit of eating the food their mothers and grandmothers cooked. Those who work at the booths go back the next day to living and working like everyone else in this country. It is at best a sentimental exercise. It is an American way of rendering harmless what were once murderous oppositions, rendering them harmless by removing the nerve of principle.

Still, the word culture retains some of its original force, so that as soon as someone raises the flag of culture, his or her cause gains a certain respect. In the past one spoke of the bad habits of kids. Now we speak of "youth culture." The former authorized the supervision and education by adults who hoped to correct them; the latter inspires attentive admiration and expectant observation, which disarms criticism. This suits the wish of all the tawdry commercial interests who pander to the "youth culture."

There are three reasons for wanting to study cultures today. The first is the old scholarly quest to satisfy our curiosity about other ways, curiosity begun in the West by Odysseus in his travels and honorably continued by Herodotus and so many others up to the present day. This is not something that has been neglected in Western intellectual life. In fact, it is only in the West that there has been such study. It stemmed from a distinction that first emerged in Greece and has not been known where Greek thought was not known, a distinction between our ways and the good ways. In other words, the Greeks discovered the danger of ethnocentrism and thought it a thing to be combated. They and their students are, contrary to contemporary allegations, the only ones who fought the struggle. The modern proponents of culture wanted to suppress this distinction because the quest for other ways weakened one's own way. The postmodern proponents want to suppress it to overcome ethnocentrism and promote study of and respect for other cultures. But such study of cultures requires the demon "objectivity," which is the target of contemporary criticism. In this case, as in so much else, contemporary critics want to have their cake and eat it. In the name of respect for other cultures they attack the rationalism necessary for respectful attention to other cultures so they can reaffirm cultures that do not respect other cultures.

Thus, proper academic study is replaced by two related partisan arguments for the teaching, not really the study, of other cultures: humiliating Western pride and boosting the self-esteem of minorities. It might be helpful to illustrate what is going on by pointing to the academic voices expressing concern about and hostility to the five-hundredth-anniversary celebration of Columbus's discovery of the Americas. In the past such anniversaries were the occasion for self-congratulation and contented reflection on the progress of civilization, the advantages to mankind at large, and the foundation of political liberty, to all of which this discovery led. But now, many intellectuals tell us that Columbus was the initiator of very great crimes, the fruits of which white Western males guiltily enjoy. Racism, sexism, colonialism, imperialism, as well as destruction of the environment are the true legacies of Columbus. Most of all, the true cultures that existed in the "new world" were destroyed in the name of rootless cosmopolitanism. So these people wish to be party poopers. Their views might be the occasion for serious philosophical reflection on the meaning and value of progress. But they are not the occasion for such reflections; they are merely dogmatic assertions, challenging democracy's liberal individualism in the name of organic and rooted cultures. The worst crime is not denying a man his natural and universal human rights, as the liberal tradition would have it, but the destruction of cultures that, of course, never recognized individual rights.

This charade has already advanced to the point where in elementary schools in the state of New York, students must be taught that the Iroquois Native Americans were the founders of the American federal system, and not Montesquieu and the American Founders. This is intended to make us grateful to the Indians, whose creative culture we so brutally destroyed, to delegitimize the American regime, to make us feel guilty, and to blunt our intellectual instruments. Of course there is nothing whatsoever to this claim about the Iroquois founding federalism. It is simply untrue. But if you are a perspectivist, then you don't have to worry about truth. There are just a variety of perspectives or interpretations and this one about the Iroquois is meant to replace the perspective of the bandits called the American Founders. The means for replacing the old view by the new one is not rational debate but the exercise of power, an exercise that will empower the Native Americans. The real political advantages of this ridiculous position are irresistibly great for those who want to give Native Americans esteem while taking it away from the old oppressive majorities. The political force of this movement is attested to by the fact that it is not only pushover institutions like Stanford and Duke who have changed curricula because of it, but such politically highly charged parts of the American polity as the public schools. Instances of this kind proliferate across the country.

A similar case is Jesse Jackson's decision to call blacks African-Americans, a decision respectfully accepted by the media. When black was substituted for Negro a generation ago, it made perfect sense, for Negro was one of those timid, pseudoscholarly devices for making something respectable that did not appear to be respectable. White and black are perfect coordinants. But the term African-American is not only a description but also the announcement of a normative program. Africanness is a description not merely of skin color, a thing unimportant in itself and irrelevant to the principles of the Declaration of Independence and the Constitution, but of the essence of blacks living in the United States. It is a demand for the recognition of a separate status for the African inhabitants of this country and an educational reform appropriate to that background. It places unclear demands on education inasmuch as what constitutes the African-American culture is extremely vague, apart from the assertion that it is not Eurocentric. It has tyrannical implications because it is not at all clear that American blacks want to be African-American in this cultural sense. I note that in a recent poll 80 percent of American blacks still prefer to be called black, but that will not stop the alliance of Jackson and the white-dominated media from trying to impose it on them. This whole thing is dangerously close to racism because it implies that centuries of separation from and utter ignorance of Africa have not altered a core of Africanness in black persons in America. The analogy to epithets like Jew-

colonization by
the left

ish-American is spurious. No serious Jew would call himself a Jewish-American. That is a sociologist's rubric. He would say that he is an American and a Jew, one who does not make special demands on the regime because of his Jewishness, but who benefits from the separation of church and state explicit in our Constitution. He would not cover over the possible tensions between the two elements of this hyphenated bastard by hiding under it any more than a Mormon would or should hide under a phrase like Mormon-American. We do speak in the universities and newspapers of Jewish-Americans, Italian-Americans, and Asian-Americans. Judaism is a religion and Italy is a country, whereas Asian-American refers primarily to race. From a constitutional point of view, religion is an important consideration, to be freely exercised and not established, national origin is utterly unimportant, and race is a problem to be overcome for the sake of individual rights.

African-American is not a religion, not a national origin, and in this formulation meant to be something above and beyond a race. What is it then? Here is where our amorphous word culture comes to the rescue. Culture is whatever those who are a part of it say it is, without having to say why it is important and right for others to respect it. It comes down practically to the insistence that blacks need black role models in order to have self-esteem, and that myths must be invented for them, as well as for others, in order to say that they have achieved a culture. I believe this is something unheard of in sound educational theory and hostile to the spirit of this regime. It is one thing to argue that there are not enough black professors in universities because they have been discriminated against because of their skin color. It is an entirely different thing to insist that there be an African-American perspective in the universities represented by African-Americans who alone have the qualities of soul to promote it. It is not so much the pernicious political consequences of this move that alarm me, but the intellectual confusion, thinness, and deceptions that are its necessary accompaniments. It stands in the way of each person's thinking seriously about his individual situation with the help of those great thinkers who have stated the alternatives. Students are made to believe, before examining them, that those thinkers are the exclusive oppressors.

 My prescription, a prescription that has no chance of being adopted, is to take those components of the college years now being given over to studies based on the idea of culture and devote them instead to studying that idea itself. That study would ask such questions as whether there is such a thing as culture, unnoticed until the nineteenth century; what guidance can we get from the idea of culture; and what alternatives to it do we have? Such a study would lead us to the peaks of the vexed and profound tension in man between his particular attachments to family, nation, and religion, and his universal vocation as a human being. I believe that this fundamental tension is evaded by the idea of culture, but we cannot be sure unless we engage its most serious proponents. The result of such a study is uncertain, but it is what we need in order to clean up our dirty little act.

Such foci, central to important public concerns and evoking intense passions, are requisite to a liberal education, if it is to engage the best qualities of heart and mind. Almost all students today are more or less consciously in the grip of the cultural interpretation of society and have real feelings about it. Professor Hancock has criticized me for not concentrating more on the American tradition in teaching American students and leading them to a heightened intellectual awareness of that tradition. I would answer that there are many ways to skin a cat. Truth is one, but the beginning points of the road to it are almost infinite. But I would argue, in addition, that young Americans live more truly in universal abstractions than in their own tradition. Even if they were ultimately to come back to a concentration on that tradition, they would have to begin by thinking through those abstractions such as culture. I have a long experience as a teacher and I keep discovering that such general questions are the ones that appeal most to the students that I, at least, encounter. Many of those students have become distinguished scholars in American things—among others Jeremy Rabkin, Nathan Tarcov, William Galston, David Epstein, and Thomas Pangle. And I would end this apology by saying that even though our particular attachments to this country are very important, the universal questions are the ones that ultimately concern us most. In this country we have the rare, or even unique, advantage that our legislators recognized this and unabashedly referred us back to such "great civilians" as Montesquieu, who happened to be French.

A final word regarding the place of a great university among religious believers. The contemporary study of classic books by believers is akin to such study by thinkers like al-Farabi, who was attached to the Koran, and Maimonides, who was attached to the Torah. Their faith was made profounder by facing all that the world can offer rather than closing off the minds of the faithful. Such study both perfects an important human faculty that one would not want to leave uncultivated and it helps us to reflect on our pasts and plan our futures. It especially helps us to cut through the nonsense of the ephemeral contemporary, particularly when it is so theory-drenched as is ours. The study of the human condition through philosophic and literary texts is far from being a guarantee of a person's morality. Common sense and experience teach us all too clearly that there are many decent simple people and many intellectual scoundrels, enough to persuade some people that intellectualism is a temptation and a vice. Moral education is largely a concern of the family, the schools, and the religious community. For persons properly prepared, liberal education can be the perfection of which I have spoken. But I also do not despair of the possibility of a person's discovering, in the company of the great princes of antiquity, as Machiavelli put it, the grandeur of the issues that confront humanity and of those marvelous and liberating writers, and becoming better for it.

Notes

1. Allan Bloom, *The Closing of the American Mind: How Higher Education Has Failed Democracy and Impoverished the Souls of Today's Students* (New York: Simon & Schuster, 1987).

Tocqueville on Liberal Education and American Democracy

Ralph C. Hancock

Allan Bloom was not, strictly speaking, the first victim of political correctness, for surely Bloom himself would concede this title to the unnamed masses of indoctrinated students whose plight he described in *The Closing of the American Mind*.[1] This, of course, was some years before the epithet "politically correct" had been made to stick in the public mind as a description of the left-liberationist establishment in higher education. Bloom himself, for all the penetrating insight and commercial success of his landmark book, had not succeeded in uttering the name (by now tediously familiar) that would make the phenomenon plainly visible to the general public.

Yet it is curious how little eager were subsequent critics of the ascendant academic dogma to acknowledge that it was Bloom who, just a few years before it became fashionable to attack political correctness, had ironically employed the term "openness" to indicate the narrow dogmatism of the academy. Why this reluctance to notice the obvious link between the politically correct and dogmatic openness? How did Bloom earn this silent treatment? E. D. Hirsch, author of *Cultural Literacy,* suggests an answer. At pains to distance himself from Bloom's offensive questioning, Hirsch has pointed out that the difference between himself and the author of *The Closing of the American Mind* is quite simple: Bloom is a "conservative" and, Hirsch presumed (wrongly, in the event), probably a Republican.[2]

In Bloom's defense, it should be noted that he seems to have anticipated the risk of an unseemly association with conservatism and to have taken some pains in his book to avoid it. Thus, as he assesses some of the social consequences of feminism and sexual liberation, he is careful to note that he is "not arguing here that the old family arrangements were good or that we should or could go back to them." And though he can't deny that the old-fashioned parental warning that it is contrary to a girl's self-interest to give her sexual favors too easily "turns out to be the truest and most probing analysis of the current situation," he presents this as a paradox, a strange accident, a lucky strike for the "tiredest and stupidest bromide" of our mothers and fathers. In concluding his rousing attack on rock music, Bloom assures the reader that his concern "is not with the moral effects of this music." If there is some connection between this music and "sex, violence, and drugs," then these are an issue for him only in their effect on "education." If Bloom wants to encourage a more respectful treatment of traditional "prejudices," especially religious prejudices among intellectuals, this is finally because "one has to have the experience of really believing before one can have the thrill of liberation" (132, 134, 79, 43).

Despite such protestations, Bloom's deconstruction of the ideology of openness was probably fated to attract the label "conservative" simply because it touched too raw a nerve. The relatively facile mocking of the "politically correct" targets new enemies of liberalism without putting its substance in question; it unmasks new orthodoxies, but does not question the habitual unorthodoxy of liberalism. But Bloom's examination of openness as "our virtue" raises profound questions concerning the status of openness itself. By observing that what we call "openness" functions (albeit perversely) as a *moral* virtue in our society, that its dominance is not to be explained so much by rational appeal as by social and political interests, Bloom has made himself a heretic. "Every educational system has a moral goal," he writes. "It wants to produce a certain kind of human being" (26). But what could be more subversive than to ask a society that styles itself "open" what kind of character it wants to produce, what way of life is best? Bloom's great merit is to have posed the *question* that shakes the foundation of contemporary liberalism, an offense that now requires the author's exile from the company of respectable intellectuals.[3]

To mitigate the offense of the question, Bloom suggests an answer in terms calculated to appeal to a liberal society. He presents himself as the champion of openness properly understood, of truly liberal education, for the good of the academy and of society alike. But to give the right answer could not wipe away the sin of having asked the question, if only because the answer is much less clear in Bloom's presentation than the question. More precisely, Bloom's advocacy of the intrinsic goodness of intellectual openness raises deep questions concerning the relation of this goodness to the good of society, of intellectual goods to moral and political goods. Bloom not only derides those we have since learned to call "politically correct," but also questions the reassuring assumption upon which most mocking of the politically correct rests, namely, that the purposes of higher education can be insulated from politics. To say that Bloom does not provide final answers to the important questions he raises would hardly be a fair criticism. My complaint, a complaint that will emerge from a comparison between Allan Bloom and Alexis de Tocqueville, is rather that Bloom does not take the problem of the moral-political setting of the intellectual life seriously enough, that he does not take responsibility for its seriousness.

Bloom, Ecumenical Philosopher

In his introduction, Bloom identifies the good or true kind of openness as openness to the good, "the virtue that permitted us to seek the good by using reason," a serious interest in knowing "what is good for me, what will make me happy" (37, 38, 41). The ancient Greek philosophers were the first men we know to represent this openness, and thus also the first to articulate the tension between such rational pursuit of the good and the necessary closedness of society (37–38). For each political community, this closedness takes the form of laws and beliefs necessary to the life of that community. These authoritative opinions not only hold the community together but shield the individual from the prospect of his own extinction, for "the most powerful passion of most men is fear of death" (277). Only the rare philosopher, according to Bloom, can rise above this passion; most men must spend their lives hiding from their own awareness of the fragile and fleeting existence of all that is dear to them: their own lives, their children, their city. Society is fundamentally constituted by our inclination to assist one another in generating and preserving illusions against this awareness.

This is a grim picture. But Bloom is cheerful, or at least serene, for the consolations of philosophy are ready at hand. As he surveys the nothingness that must overwhelm all human goods, the philosopher is "compensated" by "the intense pleasure accompanying insight" (377). Those of us whose attention remains fixed on the grim spectacle of the human condition must wonder indeed at the intensity of such an accompanying and compensating pleasure. Although Bloom cannot have been expected to convey such a pleasure in some descriptive formula accessible to every reader, his apparent lack of interest in the question of the ground and character of the good of philosophers is remarkable. Does he mean to refer us to a Platonic teaching according to which the purest and most self-sufficient pleasure accompanies the intellectual apprehension of that Good that is the ground of all knowledge and of all being? Indeed not, for this would exclude the pleasures of philosophers who believe in no such ground. Bloom wishes to be more ecumenical; he simply takes his stand on the claim that "the fulfillment of humanity is the use of reason," and doesn't care to judge between those for whom reason means "wonder at the apprehension of being" and those who claim no more for reason than "just figuring things out" (292).

To show favoritism toward any particular view of the object of reason would apparently detract from Bloom's intention to praise reason in general; his purpose is to praise the "good old Great Books approach" to education, and it would be counterproductive to begin taking sides in conflicts among their authors (344). In particular, Bloom takes a stand against taking a stand on the good old conflict between ancients and moderns. In fact, he denies that a serious conflict ever existed. "The great modern philosophers were as much philosophers as were the ancients." This is to say that they share the "philosophic experience," that fundamental insight of all philosophers that philosophy is the best way of life (268, 271). Any dispute between philosophers is after all a "dispute within philosophy," and we must not doubt that "there was an agreement among the parties . . . about what philosophy is," namely, a "rational account of the whole, or of nature," and not an account that necessarily associates this whole with some "good" (much less with some god), but that may unfold simply "for curiosity's sake" (264, 270).

The only important difference between Plato and Machiavelli, according to Bloom, was a difference of political and rhetorical strategy: "philosophers switched parties from the aristocratic to the democratic" (288). Whereas the ancients endeavored to carve out a modest social space among the ruling class of nonphilosophers by speaking the language of edification, the modern philosophers propose actually to rule society (albeit indirectly) by committing themselves to the service of the common, bodily needs of the common man. Whereas the ancients flattered the noble pretention to transcend death, the moderns harness their energies to the universal interest in putting death off as long as possible. Thus the rhetoric of the "Good" and of the "Soul" is replaced by that of individual self-preservation and of technological science— Bacon's "mastery and possession of nature for the relief of man's estate."

But only the rhetoric has changed. Neither the ancient pursuit of the good of the soul nor the humanitarian benevolence of the moderns would appear to have any standing at the core of the perennial philosophic experience, for "the philosophers in their academies have entirely different ends than the rest of mankind. The vision of the harmony of theory and practice is only apparent" (291). What we take to be the moral and political beliefs of philosophers are only their moral and political teachings. In fact, they have no moral or political beliefs, for their concerns have nothing in common with the illusions by which most people live.

Indeed, it is hard to see what teachings of the philosophers are to be taken as philosophical and not simply rhetorical and political. In order to praise all philosophers equally, Bloom is driven to reduce philosophical differences to nothing. Although he identifies philosophy with the attempt to know nature, or to give a rational account of the whole, he is not interested in the substance of Aristotle's teleological account of the whole, or in Descartes's mechanistic theory, for these accounts cannot be separated from the moral-political intentions of their authors. If every teaching that attempts to connect the goodness of the human mind with some purpose outside it (whether divine or bodily) is discounted as merely rhetorical, then nothing is left at the core of philosophy but its exemption from the illusions of ordinary people. In order to avoid intraphilosophical contention, the authors of Bloom's Great Books will have to make do, for a positive purpose, with sheer "liberation" from common beliefs. It thus appears that the only truth philosophers can hold is a truth they can all share: "the truth about death" (285).

Having exposed both the ancient and the modern—the aristocratic and the democratic—strategies for defending the life of the mind in a world obsessed with the life of the body, where can Bloom turn for rhetorical resources in defense of liberal education today? Oddly, if perhaps inevitably, he turns to these very strategies, employing now the one, now the other, as the occasion seems to demand. The modern strategy no doubt deserves a certain primacy, since it is the modern university that must be defended. "The best of the modern regimes—liberal democracy—is *entirely* [the] product" of the modern strategy, that is, of the Enlightenment. And "the academies and universities are the core of liberal democracy, its foundation, the repository of its animating principles. . . ." From this point of view, our continued security and prosperity depend upon the fundamentally technological reason embodied in the university for "keeping the machinery of the regime in motion" (259). But elsewhere Bloom seems about to fall back on a more old-fashioned, edifying defense of the academy. He seems to regret what he sees as the passing of an American tradition in which students came to the university informed by the "unity, grandeur, and attendant folklore of the founding heritage," including the Bible, the Declaration of Independence, and a reverence for national heroes and for the Constitution (54–55). He even goes as far as to say that "a life based on the

Book is closer to the truth" than one based upon relativism, and that "a vision of a moral cosmos" is necessary to serious education (60).

But Bloom's account of the unity of philosophy, as an attempt to show respect to both ancient and modern strategies, in fact makes both impossible. The modern, scientific view imposed social burdens on reason that eventually crushed it: "Western rationalism has culminated in a rejection of reason," Bloom writes (240). And when he then immediately asks, "is this result necessary?" it is hard to avoid the impression that indeed it is. This rejection is articulated most decisively by Nietzsche, a thinker "of the very highest order," and by his illustrious successor, Heidegger. Bloom does suggest the hopeful possibility that Nietzsche and Heidegger "did not take seriously enough the changes wrought by the modern rationalists and hence the possibility that the Socratic way might have avoided the modern impasse" (310). This suggestion seems intended to fix our hopes on a revival of some form of ancient teleology. But Bloom himself has insisted that these changes were at bottom cosmetic; he points to no serious difference between classical reason and modern rationalism as to the relationship between the way things are and the best way of life. Thus it is hard to see how Bloom himself can escape the "difficult position" of the post-Nietzschean professor he ridicules as "a professional contemplative holding down a prestigious and well-paying job, and who also believes there is nothing to contemplate" (314).

Bloom would like to pick and choose among the advantages of the ancient academy and those of the modern university without accepting any of the attendant obligations; he wants professors to be the heroes of society without being answerable to the needs of society. The universities ought to be "the temple of the regime . . . founded upon reason," that is, upon Enlightenment, and yet one in which "society is ministerial to the university," not the other way around, as the Enlightenment would have it (245). He wishes that philosophers could be as popular as Locke and as lofty as Plato. But in attempting to employ both the ancient and modern rhetorics in favor of education, he makes both impossible.

Bloom's Tocqueville

In a section entitled "Tocqueville on Democratic Intellectual Life," Bloom produces the Frenchman as a witness for his defense of the university as key to the health of democratic society. And there are indeed many points of contact between Bloom's argument and Tocqueville's.

Tocqueville deflates the democratic pretension to openness if anything more brusquely than Bloom, announcing in the second chapter of the second volume of *Democracy in America* that it can never happen that there are no dogmatic beliefs, that is to say, "opinions which men take on trust without discussion" (433).[4] Such beliefs are as necessary from the standpoint of the individual considered singly, he argues, as for society; for as social order implies the authority of some "leading ideas," so the individual must make use every day of many "truths" that his individual reason cannot provide him but that he must accept on trust from another. The democrat who denies any authority above himself is likely, in fact, to be more slavishly confined by the authority of public opinion than men in traditional societies were by the beliefs held by the ruling class. Whereas in traditional societies "truth" always presents itself in the distorting guise of ruling opinion, in modern democracies the very idea of truth risks being overwhelmed by the naked power of the society as a whole, that is, of the majority. This much of Tocqueville's argument seems to support Bloom's account of the "openness to closedness" of contemporary liberalism. And Tocqueville indeed goes on to recommend the cultivation of the theoretical life as a counterweight to the utilitarian drift of democratic thought. Since every tendency of American democracy leads toward an emphasis on the "practical application" or the "industrial side" of science, "nowadays the need is to keep men interested in theory," that is, in "pure science," in an "ardent, proud, disinterested love of truth," or knowledge only remotely connected, if at all, with what is useful to the body (461).

One immediately encounters important difficulties, however, in aligning Bloom's diagnosis of American democracy with Tocqueville's. As soon as one asks how this "intellectual weakness" of democracy figures in an overall analysis of the moral and political health of America, Tocqueville's path diverges significantly from Bloom's. Bloom seeks support in Tocqueville for his idea that the university is the vital core—the seat of the animating principles—of modern democracy. By maintaining the permanent questions front and center, especially in the form of the Great Books, Bloom argues, the university serves the essential purpose of curing or preventing a democratic blindness to superiority. It is thus the university that must play the decisive role in countering the leveling, confining, homogenizing power of democracy. Now it would perhaps be facile to observe that the university could not have been central to Tocqueville's analysis for the simple reason that there were no universities in Tocqueville's America. In fairness to Bloom, though, one must grant that there is much in Tocqueville's account of the life of the mind in America that may shed light on questions surrounding contemporary higher education. Still, it will be obvious to any reader of *Democracy in America* that Bloom's reading of Tocqueville as champion of a Great Books university education is very selective. Of course, Bloom is entitled, in a book on higher education, to select those arguments of Tocqueville's that bear most directly on the subject. But Bloom has written on higher education *as* the heart and soul of liberal democracy, and it is not clear that Tocqueville can be made an ally in this project.

It is notable, first of all, that his use of Tocqueville pulls Bloom's generally nonpartisan defense of the Great Books, both ancient and modern, in a decidedly aristocratic direction. We now learn that "the mere announcement of the rule of reason does not create the conditions for the full exercise of rationality." These conditions include a certain economy of the soul in which the passions are considered servants of reason, an economy affirmed by "a nobler, philosophic interpretation of reason" at home in "older, more traditional orders" and denied by Hobbes, whose view that reason is a "handmaiden of the passions" contributed to the development of the modern democratic idea (251). The perfect insulation of the enduring core of philosophy from any modification by its political strategy, ancient or modern, seems here to subside in favor of an inner connection between traditional virtues of character and the insight of philosophers. Thus, although Bloom continues to insist that "the lover of beautiful and useless things is far from being a philosopher—at least as far of the lover of the useful," (250) he allows that piety or "a respect for the contemplative life, understood as contemplation of God and the peak of devotion" is an *image* of philosophy, albeit also a distortion. These traditional images of higher things "preserve the order of the cosmos and of the soul from which philosophy begins" (251). And thus it appears that philosophy cannot be reduced to the sheer ability to digest the truth about death or to the mere exercise of curiosity in "figuring things out"; in its *beginnings,* at least, philosophy is bound up with a teleological view of nature, that is, a view of the order of the whole that has a place for the order of the human soul.

This broadly aristocratic defense of the life of the mind makes much more sense in Tocqueville's context than in Bloom's. For Tocqueville makes no pretense of avoiding partisanship as to the essential point dividing traditional from modern-democratic ideas. To be sure, he is as sensible as Bloom of the necessary failure of any particular traditional or aristocratic view of man and the world to adequately grasp the dignity of humanity. The aristocrat's view of natural perfection is always conditioned by his own distinctive ruling characteristics; the aristocratic mind peoples its cosmos with gods, heroes, or angels representing the qualities it honors most (II.i.17; II.iii.18). It is thus "confined to the particular." A people who live by courage live for courage in a world ruled by courageous gods; for the aristocrat, valor is virtue, and other human virtues must align themselves with this or lack honor altogether. But a devotion to narrow and exotic virtues is not the fate that inspires in Tocqueville a "religious dread" as he contemplates the possible future of modern societies. The danger is rather that the democratic (and ultimately, Christian) tendency toward universalization will dissolve traditional notions of honor altogether and reduce humanity to its common bodily needs (627, 632).

Tocqueville, Partisan of Human Dignity

Tocqueville's disposition toward what one might call the Great Ideas that articulate and contribute to this materialistic universalism hardly resembles Bloom's ecumenical praise of the theoretical life. In his introduction he throws down the gauntlet to the self-styled "champions of modern civilization . . . whose object is to make men materialists, to find out what is useful without concern for justice, to have science quite without belief and prosperity without virtue" (17). Seven hundred pages later, in a concluding reflection on the prospects for a decent democratic future, he inserts a final warning against those "false and cowardly doctrines which can only produce feeble men and pusillanimous nations" (705). In between he has targeted those democratic historians who deny the efficacy of individual virtue in the face of the vast general causes by which they want to explain everything (I.i.20), and he has warned against the "pantheism" that eventually issues from the modern democratic concept of unity, according to which "an immense Being . . . alone remains eternal in the midst of the continual flux and transformation of all that composes Him" (451–52). And in Tocqueville's referring to such philosophical systems, his tone does not at all suggest a detached intellectual contemplation. Rather than recommending ecumenically that we renew our souls and our polities by returning respectfully to the Great Books that made us, Tocqueville urges *against* such Great Ideas as materialism, saying that "we need to raise men's souls, not to complete their prostration" (496); he sounds a virtual call to battle against modern pantheism: "All those who still appreciate the true nature of man's greatness should combine in the struggle against it" (452).

Given the soullessness of such modern ideas, Tocqueville does not regard it as bad news that Americans have not fully mastered them, or been mastered by them. It is in fact much to the Americans' credit that they are less enamored of general ideas than the democratic mind in France. To be sure, when Americans wax philosophical one finds them

repeating the formulas of European rationalism, the formulas of an individualism and naturalism ultimately traceable to the philosophy of Descartes. But if Americans excel in the practice of individualism it is
precisely because they are not consistently faithful to its skeptical and
materialistic theory. If by their words Americans do more honor to their
philosophy than to themselves—they honor a philosophy of self-interest
that cannot do honor to human nature (II.ii.8)—then in their deeds
Americans exhibit a certain inarticulate virtue and a love of liberty that
to some degree transcends a concern for private self-interest (527, 541).
Thus Tocqueville clearly prefers the practice of American democracy to
its theory, and his praise of American Enlightenment has quite different
implications from Bloom's account. Whereas Bloom sees America, and
liberal democracy in general, as "entirely [the] product" (259) of the
materialistic philosophy of the Enlightenment, Tocqueville finds Americans indeed to be enlightened, but in the right way, and one might almost say, not too much. A lack of taste for pure theory may prevent
Americans from reaching the greatest heights of the human soul, but it
also saves them from rationalizing the soul away altogether. What lifts
the American soul is not any explicit interest in theory but, especially,
the practical experience of self-government. "True enlightenment is in
the main born of experience, and if the Americans had not gradually
grown accustomed to rule themselves, their literary attainments would
not now help them much toward success" (304). To the degree that
Americans depend for their moral and political health upon ideas reaching beyond the practical sphere, these are provided by a mild and generalized form of Christianity that reigns nearly uncontested. The roots of
American political and social order are therefore not to be sought ultimately in any modern intellectual movement, but in a practical experience that has embedded a certain aristocratic concern for particulars in
the otherwise abstract democratic mind, a living tradition of moral self-
government that has attached itself to, but cannot finally be identified
with, the rhetoric of enlightened democracy. It is this tradition that con-
nects Americans with "eighteen centuries of labor and experience" and
leads Tocqueville to argue that America succeeds as the first new nation
precisely because it has inherited so much that is old: "in the United
States, society had no infancy, being born adult" (303).

Aristocratic virtue and hierarchy, or democratic equality and progress—Bloom and Tocqueville agree that these are two perennial springs
of thought from which human beings must draw in constituting their
moral and political lives. They also agree that neither style is adequate
to the truth. The profound difference between them might be reduced
to the following: whereas Bloom believes philosophers can learn nothing of intrinsic interest from either, Tocqueville believes that both re-

flect a part of the truth concerning human dignity. The aristocrat admires greatness, or elevation and perfection, but he conceives these in a narrow and exclusive way. The democrat extends his view to encompass universal humanity, but in doing so loses the capacity to articulate human greatness. The mind of God must have the capacity to apprehend the worth of each without reducing it to the common needs of all, but the human mind cannot (II.i.3). Still Tocqueville acts and thinks on the conviction that despite these insurmountable difficulties, human dignity, the dignity reflected, however imperfectly, in both the aristocratic and the democratic mind, is real, and not merely, as Bloom would have it, an illusion projected to distract attention from our individual mortality.

Bloom attempts to defend the dignity of theory as entirely divorced from the (specious) dignity of practice. He believes that philosophy can and must stand alone, uncontaminated by the fundamentally irrational concerns of morality and politics. And Tocqueville believes no more than Bloom that theory and practice can or ought to be unified, that the demands of the mind can ever be made to match the demands of society. This would require a universally demonstrable theory of practice, a science of human dignity. But, unlike Bloom, Tocqueville understands that the unavailability of a science of human dignity, of a final and complete teleology of the soul, implies the ongoing interdependence of theory and practice, of philosophy and morality. If respect for the dignity of theory, that is, the good kind of openness defended by both Tocqueville and Bloom, saves the citizen from moral fanaticism and from materialistic vulgarity, so the dignity of theory depends in turn on a certain openness to practical greatness. This is to say that the "order of the cosmos and the soul from which," according to Bloom, "philosophy begins" is also where, in a sense, according to Tocqueville's implicit teaching, philosophy always ends, or rather keeps on beginning. The "hierarchy of words," however conditioned by the ruling interests of a given society, corresponds in some imperfect way to a natural hierarchy of goods, to "the very nature of things" (481). If the practical man ought to respect the dignity of theory, so the theoretical man can only orient himself by practical greatness, even as he conceives the never-completed project of transcending it. The author of *Democracy in America* never presumes to leave behind the practical realm because he knows that the dignity of theory cannot be defended without defending the dignity of practice.

American Liberty and Liberal Education

Let me now collect some of the implications for liberal education in America of this attempt to read Bloom's *Closing of the American Mind* in the light of Tocqueville's *Democracy in America*. Bloom has put all American educators and indeed all thoughtful Americans in his debt by boldly—and on the basis of an intimate acquaintance with the philosophic tradition—laying bare the easygoing nihilism that threatens not only our polity but our souls. But in responding to this threat Bloom seems to ask at once too much and too little from the university. He looks to the university to form and sustain the moral and spiritual core of American society, but he does not accept the obligation to exhibit a connection between the university's pursuit of knowledge, and society's pursuit of not only prosperity but also of dignity and happiness. In fact, he denies that any intrinsic connection between the highest reaches of the university and the ordinary moral and spiritual concerns of citizens is possible.

Our reading of Tocqueville would suggest, on the other hand, that the Great Books cannot be defended without defending some greatness beyond these books. This does not mean that the big questions must be taught with corresponding big answers dogmatically attached. But without a serious, respectful concern for the possibilities embodied in the answers—a sharing of the common human interest in the Good, the True, and the Beautiful—Bloom's openness to the Good becomes a mere openness to openness, just a slightly more refined or esoteric version of the specious openness he derides. If the critical examination of such problems, or philosophy, is understood as the pinnacle of liberal education, then we must not sever the ties that link it with moral, political, and indeed religious education.

I will take the argument a step further: the defense of the Great Books in *American* education depends on the defense of something great in America—or, shall I say, it depends on a certain disposition to acknowledge and defend some common goods as images of a certain greatness, as well as to acknowledge that they are only images. Rightly understood, the education this formula recommends is as far from uncritical patriotism as it is from facile debunking. It certainly does not refer in the main to American power or American prosperity. It follows from the idea that the greatest questions of philosophy begin with and never altogether leave behind the prephilosophic interest in the Good, or in the best way of life, coupled with the idea that every particular society must conceive these questions in terms initially defined by its own partial and thus partisan answers, its own conception of what Tocqueville calls human dignity. Thus the path for Americans to the big questions considered in the Great Books would begin with distinctively American notions of human greatness, that is, notions framed largely in the language of liberty and equality. This path would pass through the sources of this language in the moral-political tradition of American constitutionalism. It would explore the mingling in this tradition of biblically inspired notions of justice and equality with the rights of self-government as proclaimed in the Declaration of Independence, a mingling nowhere so nobly and profoundly effected as in the great speeches of Abraham Lincoln. Unlike Allan Bloom, who acknowledges the existence of this tradition only to ignore it (apparently on the assumption that it is dead), this liberal education would not assume that for Americans the Great Theories of the Enlightenment are a richer source of openness to human dignity than the speeches and writings, closer to practice, in which Americans have articulated their way of life. Neither would it assume that to make a more careful distinction between classical virtue and modern liberty than the Founders did would necessarily lead to a more profound or accurate view of the American character or polity.

Perhaps the most important thing to be learned from this review of Bloom's defense of liberal education in the light of Tocqueville's account of American liberty is that we cannot expect universities by themselves to salvage what may remain of the health of democracy. At best the academy might learn, without abandoning reason's critical function, to respect and perhaps indirectly to nurture whatever moral and spiritual resources—resources not derived from anything new in the Enlightenment—may still be present in America, even if Bloom does not find much evidence of such resources among his students. More realistically, perhaps the most we can hope from the progeny of the Enlightenment is that they might be persuaded to limit their attacks on these resources.

Notes

1. Allan Bloom, *The Closing of the American Mind* (New York: Simon & Schuster, 1987). Further references to Bloom's book will be indicated by parenthetical page numbers.

2. E. D. Hirsch's *Cultural Literacy* (Boston: Houghton Mifflin, 1987) defended the idea that a shared body of knowledge is essential to education; it had the mixed fortune of playing moon to Allan Bloom's sun. Subsequently, Hirsch has been at pains to demonstrate that his light was not borrowed, or at least not from that source. Roger Kimball, in *Tenured Radicals* (New York: Harper & Row, 1990), 172–76 reports that Hirsch, participating in a panel discussion at Williams College in 1989, seized the occasion to draw the line clearly between himself and Bloom. Though Hirsch himself might plausibly be accused of the youthful indiscretion of publishing a book in 1967 that attacked "radical historicism" and certain German forerunners of the presently fashionable French theories of linguistic indeterminacy—*Validity in Interpretation*

(New Haven: Yale University Press)—he assured his audience that he had the good taste to keep his distance from such company as those called the "Killer B's"—Bloom and Reagan's former secretary of education, William Bennett.

3. Postmodernists, too, attack the modern faith. But they generally know enough to do it in a way that exploits and thus finally reinforces that faith. What multiculturalist takes any nonmodern culture seriously as a way of life? Non-Western beads and braids are one thing, but who is going to ask a patriarch's permission to marry?—if indeed one chooses the (contingent) "commitment" of marriage.

4. Parenthetical page numbers for Tocqueville refer to J. P. Mayer edition (Garden City, N.Y.: Doubleday, 1966). Volume, part, and chapter will be indicated thus: I.i.3.

5

Conservatism, Liberalism, and the Curriculum: Notes on an American Dilemma

Stanley Rosen

To those of us for whom the modern epoch is a process of continuous revolutions, the ongoing debate in the American academy concerning the nature of a sound curriculum in the humanities is no surprise. We are entitled furthermore to expect that the warriors currently engaged in this latest version of the "battle of the books" understand themselves in the light of the quarrel between the ancients and the moderns. This expectation is compromised by the fact that the current quarrel has degenerated into a debate between self-styled "liberals" and "conservatives," neither of whom seem to have a firm grip on the significance of their preferred appellation.

Leo Strauss, today a hero of the self-styled conservatives, used to regularly remind his students that the senses of the terms "liberal" and "conservative" have undergone an inversion during the past two-hundred-odd years. Conservatism was once a doctrine rooted in the affirmation of a strong central government, including the regulation of the economy as well as of political, religious, and philosophical doctrine or what is today called "ideology." Liberals, on the contrary, rebelled against the subordination of theory to public dogma, as well as against a strong central government and a controlled economy.

If it is fair to say that conservatism is characterized decisively by the drawing of a distinction between the few and the many as guaranteed by nature, together with the desire to preserve the ancestral ways of doing and speaking, and therefore of thinking, then it is obvious that a conservative regime must have extensive control over the lives, both private and public, of its citizens. Conversely, if liberalism is the party of freedom, not simply for the state but for the individual as well, and if further it rejects the distinction between the few and the many or determines it to have been established by custom rather than by nature, then adherence to the ways of the ancestors makes no sense, and the best government must be one that interferes as little as possible with the speeches and deeds of its citizens, allowing them to face their spiritual as well as their economic destiny largely on the basis of their own unimpeded efforts.

The confusion underlying the contemporary debate is evident from the fact that liberals today advocate a strong central government and a regulated if not entirely controlled economy, whereas conservatives oppose these steps and favor their opposites. On one crucial point it looks initially as though the old sense of the terms has been preserved. Conservatives continue to defend the ways of the ancestors and the distinction of the few from the many, whereas liberals stand for a reinterpretation of the thought of the founding fathers on the basis of contemporary doctrines and problems, and they firmly reject any natural basis for a distinction between the few and the many.

A closer look, however, shows us that confusion obtains from this standpoint as well. Liberals are required by the force of their moral and political commitments to favor doctrines, and therefore actions, that sustain those commitments, which tend to replace the belief in natural standards favored by conservatives. At the level of action, the resources of the state are invoked to ensure the triumph of liberalist doctrine, which is thereby converted into a new interpretation of the teaching of the founding fathers, and so into a blueprint for the future. Custom indeed becomes second nature. The appearance of diversity and a new appreciation of multiculturalism is thus an easily penetrated disguise for the triumph of egalitarian values. Even if a liberal curriculum included works by Plato, Aristotle, and Saint Thomas, not to mention Chateaubriand, Leopardi, and Nietzsche, they would be (or have been) either vitiated by liberal hermeneutics or presented as specimens of fascism.

The liberal cannot attend to the voice of Plato's *Republic* without hearing there contemporary melodies of women's liberation and the democratic concern of Socrates for the welfare of all his interlocutors. To mention only the crucial point, liberation and welfare are intelligible in Plato only in terms of the natural distinction between the few and the many. Recognition that women may be philosophers has nothing to do with egalitarianism, or even with the endorsement of the abolition of differences between male and female at the political level. It is a recognition of the difference between philosophy and politics, a difference that is not blurred by the ostensible necessity for the rule of philosophers if a just society is to be established.

It would, I suggest, be better if Plato were not read at all, rather than that he be read in a way guaranteed to inculcate the debasement of all intellectual integrity. But the conservatives are not in a position to claim greater consistency on the point under inspection. This is because in the United States, conservatism during the past twenty-odd years has taken on a populist rather than an intellectual cast; the distinction between the few and the many has accordingly, despite the token references to Leo Strauss or the constant vision of William Buckley's haughty features on our television screens, come to be interpreted from the standpoint of the many. The war against unpatriotic relativism, Godlessness, and pornography, as well as the decay of praise for the nuclear family into a dialect of Babbitry, has a much deeper and more pernicious effect than to identify fashionable university professors and other intellectuals and artists as members of a decadent "cultural elite," determined to corrupt the salubrious morals of the silent majority. It degrades the very standards of nobility and high culture that have been traditionally associated with the few in distinction from, and when need be in opposition to, the many.

In a truly conservative society, whether Greek or colonial American, the moral health of the many is understood as a matter of political tactics and rhetoric, weapons that have today been transferred to the liberal arsenal. Contemporary conservatives, on the other hand, even and perhaps especially those who privately read Jane Austen and Henry James, have adopted the rhetoric of the *Lumpenproletariat*. They are therefore not in a strong position to defend western European high culture from the onslaughts of the liberal relativists, egalitarians, and deconstructors, for whom a hierarchy of values constitutes fascism, racism, and sexism. To employ once more a distinction made popular by Strauss, contemporary conservatives, in their zeal to defend the esoteric teaching of the few, have adopted the exoteric doctrines of the many.

This general description has now to be qualified by recognition of some of the peculiarities of the local, that is, American, situation. We need to factor into the general description the differences between America and Europe on the one hand and, perhaps even more crucially, between the America of the founding fathers and that of our own time. These differences are well known and need only be mentioned here. Despite the debts of the founding fathers to thinkers like Locke or even Aristotle, the United States was created largely in opposition to prevailing social and political practices of eighteenth-century Europe. On the other hand, the original republic of citizens of homogeneous racial and ethnic origin, based upon an agricultural economy, buffered by geographical isolation from most of the wars and revolutions of Europe, with the cancer of slavery diagnosed but still more or less dormant, has all but disappeared in the course of history, a history that is further

exacerbated by the explosion of scientific knowledge and technology
that brings us not only Buckley on television but global pollution and
the possibility of nuclear holocaust.

It has to be said that the liberals are right to note the difficulty, perhaps the impossibility, of applying a strict construction of the intentions
of the founding fathers to contemporary social and political problems.
The fundamental problem is plainly not the quarrel between conservatives and liberals, but how to preserve the original Constitution and
its underlying philosophical convictions under almost totally different
circumstances. And all other difficulties to one side, there is something
intrinsically ludicrous about conservatives who defend the ancestral
aristocratism of the republic against vulgar democratic onslaughts with
the mixed rhetoric of a fundamentalist preacher and the Chamber of
Commerce.

On the other hand, the conservatives are right to insist upon the political necessity of what Nietzsche called *Rangordnung,* however inconsis-
tently they articulate and defend their own standards. No liberal society
can survive that is unable to distinguish between freedom and chaos or,
less abstractly expressed, between the defense of its own liberal principles and fascism. Still more precisely, no society can survive that is
unable to distinguish between reverence for its principles and traditions,
and the just repudiation of abuses of those principles and traditions.

The problem, of course, lies in the identification of the principles and
traditions that we are being asked to revere. The intelligent and honorable liberal is convinced that his conservative counterpart is defending a
tradition of interpretation of first principles rather than those principles
themselves, and further, that the interpretation in question is no longer
applicable to radically changed social and political circumstances. The
intelligent and honorable conservative is convinced that the liberal has
no principles, or that those principles have been formed by shame in
the face of abuses of the original principles and traditions, rather than
by pride in those origins and a determination to preserve them against
injustice.

We thus seem to have reached an impasse. It is often wise, when this
happens, to step back from both of the conflicting theses in order to see
whether the problem does not lie in the formulation of the question.
And this, I believe, is precisely what has gone wrong in the contemporary debate about humanistic education. The issue has been formulated
in explicitly political terminology, and it has accordingly been vulgar-
ized, as I have tried to suggest by my remarks concerning the incoherences intrinsic to the use today of terms like "liberal" and "conservative," or their near-synonyms "left wing" and "right wing."

I do not of course wish to deny that there is a connection between education and politics. I do, however, deny that this connection can be properly understood from within the perspective of a political ideology. To say that such-and-such an education will best serve a given set of political objectives is one thing; to ask what it means to be well educated, regardless of the left- or right-leaning tendencies of the regime, is something else again. It is true that in making this claim, I am implicitly denying one thesis that is dear to the hearts of liberals, namely, that all standards of intellectual and artistic excellence are ideological or social. But I do so in the name of the liberal principle of the superiority of freedom to bondage. In my view, no properly educated person of normal intelligence is by nature a slave to some local historical perspective; and the thesis that there is no natural basis upon which to evaluate cultural perspectives simply transforms custom into nature, as I indicated previously. To descend to the banal, what is today called multiculturalism is itself predicated upon the assumption that a heterogeneous society is superior to one that has been fixed by a long-standing and homogeneous culture. This assumption must be defensible on grounds of reason and experience; otherwise it deteriorates into the tyranny of fashion, as accelerated by the inversion of the few into the spokesmen for the many, an inversion more frequently caused by shame and cowardice than by principled argument.

I am, however, also implicitly denying a thesis that is dear to the hearts of conservatives, namely, that culture is somehow synonymous with tradition, and I also deny the contemporary practical application of that thesis, according to which an education rooted firmly in the texts and artistic productions of the ancients is the best safeguard for American democracy. In the first place, there is an equivocation here on the term "democracy." As I have indicated above, the United States is no longer the same country it was in 1800, or for that matter in 1900. This is tacitly recognized by those conservatives who insist upon using the term "republic" rather than "democracy." But the equivocation is more immediately in play in the great social controversy about the separation of the rich from the poor, the transformation of the racial composition of the American population, the low level of education, the vulgarizing effects upon the political process of mass media, and other issues too familiar to require mention.

With respect to these social and political problems, there is no doubt whatsoever that they graphically express the difference between contemporary America and the land of the founding fathers. But can anyone imagine a debate between conservatives and liberals in which the former advocate radical measures designed to return to the landed aristocracy of a relatively homogeneous, slave-owning citizenry, whereas the liberals urge a frank abandonment of the present Constitution in favor of a complete reformulation of the laws and institutions of the country, a reformulation in which science and technology, physical and social engineering, a centrally regulated economy, and in sum, an all-powerful central government will mobilize "the best and the brightest" to resolve the multitude of problems that are destroying the texture of our lives?

This little thought-experiment is useful because it shows us that conservatives are on essential points liberals, whereas liberals are on other essential points conservatives. But this is mere playing with words in comparison with the main point. No such debate is conceivable, except as an exercise in fantasy. And yet, when it comes to discussions of higher education and the university curriculum in humanities, or of the nature of art and its freedom from or responsibility to political exigencies, analogous confusion and oversimplification prevail. At the lowest level of vulgarization, Plato and the Bible are brandished like totems against the rising horde of specialists in feminine epistemology and practitioners of homoerotic art. But even at higher levels, one hears altogether too much of an opposition between the eternal classics on the one hand and radical diversity and creativity on the other. This polarization is often implicit even when the actual discussion takes on a more moderate vocabulary; it is a direct consequence of the politicization of the question of education, and thus of a begging of the question of the relation between education and politics.

My own recommended principle, that education is higher than and prior to political orientation, may sound initially like the plaintive call of an alienated professor for a return to the ivory tower. Nothing could be farther from my mind. Political arrangements, however, are not an end in themselves; their purpose is to make possible the flourishing of free, just, and cultivated spirits, as the most articulate liberals and conservatives would surely agree. A flourishing free market that produces a nation of Babbits is an obscenity, but so too is a regulated market if it subordinates the productions of the spirit to the efficient functioning of its inner mechanisms. To say this in another way, a well-fed, well-clothed, and healthy populace is a desideratum, even a necessary political goal. But for those who engage in philosophical discussion of liberal education, it cannot and must not be an end in itself, since in itself, it is entirely compatible with a nation of robots.

Professional politicians must address themselves to the immediate exigencies of the actual political situation. But the angle from which they make this approach to the situation will be determined ultimately by the principles that define a nation's conception of human being. Those of us who are educators rather than politicians are in dereliction of our duty if we do not address ourselves primarily to those principles.

It would be extraordinarily useful if we could all take the first step of dropping the vocabulary of contemporary political ideology. Righteous indignation may or may not be a useful emotion for the deity, but in human beings it is a hindrance to rational reflection and clear analysis.

As a first step toward a national symposium on the question of who we are and whom we wish to be, I suggest that conservatives and liberals each make one concession to the other side. Conservatives should admit that tradition is continuously informed and modified by spontaneous creativity, and so that the quarrel between the ancients and the moderns is pursued exclusively by moderns; as Bacon and others put it, it is we who are the ancients. This can also be put somewhat more abstractly: If there is such a thing as human nature independent of historical modification, then that nature must be in principle as accessible in the deeds and speeches of the twenty-first-century Americans as it was in the deeds and speeches of the ancient Athenians. Differently stated, contemporary deeds and speeches may possibly be corrupt in comparison with those of the ancients, but if so, we perceive this corruption by our capacity to penetrate their deficiencies; and this is a capacity of reflection upon human existence, not to be derived from the close inspection of texts. For how else could we recognize the superior virtue of the ancients? No one can discover human nature by reading a book; on the contrary, books are intelligible only to those who understand human nature.

As for the liberals, I ask them to look into their own hearts, or if this is too metaphysical, into their mirrors, where they will see the hypocrisy, but even worse, the self-destructive consequences of public adherence to intellectual, artistic, and more generally, cultural relativism. One of the oldest and wisest principles of civilized humanity is that equality in the eyes of God, or before the law, is different from and compatible with an unequal level of spiritual production. It is not necessary for liberals to accept the conservative formulation of the difference by nature between the few and the many. I am asking them simply to admit that the many as well as the few are capable of producing and enjoying, each in their own way, a high culture that expresses the creativity but also the dignity of the human spirit.

Let me be very precise on this point: it is not enough for liberals to say that their recommended reading lists include Plato and Aristotle as well as multiculturalist theorists of comprehensive liberation. My point has nothing to do with reading lists; I am recommending concessions that lead to careful reflection on the nature of human being, not to the construction of book lists for humanities courses in prestigious universities. I certainly am not recommending a proliferation of seminars in academic philosophy. We require no further training in the metaphysics of modality, artificial intelligence, or the radical abyss from which Being presents itself as absent.

I am not, in short, recommending a turn away from the political arena to the domain of the academic specialists. The latter is precisely the wrong domain within which to reflect upon our common humanity. On the contrary, I believe that the question is being debated in so many different circles, of so heterogeneous a composition, as to produce what is in principle the sound and only possible forum for an issue of this sort: a kind of intellectual or discursive simulacrum of the public conversation that, for better or worse, determines a national consensus on issues of social and political urgency. My criticism is not at all of the personnel engaged in the discussion of liberal education; it is of the pervasive tendency for this discussion to be carried out in the vocabulary of political ideology.

Some will say that this vocabulary is the inevitable consequence of the inseparability of theory from practice; they will simply point to the inseparability of education from public policy, whether in democracies or aristocracies. They will ask me: How else are we to talk about human nature, if not in terms of what constitutes a good life? And how can one live the good life if not in a political community? Must we not say what type of political community is compatible with the good life, and does not the need to say this require us to employ the vocabulary as well as the rhetoric of liberalism and conservatism? Finally, in endorsing a turn away from academic specialists to some sort of public conversation, am I not myself guaranteeing the politicization of the debate?

Let me answer the last question first. My recommendation is not that the universities be silenced but rather that they take their part as one element within the public conversation, and an element that is paid to educate the public, not to flatter it. To educate is to lead out of ignorance, not to wallow in it. As to the other questions, I answer them in the affirmative. The political implications of education are obvious, but it is not obvious that we have to construct our educational curriculum in terms derived from ideological prejudices that are themselves the consequences of decay in both education and political thought. My introductory remarks about the confusions intrinsic to contemporary use of terms like "liberal" and "conservative" were designed to illustrate the politicization of the discussion about education and politics. "Politicization" is here a pejorative term. It is intended to apply both to demands that works by the ancient Greek thinkers be replaced by "relevant" texts and to claims that the salvation of American democracy depends upon the immersion of American students in "the classics" of our tradition.

Unfortunately for us, we are faced today with two separate questions:

(1) What does it mean to be a genuinely educated person? (2) How are we to preserve democracy in America? If the first question is subordinated to the second, then the answer we give to it depends upon an antecedent resolution of the question: What is American democracy? Is it, for example, the generalized views of the founding fathers, and their application to the Constitution, as those views were originally intended, and regardless of ensuing social and political changes? Or is the sense of American democracy itself a historical entity that evolves with time, thereby making necessary a constant reinterpretation of the Constitution, laws, customs, and institutions of our country?

In my opinion, both of these claims are correct, but this is why neither of them, when taken separately, can ever be satisfied except by a destruction of the country as it now exists. Stated as bluntly as possible, we are never going to resolve our political problems; survival must be understood as the constant adjudication of our rival claims. The intelligent and reflective citizen will be a conservative today and a liberal tomorrow, and for those who regard this as unprincipled, I remind them that Saint Paul identified himself as a pagan to the pagans and a Jew to the Jews; these distinctions, like that between master and slave or man and woman, are to be abolished only at the end of history, and so in paradise, but not on earth. The attempt to enforce the overcoming of distinctions in the city of man leads instead, as our immediate experience already suggests, to the radicalization of differences, or to a chaos that is accessible to tyranny from every direction.

It could be objected to what I have just said that nothing is accomplished by internalizing the conflict between liberal and conservative within the individual thinker, but I am not referring to a mere internalization of a polarized difference. My point is that neither eternal values nor radical creativity are well served by narrow-mindedness and inflexibility. And the following distinction is crucial: given the difference between theory and practice, it may under certain circumstances be the best defense of eternal values to support radical creativity. Even the vapid expression "multiculturalism" cannot be given any defensible content without some distinction between "cultured" and "uncultured." But if the conservative championship of tradition is to be our guide, then the result is a vindication of all cultural or ethnic traditions, however base; all that counts is that they are our own traditions.

It is difficult to separate the question of liberal education from the debate between what I will call the democratic and republican interpretations of the American polity; difficult, but no more impossible than to discuss one's religious doctrines apart from the quarrel between liberals and conservatives. Whether one ought to be a liberal or a conservative is a consequence of one's philosophical or religious views, not their

determining condition. The political situation in the United States, furthermore, is today in such turmoil, and the texture of social life so
rapidly deteriorating, that we are effectively in a state of national debate
that approximates to a constitutional convention. I do not think that the
term "revolution" is inappropriate to a description of the contemporary
intellectual and spiritual mood of the country. This is a time of extreme
danger, but as such, it allows and indeed requires us to raise extreme
questions.

Reference to a revolution may strike some readers as too extreme; I
therefore interpolate a reminder that the modern epoch is a state of
continuous revolution. But this fact should not lull us into a sense of
false security. It is easy enough to say that *plus ça change, plus c'est la
même chose,* but that does nothing to gain control over our own moment
in the revolutionary sun. It is never more than superficially plausible to
recommend a politics of "steady as she goes." The question before us,
at least as it is formulated by self-styled conservatives and liberals, is
whether we are to go backward or forward. I believe that the liberals
are right to insist that we cannot go backward; this was understood by
the most intelligent conservative of the past two hundred years, Nietzsche, who whispers into the ear of the conservative that man is not a
crab.

In the same epigram, Nietzsche shifts from a whisper to a shout:
"forward into chaos." This is the juncture point between the liberal and
the conservative denunciation of nineteenth-century bourgeois civilization; it also explains why Nietzsche is admired by the radicals of the
left as well as by the mandarins of the right. And this in turn helps us
to understand why our contemporary conservatives as well as our liberals are either explicit or tacit revolutionaries. In a time of exacerbated
sensibilities, moderation seems like spiritual paralysis. Otherwise put,
moderation can be made palatable only when it is adorned with the
habiliments of extremism.

As things stand today, the conservatives have managed to hold their
own against the liberal tide only by adopting the rhetoric of populism,
as I noted earlier. This is a frank admission that an intellectually aristocratic advocacy of conservatism is impotent in contemporary America,
except as a kind of music-hall satire on late-night television. What the
conservatives have failed to understand is that a radical and candid defense of the highest intellectual, artistic, and religious accomplishments
can be made effective in a democracy if, and only if, it adopts the
rhetoric of liberalism in a manner still more radical than that of the
liberals themselves.

Nor is this simply a matter of political tactics. The adulation of the
classics is already a sign of decadence; if this is too cryptically stated,

my point is that freedom of thought and expression, experimentation in art, and even new prophets in religion are also necessary to the health and fecundity of the human spirit. I understand very well that populist democracies are not matrices of high culture, and I am aware of the virtual tautology that aristocratic spiritual production is a function of a spiritually aristocratic society. But the high standards of Elizabethan poetry, for example, cannot be met in twenty-first-century America by instituting a monarchy, and neither can it be reproduced by training our children to speak in the dialect of Elizabethan English. We do not become aristocrats by imitating aristocrats; instead, we are transformed into servants of the highborn.

It is equally true that we will not produce a nation of creative individuals by disseminating the doctrines of John Dewey through our secondary-school systems, nor is philosophy raised to the level of *philosophia perennis* by turning it over to the centurions of multiculturalism, alternative lifestyles, and other practitioners of what may accurately be designated as snobbist populism. But the only way in which to break the grip of the snobbist populists is by being more radical, more articulate, and more open to genuine creativity and intellectual profundity than they are. In order to transform a revolution, one must be revolutionary, not moderate. The moderates are left lying by the wayside as the forces of history advance over their corpses.

Conservatives and liberals alike, taking them at their best, both agree that American education requires drastic improvement. This is not a political thesis—by which I mean that it is not peculiar to some ideological camp, whether on the left or the right of the political spectrum. The disagreement concerning the content of an improved education cannot be sustained, in my opinion, whether by the left or the right, against the universal attraction of the truth. To those who smile at what they take to be the naivete of this remark, I reply that this attraction is never destroyed, but only rendered temporarily inaccessible, by the brutality of stupidity. The rhetoric of populism itself, whether in its conservative or liberal dialect, is an imitation of the truth, not an outright lie. No doubt imitations are politically more powerful than originals, but so long as we are capable of producing originals we can at least regulate, however indirectly, the quality of the imitations: this is the greatest and perhaps the only political weapon of the few against the many.

I am then myself less interested initially in the titles of the books that constitute the curriculum of a liberal or humanistic education (and let me note parenthetically that I have been forced for practical reasons to oversimplify this problem by separating it from the question of what constitutes a scientific education) than in the spirit within which such lists are to be compiled. Even the right list (assuming such an entity), if taught in the wrong spirit, accomplishes nothing. I have been contending that the central question is one of human nature, not political orientation. But my argument is neither conservative nor liberal, in the popular sense that is today given to these terms; not conservative, because I regard human nature as open rather than closed, and not liberal, because I deny that the structure of openness is an artifact of society.

Everything that I have said in this essay is only the surface of a deeper problem that constitutes the root of human existence. The problem can be formulated in an introductory manner as follows: Human existence is distinguished from the mode of being of animals on the one hand and machines (such as computers) on the other because it is by its nature an attempted unification of theory and practice. But this attempted unification is itself a process, not a structure. There is, for example, no analogy between a human being and a computer because the ostensible analogy in us to a program, the genetic code, is intrinsically spontaneous or self-revising. We are free to revise the rules of the code, and we are now in the process of so doing.

On the other hand, as an open process, the reciprocal activity between theory and practice is also a disjunction or disunity; to borrow an expression from Hegel, human being is a *zerrissene Harmonie,* a disrupted harmony. Practice is partially independent of theory, but the converse is also true. Theory can transpire only independently of practice; otherwise, it deteriorates into ideology, that is, into routine. Hegel attempted to close the gap between the two dimensions of this disrupted harmony by grasping the pattern of the motion intrinsic to the process of their interaction. In so doing, however, he begged the question by assuming a conceptual structure of which the interaction is a fulfillment or closure. And this in turn forced him to suppress in advance the diremption in spiritual activity, which he interprets as an illusion or appearance. For this reason, Hegel's detailed interpretations of the history of the human spirit in all its fundamental domains reads like ideology, despite its frequent conceptual brilliance. There is an "official" explanation of every fundamental phenomenon.

The radical nature of Hegel's speculative logic is thus the surface of a deeper conservatism that requires everything to be intelligible, and this in turn leads to the preposterous thesis that art, religion, and philosophy, and therefore history in its function as manifestation of the spirit or absolute, are not only completed, but that they exhibit the necessary unfolding of his own speculative comprehension of totality, which with respect to the future is not wisdom but ideology. This is not the place to attempt a detailed refutation of Hegel; I wanted only to borrow his beautiful description of human spiritual activity while dissociating it from his systematic teaching.

We have to face the fact that the impossibility of resolving the diremption between theory and practice, although it is the very essence of our freedom, is at the same time the very real possibility of imminent dissolution. The threat of nihilism does not lie outside us but is a moment in the pulse-beat of our existence. Conservatism is thus a natural response to the recognition of this inner diremption; unfortunately, as soon as conservatism hardens into dogma, the result is an occlusion or a fatal decrease in the rate of our pulse-beat. Conversely, liberalism is a natural response to the challenge of diremption, which it understands as an open horizon; when liberalism is transformed from a response into a dogma, the result is an equally fatal increase in our pulse-beat.

If I were inclined to refer to human existence as dialectical, it would be in the sense just described: The terms of our existence are such that we are in danger of being destroyed by everything that we ourselves produce; if we cease to produce, however, we cease to exist, or deteriorate into sentient machines. I understand very well that language of this sort is anathema to the hard-headed representatives of empiricism and pragmatism, but there is a difference between good humor and denseness. The sound empiricist or pragmatic approach to the inner restlessness that is the unmistakable sign of the disrupted harmony of our lives is to acknowledge it, as did Locke and Hume, the greatest representatives of the empiricist tradition. Good humor cannot be sustained by bad faith or false consciousness.

In the last several paragraphs, I have moved considerably beyond the stated theme of this essay, but it seemed wise at least to indicate the theoretical motivation underlying that theme. All honor to the Great Books, but the destiny of liberal education will be determined by radical philosophical thought and by nothing else. If no such thought is available, whether for reasons promulgated from the right or from the left, then we are doomed to mediocrity. According to a leading spokesman of the contemporary left, reading is in fact writing, a thesis that I have described elsewhere as entailing the reduction of writing to illegible scribbling. But memorization is not intrinsically superior to scribbling; conservatives should themselves remember that Plato unites *anamnesis* to *noesis*.

6

The Young, the Good, and the West

Michael Platt

I.

From Stettin in the Baltic to Trieste in the Adriatic, all across the continent of Europe, the Iron Curtain has lifted. Behind that line almost all the ancient states of the East, with their capitals, Prague, Warsaw, Budapest, Belgrade, Bucharest, Sofia, Kiev, and their captive populations have regained their freedom. In Germany, the wall imprisoning the East has crumbled, the Germans have enjoyed their reunion, and set about the task of unification. Now far into the East the Gulag has thawed; now the specter of Soviet Communism no longer haunts the West; and now all over the world the threat of nuclear war seems to have receded.

Meanwhile, the free markets of the West and the new ones in Asia continue to produce all those goods and services that constitute progress, in such abundance as to make vast populations comfortable, beyond the expectations of desire itself and even the dreams of visionaries. Indeed, the world seems now nearly united in calling democracy the best regime, free market capitalism the best economy, and science the most humanitarian enterprise of humanity. Some speak of a new world order. Still others dream of the end of history. Investors everywhere smile.

Nevertheless, despite these welcome events, agreeable developments, and sanguine hopes, the West seems troubled.

Though wealthy, the peoples of the West are not happy; though at peace, they are haunted by the unrelenting cold war that terrorism is; though living longer and longer, they fear death more and more; and though ever advancing in technology, they feel weaker. Compared to previous generations, the people of the West, though still free, are everywhere more dependent on government, more burdened by bureaucracy, more vexed by regulation, more heavily taxed, and more deep in debt, both personal and public, yea, unto their children's children. By almost all indices, of theft, of murder, of divorce, of suicide, of how it treats its offspring, and how willing the citizenry is to defend its way of life, the West seems in decline.

Certainly we are not what our parents and grandparents once were. Though they belatedly recognized the threat of national, imperial socialism, both Hitler's new kind and Japan's ancient one, and though they needed alliance with a third national, imperial socialism to win, the great democracies called forth a supreme exertion and defeated both Germany and Japan. Yet despite the valiant work of Churchill's worthy inheritor, Margaret Thatcher, the English today are no equal to the hearty islanders who frustrated Hitler's Luftwaffe so finely. Despite the refounding achievement of DeGaulle, the French today are no match to the French who were ashamed of their Vichy betrayal, resisted occupation, fought their way to German soil, gained a place at the peace table, and founded the United Nations. And despite America's two-ocean victory, its enormous economic expansion since, and its 'victory' over Soviet Communism, the American people today are not equal to the united nation they were in World War II. For more than a thousand days and nights those men and women waged war against two mighty tyrannies. Recently a leader of the West called a tyrant, a Hitler, but ceased fighting him after a hundred hours, leaving him stronger, more able to oppress his people and, with time, more able to threaten his neighbors with mass incineration and mass plague. Except for superior arms, none of the descendants of the victors of World War II could defeat the nation they were fifty years ago.

Each of the great democracies is weaker than it was then. Weaker, sicker, blinder, blind to its own corruption—or rather indifferent to it, for although there are critics, although insight exists, although the evidence can even be presented in terms that the morally obtuse recognize, little is done. Insight exists, but not will. Everywhere sloth, sloth, sloth prevails.[1] And even to its own survival, America seems blind. Upon Communist China, with its vast Laogai system, so much more thoroughly enslaving of the mind and so much more economically productive than the Gulag—upon this tyranny, with its submissive millions, with its pervasive espionage, with its penetrating political donations, with its expansive navy and far-reaching missiles—upon this totalitarian empire, America chooses to look most favorably. Its consumers amused with trinkets, its business men dazzled with profits, and its politicians indifferent to liberty, America seems to have concluded that the world is safe for democracy, that the war to end all wars is over, and that no virile armed force will ever be needed again.

To be sure, the West has woken from slumber before. Before it beat him, the West appeased Hitler; before it defeated the Japanese, it ignored them; and for decades, before it decided to defend itself against missiles, not just deter them, the West gave ground to Soviet advances, calling retreat coexistence and then détente. Yet it rallied against Hitler, against Japan, and against the Soviet Union. Perhaps the West will rally again.

When it rallied before, the West had to recognize its enemies; now, in addition, it must recognize itself. That is a far greater task, for it requires very painful self-criticism. In what follows I will offer some, to you, my fellow Westerners. Later I will give some reasons to think we are already rallying.

II.
The Teenager

Today, if we would recognize our enemies, we must first recognize ourselves.

Sometime after World War II, a new sort of human being appeared in the West. The flat, listless, anxious, petty souls of the youth of today have been well described by Allan Bloom,[2] but their uniqueness has not been appreciated, their genesis investigated, or their plight commiserated sufficiently. There were no "teenagers" before World War II. Compare the entries in Webster Second and Third; only after the war does the adjective "teenage" become the noun, "teenager." What differentiates the teenager from all previous generations of young people is the absence of the desire to become an adult; the highest aspiration of a teenager is to become a more perfect teenager, a movie or rock star. Before the Second World War, there were youths; they grew up playing and studying, being foolish, ambitious and silly, but always wanting to grow up, to become men and women, good citizens and God-fearing souls, mothers and fathers, someone worthy of their own self-respect. Their heroes and heroines were such people; if they didn't have one nearby in their own family, they looked for one in their town, perhaps in their church, congregation, meeting house, stake, or synagogue, or in their school. And if they did not find enough good there, then they searched in their reading. Not any more; the horizon of significant adult life has disappeared for them.

The day the Teenager was created was a sad day for every youth in America. Imagine yourself young, unsure of yourself, swayed by strong passions, by turns ashamed and proud, oft shy and oft assertive, always awkward, filled with new desires and hard on yourself for having them, by desire pressed forward toward independence and by desire drawn backward toward conformity, tempted by clique cruelty, by affectation, by enslavement to pleasure, and by premature bonds, but fighting on, knowing that you want to become something better, someone capable of accomplishing good, deserving your own respect, and maybe one day becoming a good parent—imagine such struggling youths hearing their own parents saying, "Take it easy, enjoy yourself, adulthood will just happen, this is the time of your life."

You can see it portrayed in the films of James Dean. In all of them, he is an orphan, an orphan with no parents in *Giant*, an orphan with split parents in *East of Eden*, and an orphan *with* two parents in *Rebel Without a Cause*. *Rebel* imitates what was going on in the 1950s most faithfully. In it we see "Jimmy" enter a new high school and face a moral question: Should he fight if challenged? Should he risk his life, and perhaps the lives of others, to defend his honor? Should he, perhaps, do it to destroy the reputation of a teenage tyrant? Or should he ignore the foolish challenge, go his solitary way through high school, and continue to prepare to be a man? Jimmy chooses to fight, frees two former slaves of the tyrant, and wins. By so doing, he becomes a good, strong man, and even a kind of father (to the character "Plato"). Jimmy is not a rebel without a cause, but a young man with a purpose. All this, however, is achieved not only without the help of his parents but despite a contumacious mother and a pusillanimous father. The lesson is clear: in the new America, the kids are on their own. They have been on their own now for forty years.[3]

We have slid a long way since shy, sensitive, self-pitying, questioning, confused, polite, proud and gentle Jimmy Dean struggled to become a man. When I look at the blank eyes, apathetic expressions, empty faces, the hair fashioned like stegosauruses or shaven like Dachau inmates, note the leather garb, mutilating jewelry, ill-fitting tops, and shuffling pants, when I watch their cold videos, hear their music beat to the whip, and above all, when I listen to the Teenagers of today talk about their lives, the world and themselves, I grieve for them and I fear for the world. These children would rather that the world perished; they would rather you perished; they would rather that their parents perished; they would rather they themselves perished; and they kill themselves, their parents, and others in unprecedented numbers. Without desire, without pleasure, without passion, they seem to say, "I hate everyone in this room; I hate everyone I know; I hate, I hate, I hate . . . everything." "Daddy, Daddy" Sylvia Plath is their precursor, "tomorrow, and tomorrow, and tomorrow" Macbeth their ancestor, and the swine-preferring Prodigal Son their archetype. They want neither to love nor to be loved. It is a question whether any affection can ever reach them, although not a question that should stop any one from trying.

III.
The Orphans and the Great Books

Thus orphaned, the youths of the West are in the condition of Telemachus, Hamlet, or Huck Finn; they must bring themselves up. Unfortunately, today they are more like Hamlet than Telemachus and more like Huck than Hamlet. And their absent fathers are no Old Hamlets, let alone Odysseuses. For years the young people who now arrive in college have heard their parents say, "Let the kids work it out on their own," which they have rightly understood to mean, "We don't much care."

Arriving in college, these children will need some vista of greatness to satisfy the longing in their souls, or to stir it up if Allan Bloom is right about their listlessness. From time to time such students may find some greatness in their teachers, but they will only find it for sure in the great books that are occasionally still taught in the colleges. Nothing else speaks to the soul's greatest longings the way those books do. Most of the greatest minds are dead and are, thus, only available to us through the writings they have left us. Happy then the student who chances upon the greater teachers an Allan Bloom will introduce him to. That chance depends largely on the existence of a Liberal Arts, Great Books, or Western Civilization elective, requirement, core, program or major. And for most students, it also depends on meeting a teacher so formed by that greatness that he represents it vivaciously to students. Such teachers do not grow on trees. They are not watered by the affluent, but impoverished graduate schools of today. Often such teachers only spring up by getting to teach in such undergraduate programs. As Lionel Trilling once said, "Everything I am comes from the opportunity to teach in such a program."[4] Today there are precious few of them. And the best way to introduce one to a college without one might be to call it Forbidden Books.[5]

I would then, with Mr. Bloom and others, have such orphans study the two parents of the West, whose strong marriage, of reason and revelation, have made it the inquiring, the striving, and the loving thing it is. Simultaneously then, I would have them study that great movement of mind, beginning with Homer and Hesiod, including the tragedians and historians, and culminating in Socrates and all his consequences:

Plato, Aristotle and Alexander, Cicero, Vergil, and Tacitus. Nor should one neglect the four modern Socratics: Montaigne, Pascal, Kierkegaard, and Nietzsche. And I would have them study the parent of revelation, beginning with the Great Creator of Genesis, including the long story of man's choices, of steadfast Abraham, stern Moses and persevering Job, shaky Saul, and wayward David; and withal God's charitable and sagacious interventions, culminating in suffering Christ and all His consequences, including Augustine, Thomas, Francis, More, Luther, Calvin, Pascal, Newman, Kierkegaard, and Péguy.

These are the parents and their relatively distinct progeny. We in the West are one long consequence of reason, especially as the Greeks first practiced it, and of revelation, as the Jews first received it, and especially of the meeting of these two, sometimes a clash, sometimes a conversation, sometimes a chorus in harmony. We are especially the consequence of the unification of these two accomplished by Christianity. To the Jew, Christianity said, "Some of the laws are suspended by the new revelation of Christ, some strengthened by it (e.g., on divorce), and some set aside, for example, those on politics, for the "things of Caesar" are rightly governed by reason, not God or Moses or the law given by the one to the other." And to the Greek, Christianity said, "There is more in heaven than your philosophy kens of, and more on earth as well, for without breaching reason or contradicting it, or denigrating the nature it is true to, the truth of Christ surpasses it." The most comprehensive, subtle, rich and happy expression of this unification of reason and Christian revelation is to be found in Thomas Aquinas; the most deep, subtle, noble, and anxious in Pascal; and the most beautiful and sweet, in Rembrandt.

Yet the student of the West may wonder and must inquire whether these parents, of reason and Christian revelation, do go together. Is it a marriage? Various voices that a student must listen to, Tertullian and Luther on one side, and on the other, Schopenhauer and Nietzsche, agree, saying that there can be no true relation between faith and philosophy. Are they right? Should philosophy and faith divorce? And if they should, which parent should you, their child, choose to stick with? "Faith" say Tertullian and Luther. "Reason" say Bayle, Voltaire, Schopenhauer and Nietzsche, though Nietzsche adds "passionate reason." Who is right? Which will you choose? Is one right? Does reason without faith lead to liberty, understanding, and happiness. Or does faith without reason lead to righteousness, salvation, and heaven? Or are both sides wrong, and the child who is forced to choose forever maimed by having grown up in a broken home? You must decide. You must think. You must meet Socrates. You must meet Christ. Not to know them is to be an orphan of the West. For any human being, West or East, it is to miss two of the greatest opportunities for self-knowledge. As inquiring Socrates died to make us wise, so wise Christ died to make us loving.

The reminder of these deaths might teach something important to the student of the West. The founders whose marriage made and still makes the West were both put to death by the West. Has the West regretted it? Yes, and no. Athens so regretted the hemlock that it banished the accusers; Jerusalem so regretted the cross that many a Saul changed to a Paul; and Imperial Rome so regretted its Pilate that it turned Christian. Although the esteem in these regrets contributed importantly to the founding of the West, nevertheless, were Socrates resurrected, would he last seventy years? And were Christ to come again would he last thirty-three? No, if Socrates reappeared, if Christ came again, they would once again be put to death. Daily they are, have been, and will be put to death. The hemlock is always being proffered to the philosopher, approximately in proportion to his imitation of Socrates, and the Cross is always being erected for the Christian, approximately in proportion to his witnessing Christ. Nor does the fact that Socrates is somehow responsible for Aristotle and that Christ is somehow responsible for the Church mean that the combination of Aristotle and the Church that the West nearly was in Paris long ago, that that combination would not repeat the crime of Athens and the crime of Jerusalem. After all, Thomas, in whose thinking Aristotle and Christ combine as never before or since, was censured by the Church, fortunately in absentia, after he had been "absented" from this little threshing floor, streeted with straw, our earth, and was, presumably, dwelling in beatific felicity, in any case, safe from Bishop Tempier. Yet, unfortunately as well, for the Church, for had Thomas been alive and thinking when intemperate Tempier and like others condemned his teachings, Thomas would not only have refuted them but might have convinced the Church that he had, and then his students need not have gone underground for years.

This shows us something important. Though these two, Socrates and Christ, are the founders of the West, the West is far from its founding. It could not be otherwise and it will always be so. Founders are both in what they founded and immeasurably high above it. No institution is greater than its founder. *Politique* is not *mystique*, as Péguy knew. Institutions, especially countries, do necessary things and sometimes achieve fine things, things that nothing else could, but none is finer than what a noble human being can achieve. Only human beings can be friends. When countries are said to be "friendly," it just means they are not foes. Although souls need cities to be in, no city is higher than the soul. And so it is with Socrates and with Christ. Justice was profoundly important to both, yet both recognized something higher above it, eros in the one case, love in the other.

Thus we study founders such as Socrates and Christ with two disposi-
tions, with gratitude for the good in what they founded and yet with
awe for them, higher beings, and high measures of all below, including
what they founded. Thus, when the Academy is decadent, you may seek
philosophic solace in Socrates, and when Christendom is decrepit, there
in Christ you may seek ageless Life Himself. So too, when the Academy
is decadent and when Christendom is decrepit, you may reform them,
which means returning them to their first principles and purposes, by
ardently recollecting Socrates and Christ, and while reforming the institutions, endure the tribulations and suffering accompanying such reform, succeeding or failing, by dwelling with them. Time spent strolling
with Socrates and Christ gives a happiness no institution could ever
enjoy or hinder. However, even when these institutions were in the best
shape ever, nay even if they were to be in the best shape they could ever
be in, still high above them are their founders, Socrates and Christ, the
one providing an understanding few others can, and the other providing
a peace no one else ever could.

To the student of the West, these two lofty teachers enforce a second
important lesson. Do these two, Socrates and Christ, agree about important things? Do they understand things the same way? Do they provide
the same sort of peace? It is hard to discern what each teaches or thinks,
and it is harder still to see if they go together. Perhaps they agree, but
if so, is it clear where, or how, and why? We would very much like to
be present at a conversation between Socrates and Christ, yet a conversation between them might go no where, it might not even start, and
who are we to speculate about their lofty meeting? No one stays wide
awake with Socrates the night of the *Symposium*, and none of his chosen
disciples stays awake with Christ the night He asked them to. Who are
we to say we would do better than Aristophanes or Peter on the night
when Socrates and Christ converse? Raphael painted the conversation
of Plato and Aristotle as "The School of Athens." What the conversation of Socrates and Christ would be we do not know. "The School of
the West" has never been painted. Perhaps Rembrandt could have. He
didn't. We can't.

Of the West then, we are the products and also the failures, for reading the best minds of the West we cannot but recognize that in them
there is something not only vastly superior to Western institutions but
vastly superior to us. Thus time spent with Socrates and Christ is time
spent with souls whose lofty excellence is a constant personal accusation and yet whose company provides a joy few of the living, however
good, can give us, or, for much the same reason, prevent. For the record
of their time on earth we are mightily grateful to the institutions they

founded, and yet we cannot forget that they are the measures of those institutions.

Thus, although Socrates asks Athens to care for his sons and would, I presume, approve of Plato's writings, and might approve of his founding of the Academy, he would hardly approve of everything Academic since, perhaps not even the succession of civilizations, regimes, and cities that have followed, including those summed up as "the West." Likewise, although He charged His disciples to found a Church, Christ would not approve all its doings, let alone those of all Christendom, and still less "Christian civilization." (Thus, although neither Socrates nor Christ would be animated by the passion that stirred the marchers at Stanford to chant "Hey, hey, ho, ho, Western Civ has gotta go," they would not in defending such a civilization for an instant regard it as the highest thing. Nor would they approve of Western Civilization courses that failed to look higher than it, to what it has looked higher to, to Socrates and Christ, and, higher still, to what they look up to.) And although Thomas may be said to have brought reason and revelation, Aristotle and Christ, together, we don't know what either would think of the meeting. After all, neither Aristotle nor Christ speak of each other, and not at all of the consequence of the conversation their students and disciples have imagined, "the West." All criticism of the West falls short of what Socrates and Christ, just by existing, provide.

Mention of Socrates and Christ might remind us of something else about the soul's relation to greatness. It is not only true, as Mr. Bloom so rightly emphasizes and exactly describes, that the soul longs for answers to the greatest questions but that the soul wants to become great. If not deformed, a youth dreams of being some one he can respect, of doing something worth remembering, indeed of becoming someone worth remembering, someone great. Some dream of discovering truth; more dream of achieving a great good, or of resisting a great evil. Some want to be an Einstein; some want to be a Davy Crockett; others want to be an Albert Schweitzer, or a Mother Teresa; some want to be a Shakespeare or a Solzhenitsyn; and others want to be a Joan of Arc or a Lincoln, a DeGaulle or a Churchill.[6] The great books speak to these longings. Homer's heroes fired the imagination of young Alexander and young Sam Houston. Plutarch's *Lives*, which include a life of Alexander, have fired youths as well as instructed statesmen. The Platonic dialogues set the emulative soul on fire to be like Socrates. Likewise the Bible, which shows a youth the greatness in obedience of pious Abraham, beautiful David, and stern and stubborn Moses, and the greatness in love of Christ.

Nor can the soul stop at emulation. For one thing, there is more than one sort of hero worthy of emulation. Which should I choose to be like?

How can I choose between them? Why choose one rather than the others? Perhaps there was once a time when the choice was easy, when the question barely arose, when it was clear to all, or nearly all, in one's village, one's country, and one's civilization, what the best way of life is. Not any more. Perhaps it never was. Thus the student burning to be great must ask: What is great? The student wishing to be just must ask: What is just? And the student desiring truth must ask: What is true? And even: What is truth? Philosophy, at least a little philosophy, is now indispensable, at least at the beginning of adulthood. The confluence of a thousand and one 'cultures' has confused all and thrust reflection upon each youth raised in one but forced by exposure to the rest to consider all.

It is a long time since one could leave it at reading Homer, wanting to be Achilleus, or Odysseus, and worshiping Zeus. Since Julian the Apostate, no one has done more to revive the worship of Dionysus than Nietzsche and yet he and his Zarathustra philosophize far more than they dance, pour libations, or sacrifice in blood. The soft, pastel paganism of Botticelli, the multicultural paganism of Jung and Campbell—psychologists of the 'psyche' (which is not the soul)—and the aesthetic paganism of many students up until recently is effete, unheroic, and shallow, and it is impossible. Socrates is inescapable. Likewise, one cannot leave it at reading the Old Testament and wanting simply to obey the law vouchsafed to Moses, for one must consider what Maimonides teaches the perplexed; and not even in Israel, let alone Long Island, can one ignore Spinoza, the founder of both. And Christianity, in claiming that Christ is the Logos (John), that reason and its revelation agree (Pascal), requires the thoughtful Christian, such as Thomas addresses in the *Summa Theologiae*, to find out how they do agree. Faith must seek understanding.

In truth these stories of the West themselves compel emulative youth to philosophize. That Homer presents both Achilleus and Odysseus means we must consider both, perhaps choose one over the other, or perhaps compelled by the difficulty of the choice, seek some third hero beyond both, who would be their perfection and measure. Plato says that would be Socrates. Kierkegaard disagrees, saying it would be Christ. And Nietzsche once suggested it would be "Roman Caesar with the soul of Christ."[7] Likewise with the Bible. Whom should one emulate? Abraham, Moses, or David? Or Job? Or none, for perhaps the Torah forbids emulation, knows only God as great, and prefers obedience. And here Christ disagrees, saying love is higher than obedience, love for others unto death, "as I have loved you"; and yet in obedience, too, Thy will be done. Maybe emulation was not permitted until Him.[8] In any case, the diversity within the West,[9] whose many participant cultures are invisible to the angry in American Academe today, is already inherent in the West. It requires each son and daughter of the West to seek the unity of the West, to seek it for yourself, and thus to live it in your life.

Already the indispensable founding figures of the West, in Socrates and Christ, in their thinking, there is incitement to thinking. The questions aroused by Socrates' one big speech in public (the *Apology*) compel one to go on, to his many private conversations, among them none so lovely as the *Symposium* or so comprehensive as the *Republic*. What Plato's student, Aristotle, divided up into a *Poetics*, a *Rhetoric*, an *Ethics*, a *Politics*, and part of a *Physics* and a *Metaphysics*, is in the *Republic* seen together. Few, very few, other books have such a power to speak to the young soul, to provoke it into a discovery of itself, and to exercise it into a full possession of its own powers. The *Republic* is one of those books that to miss when you are young may be to miss maturity itself. From Euclid you can learn that you have a mind, but from Plato and Aristotle you can learn that the mind can reason about the most important things. (Shakespeare and Tolstoy seem to me two other indispensables, but ones that come earlier.)

Miss the experience of reason in Plato and you are likely to become a feeble drifter, thinking "It is all a matter of opinion" or, these days, a lost nihilist thinking "It is all a matter of values." Combine the many drifters and a few potent nihilists turned active and you get tyrannies the like of which were never seen until our century. Against the peculiar evil of our time, Plato and Aristotle are sovereign essentials.

So too the Gospels, whose fourfold account of Christ requires the reader to work for understanding, to reconcile the discrepancies, to harmonize the seven last words, or not to, but in any case to have sought answers to the questions the Gospels raise. The remarks of Christ, which are as witty, subtle, and deep, indeed unique, as His suffering, require the same qualities in the reader. And so too the works of discourse that follow the Gospels, the accounts of God (theologies) of Augustine, Thomas, Pascal, Kierkegaard, and others; there too Christ incites to thought. To read Augustine's *Confessions* and not carry the story through to the final, abstract discourses is not only to "not finish the assignment" but not to have understood what of it you did read. To Augustine it would be to choose "restlessness" rather than the "Thee" that true restlessness, seeking higher, would itself choose and then be at peace. Even after he had been saved, Augustine thought there was far to go. Faith *needs* to seek understanding. Thomas agrees when he addresses the twenty-five hundred close pages of his *Summa Theologiae* to pious B.A.s at Paris. And, in his way, Pascal also holds that reason and revelation can never disagree. Yet, with these discourses we must add, as their authors would, that somehow all they say is already in the Gospels, especially John's. While ancient philosophy criticized the Homeric poetry that preceded it (and refuted Aristophanes, first to quarrel with Socrates),[10] modern philosophic theology understands itself as the servant of the Biblical story and the disciple of Christ.

So far I have emphasized the founders of the West. They come first in studies but they are not all. The moderns, unto our own day, deserve attention, if only so the student is not left disoriented upon graduating. But the ancients do come first. As Lionel Trilling observed, the unargued assumption of all colleges is that you teach modernity. That is not thoughtful. Yet, even to fulfill the aim of such a curriculum, you must study more than it. Modernity is derivative, and its very claims to superiority, to bold breaks and new continents, acknowledge this however backhandedly. To examine the bold claim of a founder who boasts he is better than all that came before, you have to know the old stuff, especially when the boaster names the person he overcomes. Thus, to examine the claims of the new republican Machiavelli, you have to know the old 'imagined Republics' (of Cicero, especially of Plato, but also the "imagined" City of God of Augustine, whom Machiavelli silently and fiercely opposes). To examine the claims of the 'new scientists': Galileo, Copernicus, Bacon, Descartes, and Newton, you have to know the old ones, Aristotle, Euclid, and Ptolemy. And to examine the claims of the great critics of modernity who nonetheless renewed its designs, Rousseau and Nietzsche, you must know both the moderns they criticize, Hobbes and Locke for Rousseau, Rousseau and Hegel for Nietzsche, and also the ancients they claim as allies (Socrates for both, Sparta for Rousseau, and the tragedians for Nietzsche).

One must recognize that the tension between reason and revelation, which seemed to have reached a high harmony in Thomas Aquinas, broke out afresh. Those figures who made the Renaissance, who are the Renaissance, called for some kind of return to ancient understanding and living, and those figures who made the Reformation, who are the Reformation, called for some kind of return to pristine Christian teaching and living. Yet Erasmus and More thought these renewals were compatible. Shakespeare may have too, and what would a Great Books curriculum be without Shakespeare, whose scope includes almost all time and place, and whose beauty pleases and depth lures on the inquiring soul.[11] Looking upon the ensuing tumult and bloody civil wars, others, the founders of modernity, such as Machiavelli, Montaigne, and Bacon, claimed to see a new harmony of reason and revelation, which would dedicate the faithful, out of charity itself, to a politics of broad and inclusive goals, ones likely to be achieved and even secured forever, or at least progressively approximated: peace, freedom, prosperity, and comfort. Thus the faithful were invited to join a just war against fortune, to achieve an unconditional surrender and permanent conquest of nature, for the relief of what Montaigne called, for the first time, the human condition.

Can such a conquest be accomplished? Should it be? Is it wise? Is man wise enough to rule nature? Has he grown in wisdom since the Greeks, since the Christians, neither of whom thought the purpose of life resided in such wars? Doesn't all power over nature inevitably become the power of some men over others, some peoples over others, perhaps over the whole world, some generations over all future ones, and one species over all life? Today is there not, alas, a very immediate incentive for studying the bold founders of the modern project, at the perilous end of which we seem to live?[12] Just when the conquest of nature may mean the abolition of man, would surely be a good time to study Bacon and Descartes, who knew such a conquest to be an innovation and knew the arguments against it. Likewise is there not an intellectual provocation. Just when modern science is disappearing into black holes, bursting into a thousand particles however charming, and conceding that everything came from nothing (but not wondering if only God could create anything from nothing), would surely be a good time to examine the claim of original modern science to know the whole in principle. And what of the result of that low idealism (Marxism), namely the totalitarianism, ever advancing a war against human nature, as well as nature, and exercising unrelenting terror of against both, that has corrupted, enslaved, and killed so many millions in our century? Is this low idealism unrelated to the call for lower goals by Machiavelli? Or to the covert antitheological ire at work in him and most of his "captains," most of the subsequent moderns?

Yet is there no good in this philosophic project, the modern project, and do we not see it most in our America, in what the Framers built, the generation of Lincoln shed blood for, the pioneers filled the continent with, and what Americans have enjoyed for two hundred years? In it Machiavelli might find manifest mastery of fortune, Montaigne ease and ease of thought, Spinoza freedom of speech, Bacon warmth, and Descartes health; in it Locke might find toleration, Rousseau find innocence, Hamilton empire, Twain folly to laugh at, Whitman loafing, Cather fortitude, Tocqueville piety and liberty, and in it Lincoln might find a sign of the divine hand and the hope of humanity. Is not the good of America, mingling modern designs and Christian teachings, uniting nature and nature's God, something good and thus an argument for the partial good of the modern project? Yet even in America, some great minds have seen the end of humanity. No one has decried the ignobility of this project more penetratingly than Nietzsche. Was he wrong to? To know, you must study him, too.

Although the student should study the course of modern philosophy, it must be admitted that there is something willful and therefore not quite adequate, adequate to reality, in most of its great minds. Most are so busy changing the world that they do not see it clearly, and often ignore nature entirely, including human nature, and thus themselves. By contrast the great statesmen of the modern era, who try ever to find the good in straitened conditions, and thus always have their eye on human nature, in the fine-grained picture of it, in the shifting situations they face, and the contending characters, both adversaries and allies, seem to understand human things better. The student should come to know, in memoirs and faithful histories, a few at least of the likes of Washington, Jefferson, Hamilton, and Madison, Lincoln, Cavour, Bismarck, Marlborough and Churchill, and DeGaulle. Their brave and sagacious efforts, whether successful or not, stand out against the darkness of modernity. It is not only in antiquity and Plutarch that nobility shines in deed and speech. For every page of Heidegger read one of Churchill. For every page of Hegel read one of Lincoln.

Likewise, in contrast to the projective character of modern philosophy, stand the great poets of the modern era, Shakespeare, Goethe, Kafka, Tolstoy and Dostoyevsky; their works seem more comprehensive, more thoughtful, deeper, partly because they are not wholly modern, not rebels, but true inheritors, more akin to Socrates and Christ than Bacon and Descartes and their philosophic train. In them there is often more philosophy than in modern philosophy and often more piety than in the churches. In any case, Tolstoy's *War and Peace* is simply indispensable in the life of a growing soul. Both future philosophers and future Christians, if not future statesmen, have much to learn from this great story.

This brings us full circle, for to educate the sons and daughters of the West, a curriculum of Great Books must include the stories from which the West starts, on the one hand, Homer and his progeny, the historians Herodotus and Thucydides and the tragedians Aeschylus, Sophocles, and Euripides, and on the other hand, Genesis and its trail, Exodus, and onward to the Gospels. And such a curriculum must include the stories that carry forward the West to our time, among them the Faust story of the striving that in contending with nature will never find rest, the Don Quixote and Hamlet story of the noble man ever ready to take arms against the sins of the world, and the Don Juan story of the roving eros that never lifts its eyes above humanity. It is not accidental that the characteristic evil of our time has been best understood by a poet, Solzhenitsyn, in the "literary investigation" entitled *The Gulag Archipel-*

ago. Such poetry is not only more philosophic than history, as Aristotle said, but truer, truer than "History."

Philosophy without poetry is thin, and poetry without philosophy is miscellaneous. Maxims without examples are blind. Instances without principles are deaf.[13]

IV.
Difficulties, Objections, Vilifications

He who pursues such a curriculum will meet many difficulties, old, unavoidable, and enduring; the sides of the path have, since a generation ago, also been lined with several objections; and today straight ahead are foes vilifying the student. Such curricula are said to be white, male, and dead. Commonly this is said in enmity and in triumph. No objection, no rebuttal, let alone conversation, is expected to ensue.

That most of the great minds are dead is simply true. It always will be so. Those who don't know the past are, said Santayana, doomed to repeat it. And those who don't know the great minds of the past are doomed never to know—what they are missing. It is a vain and foolish presumption to think that because someone is alive at this hour he or she is great. Just because you are alive doesn't mean you are great, or good, or even mediocre. You should overcome such self-love, rather than lounge in it.

That the skin color of the authors of most of the great books is on the light end of the scale is true. Those who think some author with dark skin has been unjustly neglected should propose inclusion, and the proposal should be judged by the same criteria already used, not by race and quotas. Most of the great books show little interest in skin color, either prejudicially or predilectionally. To the great this natural distinction is trivial. To treat it as more is small. Those who treat race as central, such as Alexander Stephens, Arthur de Gobineau, and Adolf Hitler, are very much less than great. Nothing human should be judged by such persons. They are not fit to rule. Nor are they fit to teach. They do not belong in places of learning. The natural right of a student to study great things should not be abridged by any person, anywhere, any time. Especially not by those who are insensitive to greatness, or sensitive to it only so far as they hate it. Such hatred is of a piece with the slaveholder who found his wife with young Frederick Douglass, teaching him to read, and ordered her not to; it is of a piece with any one who would have refused Booker T. Washington entrance to Hampton Institute; and it is active in all those who institute college programs based on self-love, self-love for accidental things such as race, nation, sex, parents, or origin, and with courses in which any student with the right attitude would deserve an "A" on the first day.

Like skin color, sex is a natural distinction, but it is different. It is more than skindeep, and perhaps intrinsicate to the soul, or at least linked to it. The clear distinctions in body of male and female not only have important purposes they point to, child bearing and feeding, and fathering and whatever (for males seem less fixed, also for the same reason, less steady, rooted, fixed), but these differences seem to reach into the souls of those different bodies, so that the soul of a woman is different from the soul of a man. It is a long question, but surely we can say that men and women are enough alike so that anything the one can understand, appreciate, or discover, the other can too, but enough different to so that there is something eternally "other" in what attracts each to the other.

Whether the great minds and their works slight the eternal feminine is doubtful—think of Penelope, Emma, Mary, Anna Karenina, Natasha, all Shakespeare's witty lasses, and all the lyrical love in the world's poetic anthology—but it is true that the vast majority of authors in such curricula are men. This is either unjust to neglected authors, an expression of the natural difference of the sexes in the human species, or a consequence of conditions and causes that could be changed.

As to the first, the burden is on those who charge it, to bring forward their candidates, and for others to admit them by the same criteria that gains admission to other candidates.

As to the second, just as nature favors right-handedness, so perhaps it favors the male; perhaps nature wants men to aspire to greatness and women to goodness (for which distinction see the next section); but as with handedness in nature, the favoring of the right hand is not to the exclusion of the left, with even some coincidence, perhaps partly causal, between left-handedness and genius. Here the tricky thing in achieving justice is how to be just to the generality without being unjust to the exceptional; how to support the rule that favors the majority without blocking the way for the rare minority, whose excellence, after all, may benefit all. Let Eve Curie pursue her studies and all may benefit. Justice and the good of all lie not in the rule or in the exception, still less in exclusions or quotas either way, but in sagacity, in knowing how to arrange things so the rule rules most of the time but not always, and thus the exception gets an opportunity.

As to the third, that the number of male authors in such a curriculum is a reflection of conditions, not nature, conditions whose alteration would eventually change the composition of the great team—it is untrue to suppose that conditions make greatness, for all the great minds, although they enjoyed conditions that did not prevent their greatness shared those same conditions with thousands and millions of other persons who did not leave something great for others after their death. To be sure, for there to be great works by Shakespeare's sister, she needs to have a room of her own, but having a room will not produce such works. Sitting in that room, you may produce nothing or only something good, such as *To the Lighthouse*; this stubborn truth Virginia Woolf knew, but not many who hail her today.[14] Will there ever be a woman philosopher?[15] Maybe. The only candidate so far, that I can think of, is Hannah Arendt, she whose single philosophic coinage is "natality," surely connected to her sex, and yet despite the fact she never had a child, by her husbands or Martin Heidegger, which shows her coinage did not come from experience, but from thought. That her attitude to her gift and to her sex was not feminist, but human and proud, is illustrated by her response to one of her hosts at Princeton who asked her "Well, how does it feel to be the first woman Gauss Lecturer?" to which she replied, "That is hard for me to answer. You see, I have been a woman for so long."[16]

The objection to such Great Books curricula, that they are not inclusive enough, might be animated by an appreciation of greatness. Most such Great Books programs are Western, exclusively or for the most part. Yet to maintain that the West is not multicultural is ignorant. It is. Right at the beginning Homer regards the fall of Troy, not a Greek city, as immeasurably sad, and Homer's student, Herodotus, looks out at the ways of adjacent nations, Persia and Egypt especially. So too with the Torah, in which the honor of speaking with God and of putting the hardest questions to him, is given to Job, who is not a Jew, not party to the Covenant. Soon too Greeks, who had observed that fire burns in Persia as it does in Attica, spread the fruits of a culture founded on this fundamental human distinction, of nature and convention, to all Asia, and soon too the Christians brought the good news sprung from the Torah to the Gentiles as well, meaning *in potentia* everyone. As to the later course of the West, Rome by the time it warred itself into a Mediterranean empire, was already multicultural, perhaps to the detriment of its unity, which split into East and West. Moreover, all the later history of the West is of something unified enough to call the West, federated enough to have discrete parts, and divided enough to see many wars, many conquests, many strifes, between its parts, and many tongues spring up. The latter is especially important. To know the West well, really well, you would have to know not only Greek, Hebrew, and Latin, but Italian, French, English, German, and Russian, and to consider adding at least one of twenty other languages. If that isn't multicultural, what is? The tribe of translators are right to stress, as they do in their prefaces, how very hard it was for them to translate whatever they just have, and yet the tribe of readers and students are also right to read their translations with gratitude, in proportion to their success, which to judge well you must know the original itself. Although to know the West, you need to know a dozen languages, most teachers of the West today would be satisfied if students knew one, other than what they grew up with, by the time they left college, and surprised if even one knows one language upon entering, which was a requirement for admission to college only a generation ago.

Lest I be misunderstood, the fact that the West has been multicultural does not mean that the great minds whose study composes such a curriculum are the products of culture. Although such minds, in order to think, to teach, to write, needed certain minimal conditions, including perhaps some suffering, they were not made great by them. Almost all enjoyed the same conditions as others who imparted nothing great to humanity; and the exceptions, the sons of kings for example, who have everything you could want in the way of good conditions, seldom left any single thing great. Perhaps Alexander and Charlemagne are the only ones. Having everything you could want seems seldom to encourage greatness, or even goodness in human beings.

Yet what about the works that lie outside the West? Shouldn't they be studied? Are we not one world, one humanity, and do we not tend now to some world unification? Of course the great works of the East deserve study,[17] but I do not think they should be the first thing studied by young Westerners, and especially not by the present-day orphans of the West. What would one think of a young Japanese student showing up for your Western Heritage course who had not memorized poems from the *Manyoshu*, who had not read and reread the *Tale of Genji*, taken the teachings of the Buddha to heart, wanted to follow Basho on one of his journeys, and practiced some daily spiritual discipline, be it the arrangement of beautiful flowers or of deadly swift blows? His ardor for Western studies would be but a reflex of his disdain for his own heritage and it would be no check to his ignorance of it, and his ignorance of himself would be corrected by no study of anything foreign. In studying the West, he would never discover how the things of the East are a part of him. Living in America would be no true adventure, since no home would have been left behind.[18]

It is important for orphans, West and East, to study the great works of man. Being great, in scope and depth, they speak to the longings of the human soul. But it is fitting for the orphans of the West to study the Western instances of this greatness first. Today such students are as ignorant of their own heritage, especially its high founders, Socrates and Christ, as the young Japanese student I have imagined. Such high instances of the West are the basis of what a Westerner is, a measure of him, and also perhaps a distant cause of his orphaned state. For such orphans, meeting with their unknown ancestors will be an adventure, an occasion for self-knowledge, and a challenge to transform themselves, much as meeting his father was for Telemachus.

Another objection, more exactly an obstacle, is not that such Great Books curricula leave out too much, but that they include too much. How could a student study the works I mentioned in the last section, let alone in the languages I just enumerated, in less than a decade! Well, there is truth in that gasp. Undaunted, some souls will be happy to extend that ten years to a lifetime. The thing itself being good and desirable, why not more? Yet the longest such curricula, at St. John's (Annapolis and Santa Fe) and Thomas Aquinas College, last only four years. That, too, may seem long to some, for those four years are full, with no electives. Although such a four years is desirable for all students capable of college work—after all, something like it was the standard curriculum at almost all colleges a century ago—still, a little bit can go a long way. We teachers need not provide a perfect education to do our students good. (Nor need parents provide a perfect home and a perfect childhood.) The soul is not a glass to be filled, a stone to be carved, clay to be shaped, or a liquid to be poured into a mold by some one else. We fill, carve, shape, and pour ourselves, largely. Hence, just a few of the great books will go a long way. Lincoln needed only three: the Bible, Shakespeare, and Euclid. I think meeting Socrates and Christ indispensable, reading *War and Peace* in youth decisive, and Shakespeare good for life; add three other choices from those I've mentioned and that small ensemble will raise up a fine generation. And those who come to love such an ensemble will naturally go on to master the whole orchestra and become teachers of the next generation.

What about interpretation? Don't the great books depend on it, on good teachers, and good fellow students? Yes, and no. If the proper spirit is in the teacher, if he really regards the authors as great, then both he and the students will be liberated from his inferior authority, from the lacunae in the list, and all the surrounding diversions. Governed by that assumption held firmly and communicated vivaciously, the class discussion will proceed aright. It is probably not good, and almost impossible for a good mind, to have no interpretation of the great works if he has been teaching them for years. However, if you reach such an interpretation, such as I have reached with Descartes, that Descartes' teaching is wrong in truth and pernicious in action, then you should shut up in class, and let the students discover that for themselves, and if you cannot shut up, you should either not teach Descartes, or get a friend to substitute for you. Sure, it is desirable to read a great work aright, but they are so rich that a curriculum of them can succeed, succeed in the souls of the students, despite a lot of wrong interpretations.

Most of the interpretations David Denby came away with from his one year return, in middle age, to the Columbia Great Books core, seem to me wrong, if not wholly, then in some important way, but his book about the experience shows that such a curriculum works. He respects Homer, Homer has stirred him to thoughts he never had before, ones he cares for, which are superior to the movies he reviews, even the good ones, and so he would recommend time spent with Homer to others, and defend such reading against all who would deny any eager youth the great opportunity to do so. The great books are like language. The power of speech is so natural to humans that even if you have it very imperfectly, you do have it, enough so that it transforms your life. Thus, although parents and teachers are right to correct the errors in the child's usage, such as the letter from camp: "They told us to rite. I like it hear. I caught a fish what has whiskers. Please bring candy," yet there is truth in the child's plea against correction, "You know what I mean." Important as good writing is, and almost infinite its sky above the horizon of competency, the great abyss is between the level in such a camp letter, and autism. It is sad to see a child who will never write such a camp letter, and it is also sad to see an adult who will never think a thought provoked by a great author.

However, one must admit that it would be possible, just by surrounding the books in easygoing interpretations, whether falsely uplifting or falsely denigrating, and staffing the course with teachers, timid or stubborn, with no desire for greatness in anything, even in horses or ice cream, to construct a Great Books Lite program. But even then the books will be in the students' hands, in their imaginations, and in their minds. And even when the teacher doesn't care for inquiry, thinks himself better than the author, and tells students to "illustrate in your paper what I said about democracy in the *Republic*," still there in the book is Plato's Socrates for the student to learn from on his own. And even in colleges where there is no program with even a portion of such curricula, the majority today, there are usually individual courses, say in Plato, in the Gospels, etc. that a student can make sure to take.

And should that be lacking, a student, become aware of what he is missing, perhaps through reading what I have written here, or from Bloom or Van Doren, might still read such works on his own. Of course, it would be best to find a teacher willing to supervise an independent study and later, perhaps, a special major. If that is not possible, one might join with other similarly ardent students in an informal reading group. At Dartmouth, I used to lead such a group on Fridays, when most students were unstudiously occupied, but such a group is possible with a teacher at a distance. I once led one, on Nietzsche, for credit, by Federal Express, and later one on Shakespeare and one on Plato, via conference phone and e-mail. It is also possible to do without a teacher. In the strenuous version of such a reading group, such as we had in graduate school, all agree to read the text before meeting for discussion[19]; in another strenuous version, all gather to read the text slowly aloud and discuss it as we read; and in the vivacious form, we read Shakespeare aloud during the meeting, taking parts, reading the first half of a play one week, discussing it, and next time the second half. Old books and friendship go together. Though the one is discouraged by American Academe and the other not much encouraged, neither is yet forbidden, as they were in the Gulag and are in the Laogai.

V.
The Good As Well As the Great

The youth of America need, then, the great books that Bloom, others, and I have recommended, that a few colleges exist wholly to provide, and that some colleges provide in some measure, but being Teenagers as well as youths, the orphans of the West need as well as the great books, the good.[20]

College builds upon what precedes it, what precedes it in school, and most upon what precedes it in the family. If some experience of the good has not been in the family, if the family is broken, if the child has been turned over to day care or television care, if the child has been raised to be a Teenager, it will be hard for him or her to benefit much from a Great Books curriculum (unless his unquenchable desire has, in the middle of the desert he grew up in, found one oasis of good). Unfortunately, most colleges today no longer appreciate the good. Doubting truth, they ignore cheating; unable to distinguish liberty and license, they suborn promiscuity; unwilling to admit that pleasure can enslave, they shield drug dealing; and thinking big choices in life are just a matter of style, they offer no counsel to youth. And even colleges with something great in the curriculum sometimes do not seem to understand the relation of the good to the great.

The achievements of the intellect are rooted in experiences of the good. As the great discoverers tell us, the start of their great intellectual achievement often lies back in some childhood experience of something wonderful, in watching a fly walk on a wall, a current recoil from a bank, or bread mold, or wondering how much bigger than the starry sky is the whole, inquiries they had no words for then and supposed no one did or ever would. In any case, in all of us, the heart beats to the measure of the good before the understanding recognizes it. Such experiences begin in infancy, in the senses, in taste, touch, and sight; soon, as the child grows dexterous, agile, and exuberant, music infuses the good of order into the soul; and after that, the good may be cultivated in manners, in habits, and in the moral virtues, which we learn first by training, then by imitation, all long before we reflect upon and thereby perfect them. Later on, when the good has dwelt long in heart and mind, it may shine in the face and show in the hands. Many a homely girl, by appreciating the fine things that belong to her by desire, has become a beautiful woman. Many an uncouth boy, by practicing moderation, courage and justice, has become a gentleman and also handsome. Often the childhood picture of a notorious criminal shows it could have gone another way.

Growing up ought to include playing games, tag, hide-and-seek, and kick the can, seeing a garden through to harvest, and hiking up a mountain all day alone. While playing outdoors, an awful lot of primary good things—the sun, the sky, a stream, a tree, the stars—enter the soul, later to be recalled, in dark times, with peace. Nothing electronic will give that. Growing up ought to include having a pet, having a friend sleep over, and relatives to write letters to. The house ought to have a dark cellar, a cluttered attic, and snug beds; a fireplace, a piano and a kitchen table to gather around; and plenty of corners to sit quietly in. While playing indoors, while playing chess, while feeling, even with dread, that *that* black rook, knight, and bishop are closing in on you, you may experience a primary good entering your soul: that the rational is real. Provided with stories worth telling, growing up ought to become a good, long story itself, including many stories, all worth your retelling. It ought to be filled with a comprehensive happiness in being, sometimes sheer in its delight in the existence of this or that good thing, including yourself, sometimes diffuse, wide and wondrous, that such a whole exists at all, rather than nothing, and sometimes intense and sad, as when you love a pet who dies, lose a friend, or make a big mistake, and withal grateful for the whole. From such experiences of the good, great things can later come, the great delight that is art, the great wonder that is philosophy, the great gratitude that is piety, the great affection for family, city, and country, to be made effectual in statesmanship.

Those who miss the good that is in childhood will find it hard to make up for it later. It is hard to appreciate the good without first tasting the sweet. In the beginning the mind grows through the tongue. Mother's milk, a good bone, zwieback, apples with more tang than shelf life, good bread, ice cream you churned, meals made from scratch, in season, from your own garden or one you walked though or saw, and made in your own kitchen, perhaps by you when you got a little older—some taste of these will suffice to give memories as dear as that French cookie was to Proust. In childhood one springs away from the dinner table as soon as one can to play, but the happy memory of those meals should be the basis of judging all later ones, whether one arises satisfied from them and whether one looks forward to them with good expectations.

It is hard to discover the true without first gazing at the beautiful. The mind grows through the eye. The pattern made by the cracks in the paint high above your crib, sunlight through a window whose panes are proportioned by the golden mean, the rich design of an oriental rug you are following with a toy train or tank, a good combination of strong colors in your bedroom, not acrylic and glaring, but with a subtle palette such as Cézanne's—a few such experiences in childhood will prepare you to appreciate the elevated unity of color, shadow, line, in Rembrandt and to think about the meaning. So, too, building with a set of hard wood blocks will prepare you to appreciate Paestrum, Monticello, and Chartres. All the precious attention Rilke devotes to spoons, cups, and plates is fitting. All things in daily use, should be beautiful. The child's first spoon in its mouth need not be silver, but its surface should be smooth and its curve attractive. It is not wrong for zeks to cherish the spoon they fashioned in captivity. The superiority of each of the ancient peasant cultures of Europe to modern, homogeneous, cosmopolitan, mass, mall culture is evident in a single spoon, plate, or chair, despite the peasant's lack of electricity and an indoor toilet.

We tasting and seeing animals also crawl, swim, walk, and run. What exercise is the child set to? Not only strength, endurance, speed, agility, coordination, and health are at stake here, but self-control, grace, and courage, in other words, the soul, too. Are all sports equal? Why do the bodies and the souls of those who played one sport in youth seem so different from the others when they meet at high school reunions? And we sensible, moving animals also dance. What music does the child hear? What singing does the family do? And if daily family life were set to the music that fits it, what would it sound like? Haydn's Quartet op. 71, no. 1, or the Stones' "Paint It Black"? Music is at once the most intellectual of the arts and, despite the fact that it has almost no element of representation in it, the most moving of the soul, moving and forming. Start the day with a good melody and you will try to hear it all day, and sometimes you will.

We animals with senses are also rational. Good tastes, good sights, and good tunes naturally ready one for good experiences of the word, of logos, in its first form, stories. The good order of Scupper the Sailor Dog's cabin, everything in its place and him in his bunk bed, is an image of his confident soul, ready for adventure. Your room, too, could be so neat. Though abandoned by their own parents, Hansel and Gretel prove equal to the Witch they burn in that oven intended for them. You could prevail too. And later in life, in some dark hour, starting from a light sleep, it will be good to recall the night King Babar went to sleep troubled, how he dreamed of the ugly vices being driven away by the handsome virtues, and awoke to find it all true. Few orphans will be so fortified. Nor, as a consequence, can they reflect that they have these good stories because someone once read them aloud to them, someone who was thinking of their good before they were in being.

Few childhoods will be filled with perfectly sweet, beautiful, and cheerful things. Or can be. Parents who strive to provide perfect child-hoods will commonly pass big doses of their anxiety to their children. Or should be. Such parents misunderstand something. Sweet, beautiful, cheerful, good things do not have to be abundantly present for the soul, which naturally seeks them, to find them and flourish. One spring, one drink, will do, and sometimes one drop may suffice. Surfeit would squelch appetite. Moreover, if a childhood is poor in primary experi-ences of the good, their presence in good stories may suffice. Those who have missed such experiences may then benefit mightily from read-ing some good books, ones that give tastes of the beautiful, meals of the good, and for dessert, heroes to imitate; give them to all, but give especially to the needy, to those who haven't had many good meals, dwelt in beauty, or had a hero for a father or an uncle. For meals read *Farmer Boy* and learn what a boy should have for breakfast every morn-ing, apple pie. For beauty visit the *Secret Garden* and feel what power to strengthen a puny soul lies in a flower. And for heroes read the Land-mark books, meet Washington, Sequoyah, Nelson, Bolivar, Carson, and Garibaldi, and know that heroes do walk the earth. They really were heroes. Later on you can appreciate the more shaded accounts.

In a well-ordered country with flourishing families, young people first become good and only later perhaps great. As children they enjoy good meals before refined dishes, bread before sauce, hearty fare before haute cuisine, lots of *latte* before *café latte*, Frog and Toad before Stuart Little, the William Tell Overture before Beethoven's late quartets, and Brueghel before Rembrandt. Although we sometimes grow by spurts, and can even name the day and hour when we first discovered some-thing and were fetched forward by it, like Dante by Beatrice, still there is a progress from the good to the great that is steady, with steps that are best not omitted, or skated over quickly. As children, the well bred obey the commands of their parents, mind the laws of the land, and imitate the examples of the virtuous adults around them. Initial compar-ative weakness and ignorance makes obedience the first requirement of the child. Your young life, you might lose, unless you obey Mother. There is a snake, or a semi, or something so evil I do not want to name it to you; it is approaching swiftly, right now; obey immediately, without question, there is no time. Obedience is also the basis of later self-command. No one ever gave himself hard commands who had not first obeyed them from others. To obedience more must, however, be added. The destiny of the child is not to become a good slave, but a free adult, someone who chooses in accord with reason. Up this long ascent, the rules, indicating the wrongs to right and left, are helpful. Rule- or law-abidingness is not, however, equivalent to virtue, only something helpful to it. "Don't fall asleep at your post" is not the whole of loyalty, nor even the virtue of courage. Imitation is the way to such virtues. Moreover, although children benefit from the clarity of law, law can cover only the easy cases. Justice is far more than fairness. To decide when the rule fits and when it doesn't, there is no rule. Only sagacity can decide. Then to discern in a thicket of choices the right way and to follow it successfully, choosing the best means, prudence, the crown of the practical virtues, is required. The existence of this virtue is best shown precisely by examples, by men and women who possess it, yet it is hard to attain by imitation, since what is sagacious changes in accord with the circumstances in their multitudinous and mutually in-fluential detail. Here then nothing but intelligence will do. Odysseus is the best example in literature, but to understand why what he does is sagacious, you have to think his thoughts, which Homer never does for you, but once.

In the soul of a well-bred youth, it is emulation that is on the way to this intelligence. Good youths are known by their heroes. It is as La Rochefoucauld says: "The influence those we love has over us almost always exceeds our influence over ourselves" (*Maxims*, 525). There is a natural course in our emulation. At first, we emulate like the child who wears the same clothes as his hero; later we try to act just like that hero; and finally, only by thinking like him in service of the same purposes do we emulate well.[21] We go then from walking about dressed just like Gary Cooper, with "High Noon" whistling in our ears, to realizing that the Marshall is telling us to face the bully in our school, and on to simply asking, "What is the virtuous thing for me to do?" Only after doing that until you are thirty, so Aristotle says, will you be ready for the Great Books question, "What is virtue?" Young people need to read "a thousand good books before they read a hundred great ones," as John Senior says.[22]

Unfortunately, there are today very few brought up to be gentlemen and ladies. Ask the waitresses at restaurants in college towns. In the manners, the music, and morality of Western public life, there is no guidance for the young, and their homes have not sheltered them from public squalor. Down the TV antenna like lightning comes everything both effete and barbaric straight into their gaping souls. That novelty of our time, the Teenager, is truly someone without parents who command, parents who counsel, or parents to imitate. With intelligent, restless orphans, we often have then no range of choice; it is either the great books, great arguments, and great longings, or nothing. It is nobility or nihilism.

Fortunately, the great books do often give great examples to emulate, great arguments to engage, and great pleasures to arouse, but they are not without their dangers. It is not only that the metaphysical among them may close our eyes to what's in front of us, that the epistemological may paralyze the knowing mind, and that the tragedies among them will surely make the soul suffer, but that the very greatness of all great books can make the soul stoop. Reading them can make you melancholy; tales of old greatness can make you sad; and great ideas can make you feel small.[23] Orphans, especially the most virtuous among them, may suffer from the great books they read, and then make others do so. Those who seek the true without having enjoyed the good may make the true, the enemy of the good. I once knew a gifted graduate of a Great Books college who helped destroy a merely good college, half devoted to great books, just because it did not measure up to the college of his dreams, or rather to the perfect secondary book on a great book he had not yet written, which was also his justification for denying his wife a child.

There are some souls who regard the good as superficial, boring, or contemptible (which is not the same as hateful). If given Aristotle's *Ethics* to read, they will not say "That's pretty much what I've always thought," as Churchill did, but sum it up as "Look both ways before you cross the street." Of course, such a contemplative but unself-knowing soul may well step in front of the first semi of nihilism coming down the street; although they will not embrace it, they will not see it, or see it for what it is, and they will perish. Then there are those active souls whose idealism tramples on common and ordinary goods. Since he thinks well of himself for having high standards, the idealist is unlikely to examine himself, notice the consequences of his conduct, and trace the failure of his schemes to himself. Since he knows he is pursuing the good, he does not think he needs to do much of it. Such souls are, to be sure, dangerous, but I am not talking about them, but rather about those orphans in whom the hunger for truth cannot stomach the good. To their flashing eyes everything merely visible seems weary, stale, and ignoble, worth torching. Thinking that the world as it is, that it better were not, and the world as it should be, that it does not and cannot exist, they may try to prove it by destroying whatever in the world or out is good. "Burn everything older than yourself," as Holden

Caulfield might say and then just might include himself. And even an orphan who retains his aspirations, ones that have not grown up from a good childhood, may be cruel to whomever in whom he sees things he has not extinguished in himself.

Very often in the Platonic dialogues, Socrates confronts the opinions of some young interlocutor with knowledge, usually with the knowledge that the youngster does not know what he just claimed to know. These Athenian youths were, however, well bred; they were gentlemen; they were citizens; and they would soon rule. In Platonic terms, of course, they had grown up in the Cave, the Athenian version to be sure, but all cities are caves. We should be so lucky! To grow up in Athens where the public entertainment was provided by the three greatest tragedians the world has ever seen. The city of Pericles and Thucydides. The city of daring and endeavor. Some cave.

Today's students, the Teenagers, have grown up in no cave at all. Instead they have grown up in a pit below the Cave. Unlike a cave, this abyss gives its inhabitants nothing much to live for. Opinions these Teenagers do have, but not such as could hold a country, a civilization, or a family together. Nor do they please the youth himself. To each other and to every man and woman, such students are at best "nice," and to themselves, they are empty, or listless, as Bloom says. Most have never written a good letter, or received one. Most have never listened to two adults talk seriously for an hour. Most have never taken a walk with a friend or with thoughts. Falling in with what is critical, difficult, adventurous, and skeptical in the Great Books will not necessarily be good for such homeless ones.

Moreover, the great books often give examples to emulate that may be, in their ambiguous mixture, quite dangerous for such orphans. David, Alcibiades, Coriolanus, Augustine, Prince Hamlet, King Lear, Anna Karenina, Dmitry Karamazov—there is greatness in their souls, but you would not want someone to imitate all their deeds, or even a great many of them. To distinguish the evil from the good in them you have to be not only good already but also experienced in life. Likewise with such great thinkers as Machiavelli, Rousseau, and Nietzsche. That their great thoughts are ambiguous is clear enough from their political consequences, and even clear up closer (consider whoever in your circle of friends and teachers is taken with them), but who is thinker enough to separate the good and the evil in them?[24] In truth, it would take some soul on their own level.[25] And no young person, orphaned or not, is that soul. La Rochefoucauld is not wrong when he observes, "There are heroes of evil as well as good" (Maxims, 185).

It is well then if students of today meet not only the great heroes but the good ones as well. Most of the great stories do represent such men and women, but usually in subordinate roles, Horatio beside Hamlet, Edgar beside Lear, Desdemona beside Othello. It is well then, from time to time, to consider stories where the good are more prominent than the great. Jane Austen, Willa Cather, and Henry Fielding have given us examples. And in the greatest example, Tolstoy's *War and Peace*, the good are very much better than the great, Kutuzov better than Napoleon, indeed Pierre, Natasha, and nearly everybody better than Napoleon. The most revealing example is Andrei, for it is when he loses his worship of greatness, of his hero Napoleon, when he looks up at the great sky above Austerlitz and forgets "my Toulon," that he becomes something much better than great, namely good. So says Tolstoy, and this great man infatuated with goodness should be given a hearing. Neither orphan nor well-bred student will suffer from it.

Accompanying such good books in a Great Books curriculum might also come some experiences of the good as well. In no longer enforcing parietals, the colleges of the late 1960s gave up being *in loco parentis*. By saying to students in the dorms, in the dining halls, and in everything outside class, "you are on your own," the colleges of the 1960s imitated the parents who had created the Teenager a decade earlier. Both were wrong. And since then by, among other things, refusing to make drug arrests even of dealers, colleges have given up being *in loco policienis*, which not even the parents of today would approve of. What does it say about colleges that "drug-free dorms" and "study dorms" are touted as innovations? What does that say about all the other dorms? The colleges of today are profoundly irresponsible. "Student Life" should know that the life of a student is study. Everything outside class either supports or subtracts from it. Poor food, bad music, lack of clean, quiet places to study, and lax rules about conduct all subtract from study, and the rock music, promiscuity, and political activism (even for just causes) that rush in, all detract from study. It will be well then for colleges with Great Books programs to resume overseeing the whole of college life, and even for such programs to provide good experiences: to teach students to write legibly, read aloud, and memorize poems, and even to waltz gracefully, and identify stars in the night sky, as the Pierson College John Senior started within the University of Kansas did.[26]

They cannot, however, let these be the whole of the experience of the students. Young persons arriving at college, however orphaned in spirit, should not postpone meeting reason in the form of mathematics, reason in the form of discussion, and reason in the high confrontation of the soul with great things and great books. Nor do I think that the mix of students, immature and mature, and thus the books and experiences best fitted for each are so difficult to teach in the same classroom. After Socrates had shown him he lived in a dark cave and then dazzled him with a glimpse of the sun, then frisky Glaukon needed to hear about all the inferior regimes in the twilight between that utter darkness and that utter light. To have left him in despair or ecstasy, or yo-yoing between, would have been unwise of Socrates. Likewise, for the orphan, the greatness that is in reason, in inquiry, with its risk of settled skepticism, is necessary to the self-reliance of the future man. Lincoln had no very good childhood; the Bible and Shakespeare were his home; and later it was Euclid, reasoning closely through *The Elements*, and still later thinking through matters more important to the heart of man than your geometry, that made him a great man. Almost every class is a mix, and many students are too. The line between maturity and immaturity, between the youth and the Teenager, runs through the soul of almost all today.

For the teacher, the fundamental choice is always between speaking to the silent student who is your superior in heart and in mind, with the others enjoying the runoff from that fountain, or speaking to the higher part of the middle, with private time for the best. The good and the great are distinct; they are even sometimes at odds; but that they are ultimately harmonious is vouchsafed by the fact that those who have the most to say about the good are the greatest, Socrates on the idea of it, and Christ, its redemptive emissary, on its Creative Father and the destiny to which the good calls His best image, man.[27]

VI.
Great Places and Storm Homes

The soul not only longs for the truth, not only aspires to become a hero, but also aches for the best place, the place where things are all in order, neat, shining, shared, and happy. We long to live right with others, to march in step, to sing in a chorus, to enjoy friends without friction, conversations without strife, and festivities without exhaustion—to be part of some just, mighty, bounteous, generous, good whole. The great books speak to this desire. They tell us of singing heavens, of just utopias, of onward armies, fruitful gardens, and conversations not confined by mortal time. Eden, Phaiakia, the Republic, the Blessed Isles, Utopia, Paradise, and Heaven are their names. These places in the great books teach us to measure the world by the standards of the soul, the best soul. And they raise our souls up to their level. As the Cabby says, upon watching the more beautiful world of Narnia come into being through a transcendently beautiful song, "Glory be! I'd ha' been a better man all my life if I'd known there were things like this."[28]

Thus, the great political philosophers make the theme of the best regime central to their understanding of human life together. So, too, we want to live right with others now living, and we may even wish to be the founder, or at least the ruler, of such a place. Happily, the great books that are history books sometimes tell us of times when it was a joy to be alive; in them, the cities of the West rise again, daring Athens, beautiful Florence, holy Jerusalem, mighty Rome, savory Paris, and brave London. We need these great and distant places, those real, those legendary, and those actual to set in the soul's eye that we may measure the places we find ourselves in. All improvement of the place, the home, the institution, or the country that we find ourselves in begins with re- flection on the best place, and is then guided by successive imitation of it. Contrariwise, the great books also supply us with the worst places; their clear features help our eyes discern what's wrong with where we are. Sodom and Gomorra, Lotus-Land, the Swine City of Circe, the Castle of Kafka, the Gulag, and above all Hell are some of these worst places. The great books supply us with these best and worst measures, variously, richly, powerfully so.[29]

Children who grow up in a home come to these best places differently than orphans. When children from homes, who have some good experi- ence of place, meet the great places, they understand them to be en- hancements and perfections of what they already know. Though greater, they are commensurate. They are mere better homes and better gardens and better polities than their own, not The Home as opposed to their state orphanage, The Garden as opposed to their toxic swamp, and The City of God as opposed to the City of human, all too human, Man.

Homeless orphans, who have no experience of a good place, see these best places differently. They are likely to believe that nothing like the home they ache for will ever exist on earth. Despairing of it, they may be tempted to think that only the destruction of the homeless world they have grown up in will secure what they long for. The best places they meet in the great books may become the cause of ache, accusation, despair, and revenge in them. They will more often shake their fist at the condition of the world than set about ameliorating the portion of it that is their neighborhood. Aching globally, they will destroy locally.

It is well then that the great books also include history books, where good and bad places from the middle of the scale are found, not the extremes of best and worst. Between Heaven and Hell, between the best and the worst regime in Plato, between the palace of Phaiakia and the cave of Polyphemus, there are so many grades. These middle grades teach us to choose in the half-light that our lives are mostly lived in. Most choice in life is choice of the second or third or fourteenth choice. (Pro-choice is always wrong choice, since you wouldn't assert it, if you could put forward a good reason.) Although we will always judge by the extremes, to act best we need discernment in the middle range. From the historians, Thucydides to Burckhardt, we may learn that many grades of the bad can be endured and that many grades of the good can be attained. By giving us the middle of the great scale, they may moderate our impatience for reform, whose violence might make things worse, or they may wisely reconcile us to where we are now in that middle, for things could be worse.

It is true that every Christian is prepared to acknowledge that our home is truly elsewhere, that really we are homeless, but if we Christians have grown up in a good Christian home, we will leave the destruction of the world to God, honor our father and mother, and provide our children with a home worthy of such honoring. C. S. Lewis formulated Christian teaching well when he said that although it makes sense to die for your country, it makes no sense to live for it. The things of Caesar are worthy of the respect that is in rendering, the things of Lincoln are worthy of full-measured dedication, but to Christ alone is worship due.

Although no country, even a good one, can be as good as a friend, and not even the finest human being could be as good as the idea of the good or God, nevertheless, the soul does its best with mates and cannot do without a country too. It is not only that human beings, being political animals, need to associate to survive, but that souls need associations to be in good shape. Between us and the highest we can love, we need intermediaries to keep our affections alive. Even the solitary writer sometimes needs a clean, well-lighted café to sit, to see, and to be seen in.

Nothing is quite as good as growing up in a good home, but if you didn't, you can get some of that good from other sources, from growing up in a good town, belonging to a good parish, going to a good school, or living in a good country. An orphan is someone who, doing without a home, is in search of one. The common fancy in childhood that one is not really from this family, that later they will tell you you were adopted, suggests that the yearning is universal. What boy looking at his father's toe with hair sprouting from it, and feeling all his pink body has not thought, "We are different species." An experience in the snowbelt of America, when children still walked to school, bespeaks it. The arrangement was that if there were a great storm, one that would keep the children from walking back out to their farms, there was a family in town to whom each was assigned. That family was your "storm home." They would take you in. You met them early in the fall, before the snow; they knew your favorite foods; they had copies of your favorite books, and although they knew your bedtime, you felt they might let you stay up beyond it. Knowing of your storm home made the great storms less fearful, the anticipated homesickness less painful, and the world a better place. Knowing that you had a storm home, one just for you, some children wished for snow.[30]

Today in America it is not easy to find a good town, or a good parish, or a good school, and as a consequence (though also as a cause), America is not the good country it once was. The snow has been falling for forty years now; the Teenager is someone who has grown up knowing nothing else. They have been told there are no storm homes; and you should not even yearn for one, to be in one or to start one. Nihilism "says of the world as it is, that it better were not, and with regard to the world as it should be, that it does not and cannot exist."[31] But nature cannot be quite extinguished, and America is not as bad as it has been made to seem to these Teenagers. Moreover, in the foundation of America these orphans may find exactly the storm home their souls do still long for.

Thus, it is well for the orphans of America to learn something about the good of their own country, America. When the current scene looks like a combination of drunk Pappy, reechy Uncle Claudius, and 108 suitors on couches in your living room wooing your mom, Penelope, a recourse to the foundation in the cellar may be wise. Such a recourse to beginnings will combine a return to the home with the great adventure of meeting your father who you never knew, as Telemachus did Odysseus, and then together they restored Ithaka. In truth, it is only through such a recourse to our first principles that America will be renewed, its couches cleared of loungers and its market place of hucksters, and its houses become homes, that it might once again be more nearly good in itself and the cause of good in others.

America is not as gifted as suffering Athens, as beautiful as cunning Florence, or as aspiring as Elizabethan England, but it is good, good enough to be worthy of gratitude and obedience, even from time to time of esteem, and always of rededication. Moreover, for the orphans of America it is their own, in a way as well as a degree that the other lands cannot be, even if they have, like their unfortunate parents, grown up ignorant of it. Almost all nations need to chasten their collective self-love. The orphans of America, the generation of the Teenager, may be the first people on earth to need to strengthen their love of their own, themselves and their fellow Americans. Earlier Americans probably needed to pray "God mend thy every flaw, Confirm thy soul in self-control, Thy liberty in law." Present ones need to sing "Sweet land of liberty," honor the "brave" who have made this "home" "free," and discover what a "heart too full for utterance" is.[32]

VII.
America, the Home of Its Orphans

In the home that America is, everything rests on the Declaration of Independence; everything is based upon its dual principles, nature and nature's God; and, thus, everything either lives up to those principles or falls away. As the one principle looks back to Athens, where nature was first seen, so the other looks back to Jerusalem, where God, who created nature, was first heard.

In the Declaration, the two, though discerned as separate, are understood as related, both harmoniously and hierarchically. Thus the natural rights to "life, liberty and the pursuit of happiness" are acknowledged to be an endowment from the Creator God; they are His gifts, to His best creatures. While their violation is tyranny, while such violation justifies rebellion, separation, and new government, it only does so if prudence can say "More good will come than be lost," but if more good will come, then it will be a sacred duty, risking life, treasure, and honor, to resist tyranny and institute untyrannical government. When later secured, these rights will be, in the Constitution, among the blessings of liberty, to be handed down to future generations. Of course their exercise will ever require and confer what the *Federalist* will be the first to call "responsibilities" upon the magistrates of the people so blessed. Always these rights remain not only natural, thus inalienable, but "endowed" by God to His creatures. As a gift they will deserve gratitude, and as a responsibility, they will require all the practical virtues in the recipients. According to the Declaration, God gave rights because He wanted man to govern himself.

The four references to God in the Declaration are beautifully designed. God appears as natural Law-maker, as Creator, as supreme Judge, and as Provident Protector. Obviously, these forecast the separation and the blending of the legislative, judicial, and executive powers of government, created by the one sovereign People under God.[33] They also judge George III. The arrangement of the twenty-eight charges against him, proceeding from his legislative, through his judicial, and on to his executive abuses, shows his fundamental offense to be the attempt to unify all these powers, which only God does without being a tyrant. God creates men free because he wants them to govern themselves and because He wants them to worship Him freely. On this point, the Bill of Rights accords perfectly with the Declaration when, in the First Amendment, it protects both discussion and worship, through freedom of the former and noninterference with the unestablished latter.[34] To be sure, the ambiguity of the Declaration's phrase, "Nature's God," allows Spinoza and Aquinas to lie down together like lion and lamb in the American Ark; and it won the assent of such divers men as Jefferson and Witherspoon, Hamilton and Madison, Franklin and Adams. It was meant to. The God of the Declaration created man free, free to fall and free to stand up virtuous. And perhaps destined to. That so many men, meeting together over so many years and disagreeing so very much, should nonetheless create such a robust, enduring and relatively good regime, with so many divers federal parts, is remarkable. In it many have seen the hand of reason, and in it some have also divined the invisible, outstretched hand of reason's God.

The Declaration then is the basis of our pursuit (our practice) of happiness, the foundation of our government, and the presage of all our history. However, it must be confessed that, although it was signed by heroes, it would need heroes to make our Independence stand, and later to perpetuate it, and would always needs something heroic in the people formed by it, if only a capacity to recognize such qualities in others, nevertheless the Declaration, and even more its supplements, the Constitution and the *Federalist*, are not the kinds of things to fire emulative souls, especially orphans. Only a story could do that. Happily, and I submit almost inevitably, the Declaration has found a completion fit to educate the nation's orphans.

I say almost inevitably because the Founding Fathers intend the Declaration to begin a story. They cared for their children, for their children's children, and for the children of those children, too. Thus, in the Declaration, the Founding Fathers did not aim to institute perfection, like the Terror-izing French Revolutionaries, let alone to march toward it, like the Gulag-izing Russian Revolutionaries. Instead, they instituted something merely "more perfect," the passing on of whose blessings, such as liberty, would depend on the virtue of later generations. They left those later generations a precious gift, but also something worth doing. The American Revolution was not to be the end of the story of humanity, and if it was to be the beginning of a new order of happiness, it would only be so because new heroes, or at least new responsible statesmen, would be required.[35]

VIII.
The Story of America

The principles of America, enunciated in the Declaration, framed in the Constitution, supported by the *Federalist*, and looked to by the Founding Fathers, are the cause of the subsequent life of the United States of

America. The story of that subsequent life is a democratic epic, it is a domestic romance, and it is a bloody tragedy.

The principles of America were not America. Although America would not be America without its principles, no country is entirely its principles. Thus the America that based its Independence from an England grown tyrannical upon the principle that "All men are created equal" did not declare its independence from the slavery that their English colonial forefathers had instituted in America.[36] Thus, although the Constitution intended to wither away slavery, it also protected it. Truly the Constitution constituted a house that was divided. It was not really a home. For some it was worse than an orphanage. Which would it become? Slave or free? In the first two-score years after the founding, the motion was toward freedom, but in the next two score the South found that slavery was more comfortable than it could comfortably do without and that the tiger of slavery was larger than it could safely dismount from. So, slowly it began to justify what it liked, felt guilty about, and felt chained to. The series of Compromises made the House bigger but not less divided. Yet the repeal of the Missouri Compromise was worse; it set consent of the governed against justice; and suddenly the Dred Scott Decision made it possible, even likely, that the House itself might soon be united all slave. Then Lincoln rose up, debated Douglas, split the Democratic party, and was elected president; South Carolina fired on Sumter, and then came a war longer and more bloody than any one imagine or almost could endure. Lincoln judged it just to both sides, should it last two hundred fifty years, and judged that its grave wounds would only be bound up by rededication to the founding truths, now become propositions to be made true by the mighty labor of generations yet unborn. This refounding of the nation, this Unification of the House Divided, made it possible for the epic story of America to proceed apace free.

That story tells how, in a little over a hundred years, the fairest portion of a vast continent went from frontier, to prosperity, to refinement. In the two hundred fifty years preceding the Declaration only the coast, between the Atlantic and the Alleghenies, was settled; in the next hundred and a score years, five or six times more land was cultivated, populated, made home. Jefferson, the president who committed the nation to the Louisiana Purchase, thought it would take a thousand years to fill America with farmers from coast to shining coast, but the Revolution he helped to write and the Constitution that flowed from it opened the West rapidly; it did so by giving hope to all, land to many, and opportunity to each. Europe responded; lured by freedom, the discontented, the poor, the adventurous, the enterprising, the pious and the persecuted crossed the ocean, some staying in the cities of the East, others heading

West. Meanwhile, many born in the East, second sons seeking their fortune, or spirited first sons, and others, all resolute to prosper, became pioneers. For five or six generations young men went West, worked hard, driving cattle, busting sod, clearing forest, and then brought young women West after them.

Stand at the Cumberland Gap and watch the buffalo pass through, the Indian, the trapper, the trader, the cattle raiser, and the farmer—all but the first two, pioneers—or watch the same procession at South Pass a hundred years later.[37] Where did they come from, who were they, and what were they seeking? The answer may be read in the names the pioneers gave to the remarkable rock formations they encountered in the West: Independence Rock, Courthouse Rock, Steeple Rock, and Chimney Rock, that is—self-government, justice, worship, and home.[38] These are at once: where they came from, what they brought, and what they sought. The frontier very nearly is American history, and it very nearly is European history, too.[39]

America was always a story of the West being turned into the East. Given how much Locke's account of the state of nature shaped the self-understanding of the people who made a Revolution for the sake of self-government, one might describe this story as a continuous transformation of the state of nature into the civil state. However, neither the West nor the East, the state of American nature or the American civil state, was ever entirely Lockean. More than property, the pleasures of acquiring, and holding onto it, were attractive. The West was always for America the place of the unalienable rights of man, but in the Declaration these rights are included in, expanded to, and ennobled by the pursuit of happiness. Even more important, these rights are in the Declaration understood as gifts; men are "endowed" with them "by their Creator" so that they might govern themselves and prosper; and in the Constitution, liberty is understood as a precious "blessing," to be used well, to be defended, and to be passed on to one's "posterity." The Declaration knows of the importance of Prudence, the duty to resist tyranny, and the dignity of Honor. None of these is very Lockean. True, there in the West you will find the acquisitive Lockean man and there in the West you will also find the man of blood, who makes Hobbes so timorous, but you will also find the prudent man, the honorable man, and the virtuous man. And the prudent, thrifty, and virtuous woman.

Such a virtuous man is the cowboy. Although he appeared last in the pageant of pioneers and in any numbers lasted only as long as the great trail drives from Texas to Montana, thirty years or so, he is the epitome of the West. His adoption as the one mythical hero shared by all Americans shows you cannot understand America without understanding him.[40]

The best place to seek him out, other than to go West and seek the real thing, as he still exists here and there, is to open the pages of the most originating account: *The Virginian: A Horseman of the Plains* by Owen Wister.[41] Several real persons, many experiences, sketches, campfire tales, and much afterthought went into the making of this story, and from it thousands have been made. Here first in *The Virginian* the Cowboy leapt into immortality. The thundering hoofbeats of his horse recall knights in armor; in his eyes burns a light that through the ages lifted the souls of strong men who fought for justice, for God, and for country. Now the sons of this nameless American hero are so numberless they might as well be masked.[42]

IX.
The Virginian

Always in *The Virginian* there are the high plains and the clear air, with the lofty mountains beyond. "The sun shone warmly down, the tall red cliff was warm, the pines were a warm film and filter of green; outside the shade across the creek rose the steep, soft, open yellow hill warm and high to the blue, and the creek tumbled upon its sun-sparkling stones." Night follows day. "Coolness filled the air, and the silence, which in this deep valley of invading shadow seemed too silent, was relieved by the birds." As the narrator convalesces in the healthy Western air, so do we. We feel elevated and yet more aware of the heavens above us. Things are more beautiful, more dangerous, and more precious. Water becomes precious again as it is not in the East, where it is abundant. "Often he had added several needless miles to his journey that he might finish the day at this point, might catch the trout for his supper beside a certain rock upon its edge, and fall asleep hearing the stream on either side of him." It is to this sequestered pool high in the mountains that the Virginian will bring his beloved Molly for their honeymoon. In this refreshing West, we also meet a fine gallery of secondary characters: an intolerably upright preacher, a mortal rustler, a docile horse, and a memorable chicken. Although there is little cow herding and no trail drive in this archetypal story of the cowboy, there is just enough dust, discomfort, and hunger so that we won't be too disappointed by our first visit West.[43] Many a reader since, boy or girl, man or woman, has finished the book resolved to "go West" because, heart and soul, they are already there.[44]

Against this invigorating background, *The Virginian* provides a story of adventure, romance, and sagacity. For adventure, you have the strenuous labors of ranch life, "fighting words," a vigilante lynching, an

Indian ambush, a gun fight, and a long courtship. For romance, we have that courtship, one of matched minds and hearts—a long courtship, not because of mistakes or shifts, but because both do not want to settle for less than the best, in the other or in themselves. To promote sagacity, the novel gives us episodic instruction; first we meet the situation, we wonder what to do, and then we see exactly what a practically wise man, the hero, does do. Finally, by doing all this, the *Virginian* reflects seriously on the place of a natural aristocracy in a democracy of opportunity.

The Virginian is not only a type and, through adoption, an archetype, but an individual, with thoughts no one else ever expressed. His opinions on life and everything he meets in it are striking. Molly gives him Shakespeare to read; of Romeo he says, "I have read *Romeo and Juliet.* That is beautiful language but Romeo is no man. I like his friend Mercutio that gets killed. He is a man. If he had got Juliet there would have been no foolishness and trouble." According to him, if Shakespeare had known poker, Falstaff would have played a lot of it, and yet the Prince would have beat him. *Othello*, he tells Molly, should not have been written: "such things should not be put down in fine language for the public." Marriage and lightning the Virginian regards as the truly surprising things in life. That he himself is as truly surprising, he does not suspect. Although he must know his given name, we never learn it.[45]

Reticent, dignified, and strong, the Virginian treats good men with respect, bad men with justice, and fools with charity. In him a rancher will find a good foreman; the hands, a good boss; the animals, a gentle master; and in him a friend gone bad will find sadness and firmness, in equal portions. Time and time again we wonder how the Virginian will get out of a jam, or how he will get the best from a tricky and often risky situation. How will he treat this fool? How will he oppose this knave? How will he remain true to several duties? Again and again he proves equal. The Virginian knows when to oppose evil with guile, when to undo it with laughter, when to endure it with fortitude, and when to wipe it out with a weapon. He knows how to protect fools, how to foil knaves, and how to woo stubborn virtue. Even in bliss he remains "responsible." One has to go back to Odysseus for a pattern of like sagacity.

Yet the bent of his sagacity is democratic; situations a born and bred aristocrat might intervene in, he holds back from, observing the limit set by self-government. The fundamental democratic assumption, that each man knows enough to choose for himself, is the rule he honors, even when he breaks it, for better reason, as with Shorty and Balaam. Democracy according to the Virginian is not anarchy. It values the individual, choice, and liberty, but not utterly. Thus when Balaam abuses a horse, to the point of gouging out its eye, the Virginian doesn't stand by and watch; he thrashes him. The horse is Balaam's property, but there is a higher law, the breaking of which justifies violent intervention. The aim of statesmanship in a democracy is to keep together the choice of the people and justice. Thus no majority acting unjustly can satisfy the soul, and to resist such a majority would be just, as the big ranchers may have been doing in the Johnson County War (which Wister alludes to). It should surprise no one that Wister thought the United States derelict in its moral duty for not entering World War I after Germany gouged out the eyes of Edith Cavell and Belgium.[46]

The Virginian's sagacity is seen in the way he brings the men entrusted to him back from a cattle drive East. They would go off for gold, a kind of wealth that extracts futile effort from most, and the few it rewards, it usually destroys, since the passionate desire that drew them, the desire for easy, quick wealth, is the same desire that makes the rewards pass through their hands like water. Had no one but the Virginian been there, these cowboys would make it back to the ranch and enjoy the steady benefits a hard-working life for a good master provides them with, but since an evil man, Trampas, is also along, it is a contest as to whose teaching will prevail. By telling a taller tall tale, of the wealth to be made from raising frogs (to be sold for frogs' legs, much as cattle are raised for beef, to Easterners), and then letting his men see the passion that had made them believe his story, the Virginian wins. It is a testimony to the Virginian's sagacity that he gets the idea of a tall tale from his rival and enemy, Trampas, who has just sucked in his friend, the narrator, with one. It is as Foch said, "Great battles are won late in the afternoon, with reserves." Even better, this battle is won by imitating with improvements a stratagem the enemy sprang on one of your wing commanders in the morning. Washington and Grant, about whom Wister wrote compact biographies, would approve of the Virginian's statesmanship.

The book is also about what constitutes America; in it both the Declaration and the Constitution come under discussion. To the narrator from the East, the equality declared self-evident in the Declaration is no more than the fairness that allows all men to start the run of life without artificial impediments blocking their course to happiness. Such equality at the start is the precondition of their later distinction; some will win and some will lose and, the narrator implies, it would be unfair to interfere with the results of the game. The Virginian, who as a gambler knows this, also knows more. Life is not only a game, it is a school, and teachers such as the Molly he courts should treat their pupils proportionately to their gifts; it is pity not justice in Molly to bestow more time on the slowest, least gifted child, than on others more gifted. But

equality is not only fairness and not only proportion, it is "responsibility" as well. America allows men equal opportunity and it encourages
them according to their natural gifts, and in addition it asks the more
accomplished to look after the less. The narrator from the East forgets
that there is evil in the world; one bright morning, as the sun rises, he
praises the Western climate, its salubrity, its clarity, its wonderful sun;
meanwhile, the Virginian, paying little attention, aims at a rattler right
behind him, and plugs it. Remember, oh mortal, the sun that gladdens
you, warms the serpent too.

As the story progresses, the Virginian is given more and more "responsibility," and he rises to it. Elevated to the position of foreman on
the ranch, he forgoes the just revenge he could have enjoyed by dismiss-
ing Trampas. He does so partly because it is virtuous, partly to enjoy
the respect such magnanimity will win him, and partly so that he can
hinder the evil that springs from this evil man, something that will be
easier to do if he is in sight. He does so especially because he sees that
an innocent man, Shorty, will be more easily protected from Trampas.
It is the Virginian who first sees the good in Shorty; any man who,
despite the rough treatment he must give animals, retains his love of
them and even cultivates it, so he can gentle a wild horse and train a
good one up to the best in him—such a man has good in him. However,
the Virginian also sees that Shorty is a fool, easily misled, and not
capable of self-government. Shorty is something like Bob Carmody, the
ungifted child Molly heaps disproportionate time on, but the novel
teaches that the right relation of those who know about life to those
who do not is for the former to watch out for the latter, not hope they
will become like you. He who cannot be educated must be left to himself, in all but the direst of straits.

The word "responsibility" appears often in *The Virginian*; I count
about thirteen places where it is attended to. Not so long ago, Leo
Strauss observed that whereas previous generations in the West spoke
of virtue, we now tend to speak of "responsibility"; a responsible man
used to mean a man not crazed, now it means a man we are too shy to
call virtuous; thus a word once used to name the condition of free acts
(either good or bad) now substitutes for the good acts of a free man.[47]
Of course that would be a loss; a people no longer able to speak of
virtue and the virtues will discern them less sharply and soon practice
them less vigorously. However, need we worry about the word "responsible"? In *The Virginian*, first published in 1902, long before the introduction of the word "values" depleted our moral aquifer, the word "responsibility" means the sagacious care a good man will exercise over
his own affairs, over those of whomever he serves, and even over those
of some merely within his possible care. It is the virtue of the good

steward, the good foreman, the good rancher, the good father and the good husband; and should the man seek higher office, "responsibility" as we see it so abundantly in the Virginian would be the virtue of the Statesman. When the Virginian tells Judge Henry, who has just asked him to be his foreman, "I'll try to please you," it is as good as a pledge of sacred honor. James Madison, who coined the word "responsibility," would be pleased.[48]

When the Virginian courts a good, independent woman, he treats her with patience, improvement, and self-reliance. Locked in courtship, they prove the match of each other: in wit, in resolution, in love and in virtue. He prefers Shakespeare and an unnamed Russian novelist she gives him; she prefers Jane Austen whom she has read and reread. Their courtship is a strife in virtue; both must win the other; both must be patient and strong, even to the point of renunciation. He would not seek her unless he could assure himself that he can promote her happiness. Each, by recognizing something noble in the other, becomes the reason for the other becoming more noble. Although before the story begins the Virginian has known a number of women and although as it begins he "adulterates" with one, reading the letter Molly writes to seek the schoolmarm's position at Bear Creek stirs him to defend her honor, at some risk to his standing, since he cannot be sure others will line up on the side of chastity,[49] and at sure risk to his life, because the moment Trampas is forced to retract his calumny, he hates the Virginian. Something in her letter makes him feel that there are better things in life than what he has yet known. When she signs herself "Sincere Spinster," he divines that she is twenty and not forty. More important, he is impressed by someone who knows chastity means waiting for the best. The Eternal Virtuous draws him on.

Molly, too, must become nobler to be a match for her cowboy suitor. She is noble enough to have rejected the suit of a good man, for the good reason that she does not love him. Sam Bannett, back East, proves he is good, but not noble, when he obeys Molly's order not to mount her departing train; the Virginian would have disobeyed and won her. In Bennington Molly stands out as genuinely independent, but out West her independence is marred by airs and willfulness. Molly must put aside some of her false manners (about how one should be introduced, for example), some of her foolish conduct (dancing with married men while refusing to dance with eligible ones, for example), and her false opinions, for example, about the relation of the law and justice (for not everything outside the law is unjust). On the way to doing so, she must break with her past, not only with her foolish mother, but with all in Bennington that is genteel, calumnious, and mediocre. Bennington abhors the Virginian because he carries a gun; Bennington has forgotten its origin in a revolution; mediocre, it knows only of mediocre evils, ones not strong enough to need a gun to destroy. It is significant that when Molly saves her man, she draws his six-shooter from its holster and is ready to defend their lives from the Indians that have wounded him. She must "leave" all that was her home, before she can "cleave," and become "one flesh." She gets some help from a great aunt who has some of the old family virtue that once animated it, founded the independent Republic of Vermont, and shone in Molly Stark. She alone of Vermonters takes some Eastern pride in "making this country." This great aunt is everything younger members in a family might wish for. She alone asks genuine questions of Molly's man. Every time she reappears in the novel, we cheer.

The courtship of the Virginian and the Vermonter is a long one. Many of my students criticize Molly for holding her chivalrous man off for so long, I think wrongly. The wayward habits of his youth were not to be perfectly purged but by a long time of self-denial and a long practice of an ardor uncertain of ever attaining its wish. It may even be that this time should be prolonged, as it is with him, to the point where he must renounce her and even to the point where it will be clear that if his hope for her proves futile he will not return to the loose habits of his youth, which we see in the first chapters. That he says if he lost her he would bury his sorrow in lots of work, plus the fact that we believe he would, is a sign that he is worthy of Molly and ready to marry her. Then again, marriage is a more fateful, comprehensive thing for a woman than a man; married, she will lose many of the temporary advantages of courtship; her husband will never again be her courter. It is right then that she err in the direction of caution. Neither hero nor heroine in this novel is the worse for the delay. Indeed, both are the better, the more worthy of each other, for the length of their courtship.

When the Virginian must hunt down Steve and see him lynched, justly lynched for cattle stealing. and then mourn that he must, we realize that his life could have gone a different way. On the desolate trail after the lynching, we learn that Steve and he used to be two rogue males together when they hit town. Together they enjoyed the fornication of beasts, and, so the narrator tells us, the Virginian recalled these scenes in the language of elks and tigers. Leaving out that language, a more mature Virginian will later admit the facts to Molly's mother in a letter. In speaking of the justice of hanging Steve, the Virginian says that it is unjust for one man to put his iron on another man's calf. That remark also convicts him, for the adultery he commits in an early chapter of the novel could be described just so. Once the Virginian and Steve were friends. The Virginian might have gone the way of Steve. In life choice is decisive.

Speaking of the Virginian, Hemingway told Fitzgerald that there could be no scaling back of such illicit pleasures as the Virginian had enjoyed before Molly. Hemingway and St. Paul seem to agree: the natural man cannot reform; Wister and Aristotle also agree, but on the other side. The reform without conversion that Wister portrays does include guilt, such that it provokes the Virginian's only imprudence; consciousness of the repellent character of his earlier unchastity prompts the Virginian to write Molly's mother about it; this was a lapse of sagacity in him, for that silly woman broadcasts the story about Bennington, but it is strong evidence of the genuineness of his reform. And it is shame about those deeds that inhibits the Virginian from mentioning them to Molly.[50]

Being real man and real woman, the Virginian and the Vermonter have the kind of chaste courtship that will lead to a marriage of royal rule, as Aristotle says it should and as St. Paul seems to have advised in a letter. Yet what Tocqueville says about the "deep, regular, and peaceful affection" that democratic marriages, freely contracted by both parties, provide Americans, and thus provide America with the "domestic tranquillity" that supports political stability—all this is amply shown here.[51] All the miscreants, rustlers, and murderers are unmarried; of the good only Scipio is single. Only in democratic American will one find many such royal marriages says Tocqueville. Indeed, no novel could be more different from *Madame Bovary* than *The Virginian*.[52]

The honeymoon these two inaugurate their domestic happiness with is perfectly described, that is, modestly, without any of the details craved by corrupt imaginations; such details would prevent adult readers from thinking of whatever details from a similar happiness they have experienced and such details would be no help to young readers in discovering such details at the proper time and place, namely later, wedded and in the flesh. Of their honeymoon, in the mountains, beside the still waters of a high lake, the author merely says that they liked it so much there the first night they lingered for a week. A more chaste and also a more ardent line does not exist in literature.

The novel tells the story of how this natural diamond of a man loses his roughness, including some waywardness, through manly dedication to a lady. No knight of the *gaya scienza* was more courtly or gentle than this hired horseman. It also tells how he stays the man he is. Friendship can test a man as well as love. Out of justice a man might have to hang another who was once his closest friend, and right though he be, he will, nevertheless, suffer the pangs of despised friendship. The Virginian could have bowed out of the lynching of Steve, he could probably have arranged for Steve to escape, or he could, on the other side, have hanged him with sangfroid righteousness. He errs to neither side. He does what is naturally right and he suffers from it, nearly losing his moral balance in the lonely ride west to the Tetons after the lynching, and helped by chance bringing him a message from Steve himself. Wister and Roosevelt were not wrong to consider this the best chapter in the book.

Molly, the beloved lady, must also learn this about justice: that sometimes nature and duty suspend convention and due process. Suspensions of liberty are justified if they are for the sake of the regime that defends liberty. Lose Liberty and you are not likely to have Virtue spring up in your midst. Yet the case, one of a sober hunt and lynching, is a difficult one, because the offense is only theft and because, it might be argued, that it is not what the Constitution recognizes as a time of civil rebellion. Still, this is but another instance of the way the novel is about the American regime and also the kind of American discussions it stimulates.

Finally, Molly, and we, must also learn another civic lesson: that sometimes all must be risked or nothing will be left to love or be loved. Lose Virtue and you will lose Liberty too. There can be no homes and families without a country to surround them. The lesson is difficult because it is tied to another. Honor pursued is often a bauble, an airy nothing, and honor defended often but pride luring to stupidities. Nevertheless, the Virginian cannot let Trampas's direct challenge to his honor go unanswered. If he does, he will lose the good that comes from reputation, the power to threaten bad men and reassure good ones, for if he ignores Trampas's challenge, he will invite every swaggart to take a shot at him. This Molly learns on their wedding day, and it would have been no wedding day if she had not learned it. From this episode spins off that fine movie *High Noon*. Not all good things are the cause of the increase of goodness, but some are, and *The Virginian* is one such good procreator of good.

We sometimes hear that the Founders of America built on nothing more elevated than the pursuit of comfortable self-preservation taught by the clever John Locke. Admitting that, as Washington affirmed (in 1783), America is built on a new understanding of the rights of man, or what Publius Hamilton calls a new science of politics (*Federalist* 9), and hence on a new relation of rights and duties, and admitting that, as Tocqueville said, American democratic man strives to identify virtue and interest, still, did the Founding Fathers really bring forth something so low and wholly modern? Did they perceive the knavishness of Locke and imitate it? And if they did not, were they Locke's fools, or did they simply take the evident good in him and ignore the esoteric evil? And when Americans think back to their foundation in the state of nature, do they become poor timorous Hobbeses, cautious cupidinous Lockes, or sentimental Rousseaus, or, just as often, brave, virtuous Virginians and Lone Rangers, ready to protect life and property from designing Machiavels, and to institute self-government based on God-given rights? The account of America given in *The Virginian* affirms the latter.

The novel also tells the story of another Easterner, a wealthy New Yorker in fact. Like Molly, the narrator also becomes who he is by going West; there he, too, loses a certain softness. Both are tenderfoots, but he a tenderer one. She arrives in Medicine Bow healthy, he arrives suffering from some unnamed debility of spirit. There he convalesces, and as he does so, matures. His growth in the virtues goes along with his growing friendship with the natural aristocrat, the Virginian. Thus, during the middle of the novel, in the tall-tale contest with Trampas, the character of Scipio must be introduced so that we can appreciate the statesmanship of the Virginian through a knowing observer, but by the time Steve must be hanged, it is the narrator who is close to the Virginian, and in the ride afterwards he is at times actually superior to his troubled friend, and beneficially so. Still, there remains a difference between them; during the night before the hanging the narrator feels more for Ed, who fears death and does not die bravely, while the Virginian feels more for Steve, who though fearing death does die bravely, which the Virginian admires and hopes he will equal. Nevertheless, although the narrator acts very little in the story, only he could have told it. The Virginian and the Vermonter are perfectly matched for courtship and marriage, but neither could have told the other's part of the story well enough. Perhaps they could not even tell their own side as well as the narrator. And only the narrator has the breadth of experience that knows America contains Medicine Bow and Fifth Avenue. There is a difference between hero and heroine, on the one hand and on the other, the poet, but there need not be enmity between them.

X.
The Most American Novel?

The narrator's comprehensive appreciation of what makes up America brings us to the author, Owen Wister, and what he comprehends. Wister had an eye for all that is beautiful in nature, splendid in man and woman, and good in our nation. *The Virginian* is the most American novel I know of. Other American novels may be greater, perhaps one of them is the Great American Novel, but they seem less American. As an American, I am proud of them, but if someone asked me, "Which one gives the best account of America?" or "Which one should I read before visiting?" I would have to say *The Virginian*. If Tocqueville were alive and preparing to revisit America, this is the story I would want him to read.

Let us consider the other candidates, ones which would surely be candidates as well for inclusion in a Great Books curriculum. Like *Faust, Moby Dick* treats the Baconian project of mastering nature; it is American because Melville places that project in America; and it is great because the monomaniacal character of that project is well brought out by Melville not only in his account of the first oil industry, but in the passionate hatred of nature and nature's God that beats in the flinty frame of Captain Ahab.[53] Melville understands that it is antitheological ire that drives the modern project; his modern captain takes the question with which God answers Job: "Can you put a hook in Leviathan?" as a dare, and answers, "Damn right, and a harpoon in You, too." Unfortunately, Melville seems to share his injured hero's hatred of God. Cetology is really theology; so while Ahab fumes and harpoons, Melville cackles.[54] Melville is right to place his Baconian drama in America where, without the accumulated lets and hindrances to innovation present in Europe, the project has been carried on with a commercial fury, and Melville may be right, long before Weber and his greater teacher, Nietzsche, to link Protestantism with the spirit of this imperial capitalism, but Melville stands outside America. Maybe he understands America better than Americans understand themselves, but he does not first understand them as they understand themselves.

Not so Wister. The religion of his West is that recommended by Washington, lauded by Tocqueville, most deeply meditated by Lincoln: firm, unceremonious, believing in the Creator, emphasizing conduct in this world more than salvation in the next, rejecting wickedness as much as those preachers who say we are all wicked, and not very established. For the Virginian, the most important of God's attributes is Justice: "If I can't do nothing long enough and good enough to earn eternal happiness, I can't do nothing long enough and bad enough to be damned. I reckon He plays a square game with us if He plays at all, and I ain't bothering my haid about other worlds." This is not the faith of Pascal, nor his persuasive Wager, or the faith of Lincoln, with its acknowledgment of painful mysteries, but it is the faith of the land of Lincoln. The God who presides (I select this word deliberately) over this spacious land is much like the man the Virginian says he has gained the most from, the man who says more by his noble example and few words, which make one ashamed, than by garrulous threats. The God of the Virginian is a God who prefers to instruct gentlemen than to command servants. The democratic consequence of this aristocratic disposition is well spelled out by Judge Henry: "As soon as you treat men as your brothers, they are ready to acknowledge you as—if you deserve it—as their superior. That's the whole body of Christianity, and that's what our missionary [McBride] will never acknowledge." McBride is a Christian moralist. Since he is righteous, he does not include himself in his account of human nature; the standards he appeals to, he identifies with himself, instead of seeing them above himself, judging him as well. Being punishments of others, his speeches do not persuade.

In *The Virginian* McBride is directly countered (by the Judge) and narratively surrounded by the story, when the Virginian mimics the reformation of a sinner, keeping McBride up all night, and making him such a laughing stock that he departs in haste and indignation. Does McBride show how evil it is to believe in good and evil, in anything based in metaphysics, in Platonism, and in Christian morality? No. The answer to moralism is not relativism, but morality.[55] And pity, "toleration," and state welfare would be no replacement for the charity that morality also calls for.

It is significant that the first thing the new community at Bear Creek sets about establishing is a school; in the country constituted by the Constitution and its First Amendment it is no surprise that respect for Washington is taught explicitly and the common tenets of Christianity tacitly. All preachers are welcome at all good ranches and homes, and denominational differences belong in the homes and the various churches. And perhaps it is significant that Judge Henry's understanding of the reason the Virginian must face Trampas is better than the Bishop's advice on the question. Of course, the same question, When should I fight? will be the one Jimmy Dean will face in *Rebel Without a Cause*, without Bishop, Judge, or parents.

Yet in Wister's judgment the moralism of the preachers is less dangerous to the Republic than the moralism of the democrats, their resentment of distinction, their substitution of pity for charity, and their inclination to think no majority wrong. This *The Virginian*, like the *Federalist*, leans against. Not yet in Wister's time had the democrats extended the scope of their equalizing passion to truth, first holding all views equally true (relativism) and then equally untrue (nihilism).

The two other candidates for most American novel concern slavery. The first, Faulkner's novella, really a brief epic, "The Bear," shows how the education in the wilderness Ike receives from the Bear must be supplemented by reading, especially the ledgers whose scrawls, when deciphered by imagination and experience, tell the tangled story of slavery. However, the lesson Ike and the author draw from these two books, of nature and history, leads Ike to imitate the Bear, to refuse responsibility and live "childless, kinless, heartless," not unlike Polyphemus.

True, Ike is gentle, but he is no statesman, and maybe not a man. Man may endure and even prevail, as Faulkner disappointed his dour, avant, Existential French admirers by saying in Stockholm, and even endure through the virtues he named, but not through the reason, the practical wisdom, and the sagacious unification of natural right and consent of the governed that America in crisis will require of its saving statesman, which Faulkner did not mention and nowhere portrays in the dark country of Yoknapatawpha. What is great about Faulkner, his attention to suffering, constitutes a criticism of all Southern nostalgia, whether magnolia or wounded, all racism, and all commercial optimism.[56] It is based on the principles of America but does not share its confidence or dedication.

The other candidate would seem to be *Huckleberry Finn.* Its treatment of slavery is surely part of its claim. The way Huck comes to see Jim as his benefactor, his protector, his friend, and therefore deserving of justice, and even sacrifice, is worthy. But Twain makes this discovery of natural right and its opposition to conventional right (for slavery is lawful) coincide not with a criticism of Christian hypocrisy, but a puerile ridicule of Christianity itself. Huck will help Jim even if it means going to hell. "Greater love hath no boy but that he risk the fires of Christian hell for his friend," is Twain's derisive teaching. Thus does Twain place just love of others and love of God in opposition. Twain's hero is a boy, an orphan, who is happy to remain an orphan. Civilization and everything that is connected with it seems to be the target.[57] Civilizations can benefit from such an attack as a smart man like Twain can supply; democracies need to license a Fool to sting their complacency; but they can be excused for not electing them to represent them. The prototype of Huck, we hear, became a sheriff out West—perhaps he became the Virginian, but Huck never does; Twain never has him grow up, and there is little room in *Huck Finn* for the founding principles of America, or the virtues it requires of its leaders.[58]

Intelligent, gifted, and even great as Twain and Faulkner and Melville are, none would make a fine president, governor, or senator. Are their principles the principles of the country? Only partly, I think. If not, that leaves *The Virginian* as the only candidate that deals with the character of democracy and human nature, hence with an aristocracy of virtue, with nature, and with nature's God, all in a way that accords with the founding, with its perpetuation by Lincoln (both of which are mentioned), and with the common sense of most Americans, however uncommon the reach of the author's understanding. Thus, it should not surprise one that it is easy to imagine the Virginian as president of the United States and therefore also possible to imagine the author of *The Virginian* as president.[59] Wister was a friend of Theodore Roosevelt;

the book is dedicated, and then in 1911 rededicated, to our twenty-sixth president, who was soon to run, as a Bull Moose, to become the twenty-eighth. Later Wister wrote *Roosevelt: The Story of a Friendship.*[60]

The great rival of Wister, for the title "the American novelist who wrote best of America," is seldom considered with the rivals I have mentioned. Yet no one has written so well and so much of the frontier and the pioneers of America as Willa Cather. Alexandra, Tom Outland, Antonia, and Archbishop Latour are pioneers. Their stories are the story of America. And so are Cather's stories of the lost pioneers, Claude Wheeler and Mrs. Forrester, persons who are lost without the frontier but who have also lost it, through nature or choice. Of Willa Cather it might be said that she was so good, such a vital fountain of good—gusher, arc, splash, and basin—that she was great.[61] It must be conceded, however, that none of her pioneers, even Archbishop Latour, would make quite as good a president as Wister's Virginian.

In *The Virginian* the West unites the old South and the old North by returning to their natural origins. The vantage point from which the flaws, vices and defects of America are seen by Wister is not a Southern farm (as with the Agrarians), a Chartres Cathedral (Henry Adams), a café in Paris (the very lost generation), or a future never-never land (Marxist or Sci-fi-ian), but a high range in Wyoming, or anywhere there are men and women. The vantage point is not history, either some historical epoch or some future historical state, but the virtues, and especially the natural right that shines in nature and must shine in the Republic founded in nature and in nature's God, if we are to keep it.

In conclusion, let me share with fellow teachers of American literature and government, thinking of teaching *The Virginian*, the reports of two students. Intelligent, yet struggling, sometimes even displeased-to-be-pleased, but gutsy, this Honors student at North Texas wrote in one of her journals, "I didn't get it when we read Plato in the fall, or the *Federalist* this spring, but I do now; yes, I confess it, I have lost two nights sleep since I deigned to pick it [*The Virginian*] up and have only now finished it, so that my life may continue." Another Honors student tells me that she insists that before he proceed further any suitor must read *The Virginian*. Since the maiden does the insisting, I think this is even better than the three caskets the father of Portia set in her suitors' way.

XI.
The Union of the Great and the Good

So far, I have said, you will have noticed, nothing about the criticism that this book, *The Virginian*, and the America for which it stands might be subjected to. The best criticism would come from the point of view of the body or Marx, of the soul or Plato, humanity or Goethe, technology or Heidegger, and nobility or Nietzsche.

Brief let me be. To the first, it might be said that the envy of the great and desire for ease in the Shortys of America may always be exploited by the Trampases unless the Virginians watch out.[62] To the second, it might be pointed out that the protection of property in America and the right to inherit it will always allow a few sons of the wealthy the leisure to survey the whole American scene, as the narrator does, and thus might one day support a philosopher. To the third, one must concede that anxiety about natural death could indeed bankrupt America and, on the way to it, make Americans into nothing but patients, litigants, and tourists. Thanks for the warning, faint advance clouds of which were only on the horizon of *The Virginian*, Herr Goethe. As to technology, the novel shows that the people who first change the face of nature in the West, wasting much, are pretty much the same ones who come to appreciate it, in the next generation, of which Wister's Western-and-Eastern friend, Teddy Roosevelt, was the leader, who saved the West, its lands, its flora, and its fauna, especially the buffalo. "Clean up your own mess" is a good maxim, which all business men once heard their mother say; Nature, too, is a blessing to be passed on to your posterity; and the causes now called environmental are fundamentally conservative. Conservation of nature is conservative. So, when you see a business gouge out nature's eye, hit it as hard as the Virginian does Balaam.

And toward the fifth, let one riposte suffice for now. At a dinner in the White House of Teddy Roosevelt, which Wister attended, the question arose, "How many of the people are knaves and fools?" and after many had spoken upping the percentage, Roosevelt or'lept all by declaring "eighty percent."[63] The judgment, which is surely also present in *The Virginian*, is nearly as critical as Nietzsche's might be, yet it did not mean for a minute that Roosevelt was not dedicated to a government of fools and against knaves, and thus for the good of persons who were all pretty much his inferiors. We find the same appreciation of human nature democratically arranged and yet cheerfully served in the Virginian's service to Shorty, his foiling of Trampas, and his wooing of Molly.

In sum then, Owen Wister's *The Virginian* gives an elevated account of the American regime, its appreciation of liberty, the importance of property in it, its understanding of justice, of equality, of race, of marriage, and its encouragement of some peculiar virtues, without which none of the blessings of liberty can ever be bequeathed to our posterity. The elevation of this account encourages a reasonable patriotism, condemns whatever then or now falls below the mark, and also inspires good young men and women, like the Virginian and Molly, to grow worthy of each other. Even to a generation suborned to promiscuity, this book has the power to present the pleasures of courtship. *The Virginian* is the most American novel I know of. The most about America, by an American, for Americans, about Americans, and the most likely to promote the good of America and Americans.

Still, it must be conceded that good as it is and good for orphans as it is, *The Virginian* is not great. Its hero bears some resemblance to Shakespeare's Henry V, but not to those of his heroes who suffer greatly, Hamlet and Lear. In addition, the way Wister has the Virginian come into some property, through a grant from the Judge, avoids the thorny issue that erupted in the Johnson County War, which Jack Schaefer in *Shane* faces so finely. Neither the Virginian nor Wister thirst for supernatural truth as Pascal did, reach for a greater stage to test their virtue as Sophocles does, or write as sweetly as Keats. Wister is not Stendhal, Halifax, or Leopardi. *The Virginian*'s deliberate rejection of such greatness is indicated by its hero's strictures against the public exhibition of a story such as *Othello*. These are appropriate to his virtue and the book's goodness, but also a confession of its inferiority to greatness. One might say that when he reaches thirty, the Virginian would benefit from a Great Books program, that he is one of the good students unlikely to be hurt by one, and also that he probably would not choose one.[64] Neither Socrates nor Christ are on his must-read-soon list. This, of course, the author knew.[65] They weren't on Wister's list either.

So far there has been only one great American story. The Declaration is, as I said before, the foundation of our pursuit (our practice) of happiness, but it also contains, as the opening of a tragedy, the makings of our greatest suffering. The generous abstraction "All men are created equal," so rightly "all praised" by Lincoln, might have led to a withering away of slavery, which the Constitution so prudently never names. Instead it led to compromises that, while staving off, also led to, a civil war, longer and more terrible, and yet just if it had lasted two hundred and fifty years rather than five, a mighty sacrifice on the altar of freedom, made greater still by the assassination of Lincoln, the greatest blow to the Confederacy according to Jeff Davis, since it substituted a vengeful reconstruction for the merciful peace magnanimous Lincoln alone might have secured.

Wister did not go on to write a novel about the Civil War.[66] The contrast that the Judge in *The Virginian* draws between the lynching of an innocent Negro in the South and the stringing up of a known rustler in the West suggests that he understood the gravity of the issues.[67] To write that novel one would have to treat Lincoln. Perhaps Wister thought himself unequal to the task or perhaps he reflected on the fact that Lincoln himself had done it already. What man ever had greater gifts of expression, narration, and comprehension than Lincoln? Who but a Shakespeare would essay to add to his words? That Lincoln wrote no drama should not hide the great role in our Globe's pageant he played; that he wrote no novel should not distract us from the story he told in the hearts and minds of his countrymen forever. No other novelist has had his words memorized by schoolboys and a temple erected to him in Washington. Lincoln is one of the few great men who was also good.[68]

His, then, is one of the stories that the novel mutant of our time, the Teenager, an orphan in his own land, an outcast in his own country, ignorant of both his Western and his human heritage, might take heart from. After all, when you consider Lincoln's life, he was a kind of orphan; in narrow circumstances and with meager means, he took responsibility for his own growing up. In that education he gave himself we find both the great, Shakespeare, the Bible, and Euclid, and the good, Parson Weems's *Life of Washington*. Lincoln thought about heaven and found in the Founding a kind of home. Something like this discovery, we may finally reflect, was also true of Wister's unnamed Virginian, the story of whose life bears some distant resemblance to Lincoln's. He too was a kind of orphan, he too educated himself, and chose Shakespeare as his teacher. Perhaps the Virginian's name was Lincoln, one who got his Ann Rutledge, who had to be a natural right lawyer, and yet needed to oppose no Trampas on the national scene because after Lincoln the House was no longer divided.

XII.
Truth, Reformation, and Politics

America and the West it leads are not in good shape today. Divided in a hundred ways, bitterly contentious on ten profound moral questions, which many deny are moral questions, living on the moral credit of its ancestors and the financial credit of its own grandchildren, and blind even to its own survival, or where not blind, as with terrorism, unwilling to carry the punishment of it to the governments that support it, far worse than Trampas, and thus soon likely to experience plagues, famines, and devastations on a scale not seen even with the Black Death, or if yielding to the treats of such, soon occupied and enslaved, today the West is in deep trouble. Yet it is well to remember that the West has rallied before, both to external danger and to internal, which today is more threatening than the external, and whose recognition must come first. Thus, a century and a half ago, just before it rid itself of slavery,

America was spreading it to every territory, soon would have spread it to every state, and was near to declaring it a matter of indifference. Yet America rallied; it refused to regard slavery as other than a moral evil; it would not acquiesce to the spread of it, and when slaveholders, defeated in ballots, drew swords, America rid itself of slavery, as no other nation has: by shedding its own blood.

Perhaps America will rally now. A salty remnant has refused to yield to the complacent slaughter of innocent life, whose protection was once the pride of liberalism and remains one of the three things Christ says He is ("the way, the truth, and the life"); a growing number of fathers and mothers have chosen, despite the subtracted income, to fulfill at home the natural duty of all parents to raise their children up right; and citizens of America's most populous state have reaffirmed the self-evident truths of the Declaration, so bloodily secured in the Thirteenth, Fourteenth, and Fifteenth Amendments. Honesty, moral reformation, and political courage are possible. The people who practice them might wax mighty again, God, the Supreme Judge of the world, willing.

Notes

1. William Bennett, *The Index of Leading Cultural Indicators* (New York: Simon & Schuster, 1994); several years ago the author identified our vice, correctly, as sloth; then, after publishing on virtue, becoming a millionaire, and thus being in a position to seek high office, he chose not to, and instead supported candidates whose pro-life views were, at best, not very lively.

2. For further thoughts apropos of Allan Bloom's fine book, see my "Souls Without Longing," *Interpretation: Journal of Political Philosophy*, 18, no. 3, (1991) 415–65.

3. These remarks are drawn from my little book, "The Teenager and the West," forthcoming one day, I hope, a precis of which appeared as "The Myth of the Teenager" in *Practical Home-Schooling* ed. Mary Pride, V1, no. 2 (summer 1993): 19–21 (her title). On the music that "rocked" youths into Teenagers, see my "A Different Drummer" in *Fidelity*, ed. E. Michael Jones (Fall 1996) (published title altered without my permission or knowledge). For how this drummer was received by faculty at Brigham Young University, see " 'Elitist!' 'Paternalist!' 'Eurocentrist!' " *Measure* (Bulletin of the University Centers for Rational Alternatives) no. 100 (November 1991), 6–8.

4. To the author; see *Dartmouth Review*, 10, no. 15 (14 February 1990): 7.

5. How unlikely such a restoration might be, I learned from a Duke professor. At a conference lunch, he related how he was thinking of offering a course called Forbidden Books at Duke. "Did he mean the Bible, Homer, Shakespeare, Plato?" the looks exchanged around the table asked. No, he explained, he meant DeSade, and so forth.

6. Do young people today want to be a great scientist? If so, who? After

Einstein, who would they set their sights on? "Great" as was their discovery, who would want to be Crick, let alone Watson, after reading Watson's *Double Helix*?

7. *KGW*, 7:2, 289; this leftover (*Nachlass*) belongs to the period Sommer-Herbst 1884. Nietzsche's sister put it in her fraudulent arrangement of his left-overs, *The Will to Power*, as No. 983. The detailed story of this fraud can be found in the preface Walter Kaufmann provided to his translation of *The Will to Power* (1968). Because it is a fraud, I print the title to this non-book with strike-through marks. Nietzsche did consider writing a book with this title, which does justify Heidegger's attention to it, but as Mazzino Montinari estab-lished, by early September of 1888 Nietzsche had abandoned the idea of such a book (and all twenty-five plans that exist in his notes): "Nietzsches Nachlass von 1885 bis 1888 oder Textkritik und Wille zur Macht" in his *Nietzsche Lesen* (Berlin/New York: Walter de Gruyter, 1982), 92–119. Those who cite *Will-to-Power* as if it were a book by Nietzsche, whether to assail or (lately) to celebrate him, show they do not appreciate what a book is and what splendid ones Nietz-sche wrote. That only now, years after the French and after the Italian editions, is a translation of the faithful Montinari-Colli edition of the *Nachlass* in the offing (thanks to Prof. Ernst Behler and Mr. Robert Looker) does not speak well for the intellectual probity of the English-speaking Nietzsche scholars, especially those who cite what Nietzsche never presented as a book right beside what he did.

8. For further thoughts, see "Only Christianity," in *Saints, Sovereigns, & Scholars: Essays Presented to Frederick D. Wilhelmsen*, ed. Fr. James Lehr-berger, Robert Herrera, and Mel Bradford (New York: Peter Lang, 1993), 211–30.

9. See, for a beginning, Michael W. Tracz, "The Multicultural West: Ethnic-ity and the Intellectual Foundations of Western Civilization," *Intercollegiate Review*, 33, No. 1, (1997): 10–17.

10. Consider however the argument of M. B. Foster, that Plato and Aristotle are the fulfillment of Homer, in *The State in Plato and Hegel* (Oxford: Oxford University Press, 1934), and the exceeding fine and deep interpretations of Homer as calling for a Plato, and Plato fulfilling the call, by Seth Benardete, especially *The Bow and the Lyre: A Platonic Reading of the Odyssey* (Lanham, Md.: Rowman & Littlefield, 1997).

11. For my introductory appreciation, the reader might turn to "The Seven Wonders of Shakespeare" often delivered, in abbreviated form, as a lecture for the Intercollegiate Studies Institute, and currently awaiting publication.

12. That we live at the end of modernity was first, I believe, understood by Kierkegaard, Nietzsche and Péguy, the first welcoming it as a test of the Chris-tian, the second viewing it more joyously than fearfully, and the third more fearfully than apprehensively; all understood it as the waning of Christianity. For more, in addition to these three, see Romano Guardini, *The End of the Modern World* (New York: Sheed and Ward, 1956). The understanding of this grave change is in the movement of intellectuals called "Post-Modernism" su-perficial at best. Discontent with modernity is hardly liberation from it. Not that

one should be discontented with such modern phenomenon as America, the good of whose founding and living reality is so justly appreciated by Tocqueville, who also justly lamented that it was not great, no room for a Pascal.

13. I am aware of the argument, which begins with Plato, that poetry is quite inferior to philosophy, its reassertion by Rousseau in the name of morality, and by Simone Weil in the name of goodness. I submit, however, that there is no ascent from the cave that does not start with a cave, that morality begins with the heart, and that, pace Weil, not all poetry fails to portray the good soul. The Teenager has no cave; the "death of God" is, as Nietzsche says, a murder, and it is a suicide of the heart; and when Tolstoy says of Natasha at her first ball, "She was so happy, she could not sin" or when Willa Cather poses high choices that only good persons, such as her Bishop Latour and her Thea Kronborg, even discern, a lost youth might learn something about the good soul. Students who elect philosophy and neglect poetry are as narrow as students who elect poetry and neglect philosophy.

14. In her *A Room of One's Own*, Virginia Woolf imagines not only Shakespeare's sister but takes from her shelf a novel by a fairly good but not great authoress. This she allows us to understand is herself. She did not claim to rank with Shakespeare, or believe that conditions of freedom guarantee anything great.

15. Nietzsche suggests the question; for my interpretation of his answer, in the "you are going to woman, then remember the whip" advice he attributes to an old woman, see "Woman, Nietzsche, and Nature," *Maieutics*, no. 2 (winter 1981), 27–42.

16. Hannah Arendt, in conversation to me, upon her visit to Dartmouth to receive an honorary degree, which I had proposed her for, and also lamented that in the ceremony she was not asked to give a speech, for the administration, fearing another antiwar speech from a graduating senior, had opted for a speechless commencement. About Simone Weil, I do not know enough to judge her candidacy.

17. There is an M.A. program in Eastern classics at St. John's (Santa Fe) in summers.

18. For additional arguments for the primacy, in the order of study, of the West for Westerners, not without remarks on the emptiness of most claims for non-Western books and advocacy of them in the name of openness, see the last part of Allan Bloom's "Western Civ—and Me," *Commentary* (August 1990), also reprinted in his *Giants and Dwarfs* (New York: Simon & Schuster, 1990). For the chant at Stanford, "Hey, hey, ho, ho, Western Civ has got to go," see endnote No. 50 to my "Souls Without Longing," cited above, plus these subsequent discoveries: that the alternate course the Stanford students were marching for was designed by Prof. Clay Carson, editor of the M. L. King papers, whom the *New Republic* reported as long denying the evidence of King's plagiarism in the thesis he submitted for the Ph.D. degree at Boston University. That the plagiarism was massive, gross, and obvious is suggested by the most extensive publication of the evidence, in parallel columns, in *Chronicles of Culture* (January 1991).

19. Meeting every weekend, our reading group was a great contrast to, great substitute for, and a great solace from the poor, weary, listless teaching in graduate school courses. Once one of our teachers joined us. At the end he said sadly, "We used to do this."

20. In my opinion, the best book on such a program remains Mark Van Doren's *Liberal Education* (New York: Henry Holt, 1943) and the best examples, St. John's (Annapolis and Santa Fe) and Thomas Aquinas (California). For my attempt (with friends, Cary Lord and Dain Trafton) to introduce such a program, see "A Road to Travel By: A Liberal Arts Curriculum for Dartmouth," *Dartmouth Review*, 10 no.15 (14 February 1990, 8–9; for what happened, see "Two Roads Diverged in a Wood," *Dartmouth Review*, same issue, p. 7 and Charles Sykes, the *Hollow Men: Politics and Corruption in Higher Education* (Washington, D.C.: Regnery, 1990), 190–191. However, a version of this program instituted at Queens College by Hilail Gildin exists to this day. And so do I, I who benefited from the chance, so important in the beginning, to teach a pilot course of it, thanks to John Kemeny then president of Dartmouth. For my contribution to an effort to bring something of such a program to a junior college for girls and horses aiming to become a four year college mainly for Mormons, see the curriculum and mission statement in the Southern Virginia College catalogue for 1996–97.

21. For more on emulation, see my "To Emulate or To Be: Aeneas and Hamlet," in *Law and Philosophy: The Practice of Theory* [Essays in Honor of George Anastaplo], ed. William Braithwaite and John Murley (Athens: Ohio University / Swallow Press, 1991), 2, 917–36.

22. See Senior's *Restoration of Christian Culture* (San Francisco: Ignatius Press, 1983) for fine remarks on what's good for the young soul, and not only the young soul; this book is so graceful and rich that half way through the first chapter, you may find yourself, as I did, knowing you will reread it soon.

23. When decline at a school I once taught at began to manifest itself in a rash of suicide attempts and I mentioned the fact to the departed founders, they explained, "We always knew that reading great books makes you melancholy. That's why we did it together." Indeed, when they did, it was a Platonic regime, with the best teachers the rulers.

24. It is so rare for a scholar to love what he studies—enough to ask himself "What would Machiavelli have me do?" or "What would Rousseau have me feel?" or "What would Nietzsche have me will?"—that one hesitates to criticize. Such questions make a scholar more than a scholar. Nevertheless, to emulate whom you study may not only not be wise, it may not be to be. For the distinction between emulating and being, see note 21 above. Maybe at the Last Judgment such a scholar will be shown "how truly splendid, deep, and wise you would have been if you had not spent time impersonating some one else, however great."

25. What is the relation, according to natural right, of the great and the good? At Schulpforta Nietzsche was not ranked first, but third or so, in the A –/B + range. Later, to his school friend, Paul Deussen, he said that that was right, meaning that no school, or polity, can do otherwise than to aim for the good of

the good ones. From another point of view, one might also observe that the great are not always entirely competent. On another level, Jacques Barzun observes that giving "objective" exams changes the ranking, so that the true A students come out B +, and the B + s come out A. For further thoughts see my "Hard to Satisfy, Easy to Please," forthcoming sometime, I hope.

26. Despite concentrating on how the program was destroyed, Robert K. Carlson's *Truth on Trial* (South Bend, Indiana: Crisis Books, 1995) gives a sketch of it, in the early chapters; Appendix A reprints a brochure; and essays by the founders are in *The Integration of Knowledge* (Lawrence, Kansas: Integrated Humanities Program, 1979). See *Modern Age* (Winter, 1999) for my review, "Truth Untried," of Carlson's book. For some of the thinking behind it, see Senior's *Restoration of Christian Culture*, mentioned above; even his strong criticism of discussion as a way to learn is gentled by his acknowledgment that good things are learned in some discussions, perhaps a loyalty to classes with his teacher, Mark Van Doren. However far Senior has traveled from his beginnings, he has not forgotten them.

27. For an attempt to distinguish the great and the good, despite their overlap, and how we are related to both, see my "The Good, The Great, and the Small" (on *Sum. Th.* I-II, Q 94, a. 2, c.), to appear in *Faith and Reason* in 1998.

28. C. S. Lewis, *The Magician's Nephew* (New York: Scholastic, 1995; orig. 1955), 107.

29. What a human being thinks the best place is tells you a lot about them. W. H. Auden says every critic owes it to his audience to say what he thinks such a best state of human things is. For his own "Eden," see *The Dyer's Hand* (New York: Random House, 1962), 3–12.

30. The true, historical, comical tragical-poetical source for this practice is a Garrison Keillor story on the Prairie Home Companion (n.d.).

31. Nietzsche, *Musarion Ausgabe*, XIX 79; Germanless readers, who still (1997) have no English translation of Nietzsche's *Nachlass* (leftovers), may find it as No. 585a in Kaufmann's translation of *Will-to-Power*.

32. The verses come from "America the Beautiful," the "Star-Spangled Banner," and "We Are Coming, Father Abr'am."

33. I owe this wonderful observation to George Anastaplo. For my full interpretation, watch for my "The Declaration of America" beginning serial publication in the fall of 1998 in *Practical Home Schooling*, edited by Mary Pride.

34. I owe this point to Harry V. Jaffa.

35. Thanks to Harvey C. Mansfield, Jr.'s address to the Brigham Young Conference for the Pike's Peak vista from which this paragraph swam into view.

36. See the remarkable sermon by Nathaniel Niles, designed to move the congregation to oppose George III; it reminds them, in the very conclusion, that since they oppress their slaves they may deserve oppression by George III; in Charles S. Hyneman and Donald S. Lutz, *American Political Writing during the Founding Era* (Indianapolis, Indiana: Liberty Press, 1983), 1: 258–76.

37. I epitomize a passage in Frederick Jackson Turner's *The Frontier in American History* (Mineola, N.Y.: Dover, 1996).

38. This wonderful observation is Elliott West's, in his judicious *Growing*

Up With the Country: Childhood in the Far Western Frontier (Albuquerque: New Mexico, 1989), p. 27; I vary the interpretation.

39. The former is Turner's view, the latter Walter Prescott Webb's, in his *The Great Frontier* (Lincoln and London: University of Nebraska Press, 1986; originally 1951).

40. Other such stories that have become "myth," through such repeated re-telling as makes them almost authorless, are, for modern civilization, the story of Faust, a man who traded all for the conquest of nature, and the story of Don Juan, a man who traded all for the conquest of woman. To these we might perhaps add *Don Quixote*, the story of a man who acts as if the good could become fully actual, and *Hamlet*, the story of a man who reasons about revelation. Such stories propagate themselves. Thus, there are so many Faust tellings that you have to distinguish them by the author's name, so many you can speak of a new author "writing a Faust." Likewise, Don Juan. The other stories have sons instead. Don Quixote has the Idiot of Dostoyevsky for a son, and Hamlet, Goethe's Wilhelm Meister.

41. For my own meeting, see Part III of my "Leisure, War, and Festivity," which appeared as "A Long Day West," in the *Concho River Review* Vol. 8, no. 1 (Spring 1994), 61–9.

42. Here I adopt the language in which the Lone Ranger used to be intro-duced on the radio, with the "thundering hoofbeats" of the William Tell Over-ture. For the remarkable connection between this natural lawman and American foreign policy, specifically the Korean War, see Fr. Raymond L. Bruckberger, *One Sky to Share*, trans. Dorothy Carr Howell (New York: Kennedy, 1952), 209–13, and also Henry Kissinger's characterization of himself as a cowboy, to Oriana Fallaci, *New Republic*, 167, no. 23 (December 16, 1972), 21.

43. For plenty of herding and one long trail drive, read Andy Adams, *Log of a Cowboy* (1903; reprint Lincoln: University of Nebraska Press, 1964) and dis-cover why the unrelenting responsibility, day and night, from Corpus Christi in April to Miles City in September was exhilarating. Doing it as a boy, Adams became a man, and twenty years later a writer. Except for reenactment, the drives are gone forever. For a living example of ranching, one might look at *Watt Matthews of Lambshead*, by Laura Wilson, Intro. by David McCullough (Austin: Texas Historical Association, 1989), or up until this past spring (1997), meet him; see also *Interwoven* (1936; reprint College Station: Texas A & M Press, 1982), the memoir of his mother, Sallie Reynolds Matthews, who arrived on the open plains, aged 7, in 1867. And for a remarkable festivity based on these memories, visit the Fandangle some June in Albany, Texas.

44. Years later Wister received a letter from a couple who had moved west to live after reading *The Virginian*. Upon receiving Wister's cordial reply, they declared a holiday for the ranch.

45. Molly knows the Virginian's given name and the narrator must, Steve calls him "Jeff" because he is from the South (Jeff Davis), but we never learn it. Someday some wag will suggest that the Virginian left home at fourteen to escape the name Marmaluke or Sarsaparilla. Like the Lone Ranger, who hid his name, or Odysseus, who said he was "No Man" to the Cyclopes, there is some-

thing right about a hero having no personal name you can handle him by, or say aloud, even with a smile. Perhaps all Wister's hiding is meant to leave us thinking, he is *the* Virginian, someone who fitly inherits the excellence of the great Virginians who did so much to found America, Washington, Madison, and of course Jefferson, the original Southern Jeff. Or perhaps it is to encourage our identification with the hero, as it partly is with Conrad's young captain in "The Secret Sharer." Certainly it is not as in Ralph Ellison's fine *Invisible Man*.

46. The eye-gouging of a horse, by a Wyoming rancher, Wister's host, was an important start of *The Virginian*. Sickened by the deed, ashamed of not intervening, Wister invented the Virginian to act right in the story, as he had not in life. Cf. the entry in Wister's Western journal for 18 June 1891 with the chapter; *Owen Wister Out West: His Journals and Letters*, ed. Fanny Kemble Wister (Chicago: University of Chicago Press, 1958). For Wister on World War I, read *The Pentecost of Calamity* (1915).

47. Leo Strauss, "Liberal Education and Responsibility," in *Liberalism Ancient and Modern* (New York: Basic Books, 1968), 9–25; consider the remark: "being responsible is so far from being the same as being virtuous that it is merely the condition for being either virtuous or vicious" (10).

48. When Madison first coined the word and employed it in the *Federalist*, it was indeed, as Mr. Strauss says, a condition of virtue or vice, yet it was no evasion, shy or sly, of virtue, but rather one thing that might allow men to resist passionate, short-winded errors and plan long-winded goods; where once the word meant the condition for virtue and, given popular government, the chance to turn out those unworthy of further responsibility, it (at least the adjective) means "worthy of responsibility"; in the immediate case, as *Federalist* 63 makes clear, it was part of an argument for a senate; see Douglas Adair, *Fame and the Founding Fathers: Essays* (New York: Norton, 1974), 257 and the footnote. American usage of the word in accord with the Framers is to be found in Coolidge, who writes of the government course he took at Amherst, "The whole course was a thesis on good citizenship and good government. Those who took it came to a clearer comprehension not only of their rights and liberties but of their duties and responsibilities." *The Autobiography of Calvin Coolidge* (Rutland, Vt.: Academy Books, 1929), 62. (For a tip on Responsible Madison, thanks to Prof. Harvey C. Mansfield, Jr.)

49. Indeed, he feels "convicted of decency."

50. I do not know where I read Hemingway's remark. I am fairly sure he did not use the word "illicit."

51. *Democracy in America* (Part III, Chapters 8–12).

52. See "Nietzsche on Flaubert and the Powerlessness of his Art," *Centennial Review*, 20 no. 3 (summer 1976), 309–13.

53. One might also wonder whether the atheism of Twain and Melville also disqualifies them, or detracts from their candidacy. The fact that cetology is theology and that Melville is, therefore, constantly appreciating the cleverness of his own atheistical jokes mars the book, I think; the cackle-cackle hilarity of Voltaire or a Bayle is tedious; in any case, their kind of mocking puts Melville

beside the main stream. In the Christianity of Faulkner, if that is what it is, I find it hard to discover political virtue: although there is much virtue in Dilsey, Ike, and the Bear, they only endure, they do not prevail. There is nothing of the Statesman in Faulkner.

54. See Lawrence Thompson's *Melville's Quarrel with God* (Princeton: Princeton University Press, 1952).

55. I adopt the felicitous phrase and firm retort of Robert Eden, at our conference at Brigham Young University, to a teacher from an elite center of deconstruction. Whether, as Tocqueville, Nietzsche, and others doubt, this morality cannot last long after the God above it disappears, Wister does not ask, except perhaps in the fine story "Padre Ignazio."

56. See the fine essays "Why the Modern South Has a Great Literature" and the title essay in Donald Davidson's *Still Rebels, Still Yankees* (Baton Rouge: Louisiana State University Press, 1957).

57. It is hardly accidental that the transforming event in the boyhood of the future H. L. Mencken was reading Huck Finn. For the way this American Nietzschean looked at the principles of democracy in America, see his piece on Lincoln. Mencken's pen was pungent, but often poisonous.

58. For a different view of the American novel and the American regime, by someone with many of the same concerns, see Catherine Zuckert, *Natural Right and the American Imagination* (Savage, Md.: Rowman & Littlefield, 1990).

59. Were the Virginian President, who might he have as Secretary of State? The Lone Ranger. And as Secretary of Defense? Shane. In the story of the Lone Ranger the masked man represents natural right, Tonto represents nature, and the Sheriff represents conventional right or law. The setting is always on the edge of civilization; the outlaws are always quicker, stealthier, and crueler than the lawmen, but also no match for the skills of the naturally right man, whose courage is supercivil and as a consequence more capable of protecting civility; being less attached to human things (not married), the Lone Ranger is better able to care for them; come to think of it, the Lone Ranger seems a priest of natural right. So, too, is Tonto's knowledge of nature based on something outside the polity; he knows how to track a bad man better than any one else because he has spent as much time in nature, with the animals, as with men. Aristotle says, "That man who lives outside the polis must be either a beast or a god." Forgetting Tonto and the Lone Ranger; the man who knows nature and the man who knows natural right, without which life on the frontier would be "poor, solitary, nasty, brutish and short." However, natural right is rightly suspect; the conventional right, which natural right suspends and even breaks, exacts its toll; the Lone Ranger wears a mask and pays his homage to civility by thinking it is right to.

60. That it was a friendship is shown best by Theodore Roosevelt's fourteen-page letter on Wister's novel, *Lady Baltimore*, criticizing the author's sympathy for the Charleston folks who had attacked Roosevelt for appointing a black skinned man, Dr. William Crum, collector of the port ("you must see that I can't close the door of hope to a whole race"), the folks who denounced and opposed "the men who are doing their best to bring a little nearer the era of

right conduct in the South" such as Booker T. Washington, whom Roosevelt invited to dine at the White House; see pages 248ff. of *Roosevelt: The Story of a Friendship* (New York: Macmillan, 1930). There was no break in their friendship and in a later edition Wister is said to have moderated these sympathies, but not his view that Reconstruction was unjust. So one learns from Darwin Payne's *Owen Wister* (Dallas: Southern Methodist University Press, 1985), 233, which is packed with information and quotations from Wister's papers. Good on the writings is John L. Cobbs, *Owen Wister* (Boston: Twayne, 1984).

61. For more, see my "The Happiness of Willa Cather," in *The Catholic Writer*, ed. Ralph McInerny (San Francisco: Ignatius Press, 1991), 129–50.

62. If you visit Medicine Bow today, you will find a hotel called The Virginian; of course, it was built after the novel. And down the street, you will also find a motel, called The Trampas.

63. See Owen Wister, *Roosevelt: The Story of a Friendship*, 46–7 for this conversation and for Roosevelt's opinion as to how long the Republic would last.

64. See "Tradition and the Individual Soul," *Intercollegiate Review*, 17 no. 1 (Fall/Winter 1981) 47–51.

65. In profile, Owen Wister, Harvard summa cum laude in music, Easterner, old Philadelphia banking family, traveling fellowship to Paris, connoisseur of fine things, known in the best restaurants of New York and the best homes of Charleston, might suggest a precursor of the class of persons later called intellectuals. Yet he differs quite a bit, especially in his appreciation of the virtues of the Virginian (and the real man he was modeled on), for intellectuals seem, as a class, to question the existence or the importance of the moral virtues (often while censuring others for not having them and not asking whether they themselves lack them). Intellectuals are, then, the opposite of the good juror, someone who is firm on principles, skeptical on evidence, and thus slow to judge the accused. While the intellectual dreams of a society made good by social engineering, he is likely to deny the existence of heroes, either chivalric or responsible, which he would otherwise be judged by and called to emulate. As Péguy said, an intellectual is someone who denies there can be saints or heroes.

66. Although Willa Cather's last novel, *Sapphira and the Slave Girl*, never portrays the Civil War, it manages to show why slavery is wrong, why the removal of it would be good, and nevertheless why the sympathetic disposition of Lincoln toward the slaveholders was magnanimous.

67. Yet although Lincoln surely appreciated the danger posed to Republican government by failure to provide the citizenry with the protection of the laws, I doubt that he would have accepted Judge Henry's reasoning; I judge from what Lincoln says about the evils of acting outside the law in his "Speech to the Young Men's Lyceum"; to enjoy the benefits of law one must accept the wrong decisions of juries, even from ones that may be corrupt.

68. After his one meeting, late in the war, with Lincoln, William Tecumseh Sherman said, "Of all the men I ever met, he seemed to possess more of the elements of greatness and goodness than any other." I cite from Geoffrey C. Ward, Ken Burns, and Ric Burns, *The Civil War: An Illustrated History* (New York: Knopf, 1990), p. 364.

7

The Religious University and Liberal Education

James Nuechterlein

The religious university is the place where, in the language of Tertullian, the second-century Latin Church father, Jerusalem encounters Athens, where faith and learning discover what, if anything, they have to say to each other. Tertullian himself, it is cautionary to remember, thought there was not much at all. Conversation with Athens, he concluded, was neither necessary nor beneficial to Jerusalem. The religious university of today must, by its very nature, be more sanguine than Tertullian about the value of the conversation, since it otherwise has no reason for being. But while the religious university may be hopeful concerning the fruits of the conversation it certainly has no grounds for optimism.

When Father Theodore Hesburgh resigned the presidency of Notre Dame several years back, he left an institution that, he said, was at once more Catholic and more academically distinguished than it had ever been. That may well be true (though my experience is that opinion as to the state of Catholicism at Notre Dame varies radically even among those intimately familiar with the place), but if it is true, it represents a notable exception to the dominant pattern of development in American higher education.

Until well into the nineteenth century, higher education in America remained primarily a function of the church, as had always been the case in Western civilization, but in the years since, the paradigmatic path for even church-related colleges has led in the direction of ever greater secularization. As Richard Hofstadter noted almost forty years ago, "There are several major themes that command the attention of the historian of American higher education, but among those the oldest and the longest sustained is the drift toward secularism." The general pattern has been from specific denominational affiliation to generic Christianity to generic religiosity to outright secularity.

That drift—which of course parallels in many ways a drift in the wider culture—has been most marked in academically elite institutions. The prevailing assumption in academia has been that scholarly excellence and religious affiliation and subscription stand in inverse ratio to one another. Thus many of our most distinguished universities practice a studied and rather embarrassed distancing from their origins. The most notorious case is that of Harvard, whose original motto *Veritas: Pro Christo et Ecclesia* has been abbreviated to the simple *Veritas*. That institutional self-editing reflects the general belief that the fullest pursuit of truth can only be conducted for its own, entirely secular, sake, and not in the service of the church and its faith.

Universities that aspire to scholarly recognition must do so according to the prevailing norms of academic life, which means that those schools that do so aspire, and yet want to take seriously their religious identification, function under continuing burdens of suspicion and intellectual tension. An institution that bears the dismissive label of "Bible College" not as a term of opprobrium but as a badge of honor—say, a Bob Jones University—experiences no crisis of identity or conflict of purpose, but a Notre Dame or any university like it lives with those crises and conflicts as inescapable conditions of existence.

Such a university has to maintain an intricate and delicate balance in its dual nature as a community of inquiry and a community of conviction. The university is involved in an endless, and presumably ever-open, pursuit of truth, while religion—certainly Christian religion—must, if it is to remain true to itself, in some sense claim to *be* the truth. The community of faith speaks necessarily—if, one hopes, cautiously and with humility—of orthodoxy and heresy (after all, no heresy, no orthodoxy); in the community of learning such ideas are considered anathema, as the current storm over political correctness most recently reminds us.

In the university, reason must have unlimited sway, and it cannot do so if those whose job it is to safeguard orthodoxy attempt to act on their knowledge of reason's potentially corrosive effect on faith by putting it under restraints and prohibitions. John Henry Newman, who surely understood reason's limits and dangers, nonetheless also understood that a university must live with the risks of reason run loose: "If we invite reason to take its place in our schools, we must let reason have fair and full play. If we reason, we must submit to the conditions of reason. We cannot use it by halves. . . ."

The nature of the religious university is such that the balance of forces in the Athens/Jerusalem tension always pulls in the direction of

Athens. It is reason and learning, after all, that is the essence of any university's nature. Even a church-related university does not suppose that it exists primarily for the purpose of providing a kind of postadolescent religious day camp, and if it cannot do what it purports to do— offer an at least adequate education—it has no excuse for staying in business. No one in his right mind, after all, would place himself in the care of a hospital where the members of the medical staff had rich devotional lives but were not quite up to speed on recent developments in health care.

This is not all that tips the scale of the religious university in favor of Athens and against Jerusalem. As the faculty members of a religious university improve their scholarly credentials, two things typically occur. First, faculty members shift the focus of their energy and interest from teaching to research, which is what the weight of their graduate training leads them to do in any case. As faculty focus more on research than on teaching, they also tend to focus less on the distinctive religious preoccupations of their institution, since those preoccupations are more likely to be relevant to the classroom than to the ever more specialized and particularistic tasks of professional scholarship.

It is similarly the case that professionally ambitious academics direct their commitment and loyalties more to the disciplines in which they work than to the institutions at which they happen to do that work. They are attached first of all to the scholarly guild and its standards and norms rather than to the concerns of their place of academic residence. Again, the socialization of graduate training leaves its mark: it teaches scholars to aspire single-mindedly to professional excellence and thus to insist that in academic matters like hiring of new faculty nothing other than scholarly promise should come into play. Intrusion into these areas of questions concerning religious commitment or dedication to the particular purposes of the institution seems to them at best parochial and irrelevant, at worst a betrayal of the academic calling.

One other factor enters the picture here. Faculty members at religious universities are often somewhat defensive concerning their religious commitments, at least when they are off campus and moving in the larger academic world, which tends to an uncompromising secularism and thus to instinctive suspicion toward members of the academic guild who have firm and public religious loyalties. Religious academics are anxious to prove to their nonreligious colleagues that while they may be religious, they are most emphatically not religious in any sort of yahoo fundamentalist fashion. It is their self-assumed burden to demonstrate that if, for example, they are of evangelical persuasion, theirs is not the evangelicalism of a Jerry Falwell or even a Billy Graham. It has been my experience that faculty members at conservative religious institutions will often go to quite extraordinary lengths to prove that, religion aside, they are in every other way models of political and intellectual correctness. And even in religious matters, they will strive mightily neither to obtrude nor to offend. They tend, shall we say, not to make their loyalty to Jerusalem a cause of scandal.

All this and more, then, makes it difficult for religious universities— especially, again, religious universities with scholarly pretensions—not to let their duties to Athens reduce to the vanishing point their loyalty to Jerusalem.

I should note here that while I worry about the long-term ability of the religious university to remain faithful to itself, as a Lutheran I am neither surprised by nor even particularly concerned about the perpetual state of dialectical tension and ambiguity in which the religious university operates. Lutherans naturally think of the relationship between faith and learning—or, in H. Richard Niebuhr's classic formulation, between Christ and culture—not in terms of transformation or integration but rather in terms of paradox and tension.

Most American religious universities have been Christian, and perhaps the most venerable view of the Christian university sees its essential work as what has been called "the fusion of high intelligence and high religion." But in the classical Lutheran view, that idea is one of those commonplaces that many of us give casual assent to but that do not necessarily stand up well under close analysis. In the Lutheran perspective, faith and learning (Jerusalem and Athens), while they are not ultimately irreconcilable and while, indeed, they must for their mutual health inform and instruct each other at certain points, are incapable of essential fusion or total integration. It is not, finally, learning that leads to or sustains faith, and learning, for its part, does not rest on faith or require it for its justification.

This is not the place for a full theological elaboration of the Lutheran position. I will note only that it finds its anthropological roots in Luther's conception of the human condition as essentially *simul*. We are at once, Luther insisted, fully sinners and fully saints, enemies of God and yet wholly redeemed participants in his eternal glory—and that paradoxical condition pervades all of human life and culture. Thus Luther's ambivalent view of everything human.

In that ambivalence, Luther, who had more than a touch of Tertullian in him, could speak extraordinarily harshly of reason insofar as it exists in respect to faith and as part of a fallen and demonic existence. Reason, Luther said with characteristic moderation, is "the devil's whore," "a beast," an "enemy of God," a "source of mischief," "carnal," and "stupid." But he truly was ambivalent, not simply condemnatory. Within its own sphere and as part of the created order, Luther suggested, reason is God's greatest, indeed inestimable, gift. He in fact personified it as "the inventress and mistress of all the arts, of medicine and law, of whatever wisdom, power, virtue, and glory men possess in this life."

Given the tension here suggested, Lutherans are skeptical of ideas not merely of Christian physics or Christian chemistry but also of Christian economics, Christian history, or Christian political science. Lutherans, then, entertain a more modest conception of the religious university than do many other religious communities. But even Lutherans are not totally skeptical of the Christian intellectual venture, and they do not consider the term religious university an oxymoron. How then might a modest conception of the idea of a religious university and its contribution to liberal learning proceed?

We might begin where so many discussions of university affairs begin these days, with the matter of values. We have to be careful here. There is in many Christian circles a kind of triumphalist arrogance that appears to assume that religious people are the only ones concerned with moral values or equipped to deal with them. From that questionable assumption there easily develops the notion that religious universities hold some sort of patent on "character formation" or concern for the "whole person."

The temptation of such universities to so view themselves is compounded by their knowledge that it is precisely these matters that currently preoccupy parents and alumni. It is embarrassing but true that a significant part of the constituency—actual and potential—of religious universities is concerned less about their academic standing than about their capacity to ensure the moral sturdiness and/or theological orthodoxy of the coming generation. Indeed a number of religious universities formerly lukewarm about their religious affiliations have recently taken to reaffirming them boldly, not so much from an excess of religious enthusiasm as from a recognition of sound marketing strategy.

But if religious universities must be cautious here, they need not be apologetic. If they are not unique in their concern for moral values, they do hold an advantage over secular institutions in that they operate from a more-or-less unified core of values that secular institutions do not share or, even if they did, could not claim.

It is essential to keep in mind that most Americans, unlike the cultural elite, still anchor their moral values in religious beliefs. Peter Berger has made this point nicely. Societies, he says, can be ranged on a spectrum from the very secular, like Sweden, to the very religious, like India. The situation of America, Berger says, is that it is a nation of Indians presided over by a cultural elite of Swedes. Religious universities can talk about the relationship between religion and morality in ways that secular universities, for obvious reasons, cannot.

Religious universities are religious communities; they are communities of religious learners. What is it that most fundamentally defines a religious university? A religious university is a place populated by people of a particular religious belief who are engaged in liberal learning informed by religious faith.

Theirs is a value-laden enterprise, and for them the question of values is not dissociated from the intellectual life of the university. Religious universities, because they operate within a coherent frame of values, can place learning in context and perspective in a way that students seek and that, again, secular institutions find it difficult to know even how to approach. Students, like all the rest of us, are meaning-seeking creatures. Because religious universities are openly concerned with questions of ultimate purpose and transcendent value, such universities can respond to student concerns about questions that public institutions, when they recognize them at all, can only relegate to the realm of the personal.

The secular intellectual elite in America marginalizes religion not so much by open repudiation or disparagement of religious concerns (though there is some of that) as by other means. The fundamental problem is not that religious answers are rejected—it is rather that religious questions are not asked in the first place. Religious universities *ask* those questions. They proceed on the assumption that any serious inquiry into the Good must at least include the question about God. Some religious academics would raise the stakes very high indeed: my fellow Lutheran Robert Jenson has said that "the reality of God is the necessary condition of an act of mind where choice of the good is also knowledge of the fact." Whatever one thinks of that, the point remains that while secular universities are inclined to talk about religion only in historical, clinical, positivist, or otherwise reductionist ways, religious universities have the great advantage of being able to talk about God without changing the subject. And because they can talk openly about God, they can talk unselfconsciously about values.

Stanley Hauerwas has raised the issue of value inquiry as it relates to the intellectual life of the university in an intriguing way. Much of the teaching life of the modern university, Hauerwas says, proceeds according to the Socratic method of critical inquiry, which claims a moral value of its own. The task of the university, in this view, is not to provide students with answers but to make them unrelenting questioners of all unexamined assumptions or items of conventional wisdom. That process takes on moral stature as it makes students practitioners of the examined life and thus, presumably, more self-conscious and perceptive moral agents.

What is generally overlooked, Hauerwas claims (in an argument borrowed from Martha Nussbaum), is that the Socratic method can itself lead in dubious moral directions. If placed in the hands of those lacking a secure moral foundation, the Socratic dialectic can turn its practitioners into cynics adept at undermining all forms of conventional morality (insofar as they cannot be empirically justified) but with nothing to put in conventional morality's place. According to this view, Socrates was dangerously indifferent to the antecedent moral training of those he engaged in dialectic. He gave intellectual weapons to those who, lacking habituation in the moral virtues, could easily come to mistake intellectual cleverness for moral perception.

The Hauerwas/Nussbaum argument certainly corresponds to much of what I experienced in the university classroom, especially with my better students. It is all too easy—it may, indeed, be a natural stage in intellectual development—for bright students to go through a debunking and skeptical phase, one in which they meet Oscar Wilde's definition of the cynic as the person who knows the price of everything and the value of nothing. At a debased level, the Socratic style of relentless questioning contributes to the abiding sin of most students I encountered, which is not the blind dogmatism or even bland indifference that their professors habitually complain of, but rather the maddening, mindless relativism that debases tolerance and that manages to avoid serious engagement with substantive moral and intellectual questions by instant retreat to the impregnable fortress of "well, it all depends on your point of view." And there is, of course, nothing to be said about competing points of view other than that they are all to be equally tolerated and equally valued. Here indeed one encounters nihilism without the abyss.

Religious universities are better positioned than secular ones to avoid or at least know how to deal with this form of corruption of youth. The point, of course, is not to discard the Socratic method but rather to undergird dialectical inquiry with the presumption that one is asking questions not simply in order to uncover intellectual weaknesses, expose unexamined premises, and probe traditional authority but in order finally, having done all these things, to be led in the direction of dependable answers. And one can only lead students to find answers if one believes oneself that answers do in fact exist, and exist at a level somewhat more substantial than that of "whatever works for you."

One last, brief, hortatory note.

If any religious university is to succeed in its particular purposes, it will have to remain continuously and actively self-conscious as to what it is about. The moral of the story of the decline and fall of the Christian college in America is clear: the road from religion to secularity was paved with massive institutional forgetfulness and disastrous good intentions. The movement from religious commitment to secularity was the result most often not of any secularist plot but rather of a fit of absence of mind.

One American university after another was created Christian, stayed Christian for a long time, assumed that the inertial force of faith was such that it would always remain Christian—and woke up one morning to discover it was no longer Christian, or was at least so far down the road past serious Christianity that no return was possible. The historical record shows that the critical steps down the slippery slope to secularity were almost always initiated by administrators and faculty members who did not intend secularity at all. They wanted to improve their institution's academic standing (and, not incidentally, find wider and more generous sources of funding than were to be found within their church body). They wanted to move beyond sectarianism and parochialism— and control by church authorities—in the direction of greater acceptance in the scholarly community. Almost all of them lost their religious identity incrementally and by inadvertence, not by one fatal step or by conscious policy.

For religious universities to be self-conscious about identity is to be actively concerned with church affiliation (there is no Christianity in general), with curriculum (a move from a Department of Theology to a Department of Religious Studies is a sure sign of degeneration), and perhaps most of all with recruitment of faculty and students (there is no intelligible way in which, say, a Methodist university can remain Methodist if it is not predominantly populated by Methodists). Religious universities need to be staffed, not by pious solipsists of course, but by sophisticated provincials—people who know the alternatives and have faced up to them and have managed to find their way back home.

And even given all this, the odds against such universities will still be high. They will only find secure consolation, perhaps, in the sentiments of T. S. Eliot:

> There is only the fight to recover what has been lost
> And found and lost again and again: and now, under conditions
> That seem unpropitious. But perhaps neither gain nor loss.
> For us, there is only the trying. The rest is not our business.

Conclusion

Of Liberty and Liberal Education

Ralph C. Hancock

All of the essays gathered in this volume are concerned more or less explicitly with the relationship between the "liberty" at the heart of the tradition of liberal education and some other, more common, meanings of liberty. What is the freedom aimed at in liberal education, and what has it to do with the freedoms proclaimed in various forms of political or religious discourse?

Our authors are in general certainly more concerned to emphasize the differences rather than continuities between the freedom of the educated mind and any more immediately practical or political notions of freedom. Thus Michael Gillespie criticizes deconstructionist postmodernism for effecting a mere reversal of the alleged dichotomies of traditional Western thought, a reversal grounded not in philosophy but in ideology, and motivated not by the much proclaimed love of "the other" but by resentment of "the same." He also criticizes traditionalists for uncritically presupposing a connection between political order and virtues of character on the one hand and the great conversation of Western thought on the other. The Great Books, Gillespie insists, do not represent a substantively unified tradition productive of definite moral or political ends, but must be considered instead as a "great conversation." Somewhat similarly, Timothy Fuller worries that "liberal learning" today tends to identify itself too closely with the political aims of modern liberalism, and so he emphasizes the distinction between the freedom of the conversation of learning and the more political meanings of freedom. Allan Bloom, for his part, grants that there is an important sense in which "all education is political," but denies, in opposition to the forces of "political correctness," that this recognition

153

of the pervasiveness of political questions excludes the possibility of "the pure love of truth." The pursuit of truth regarding cultures must not succumb to the political and ideological pressure to "act upon" cultures in one way or another—honoring them, granting them rights, or whatever. It is only the possibility of an aspiration toward truth itself, a truth apparently independent of all "cultures," he argues, that can ultimately justify the existence of universities.

Stanley Rosen seems to be on the same wavelength as he deplores the intellectual confusion that now besets "conservatives" as well as "liberals" in America, a confusion he believes prevents both ideological parties from grasping the meaning of the freedom implicit in the term "liberal education." To grasp this meaning would be to see that, although education and politics are necessarily closely related, the philosophical ends of liberal education—the forming of "free, just, and cultivated spirits"—must be understood to be higher than and therefore prior to the material ends of politics: Whether one ought to be liberal or conservative should follow from one's philosophic or religious views, and not the reverse. An adequate understanding of the ends of education would confront both conservative traditionalism and liberal relativism with the openness of human nature itself to truth. This point of Rosen's would appear to be compatible with Michael Platt's observation that the Founders of the West are not reducible to the historical tradition of the West. Rather, Platt argues, these Founders accuse and invite this tradition from somewhere above it. And James Nuechterlein, in focusing on the status of liberal education in religious universities, likewise emphasizes the independent integrity of the rational pursuit of truth as distinct from the demands of religious conviction: reason must be given full rein in the university; it cannot be used "by halves."

In this brief review I have so far passed over my own essay, which might be said to be more concerned with what I argue is an inevitable linkage between liberal education and moral-political liberty, or between "theory" and "practice," than with their distinctness (which, I hope it is clear, I am also eager to affirm). If Tocqueville (as I write) indeed recommends "the cultivation of the theoretical life as a counterweight to the utilitarian drift of democracy," he seems to situate this cultivation within the larger aim of upholding "the true nature of man's greatness," a greatness that he nowhere attempts to reduce to the life of theory or contemplation alone. And if we now reconsider the other essays as they bear upon the relation between theory and practice, we can see that the independence of philosophical from political liberalism is by no means as obvious or straightforward for our authors as might first appear.

For example, when Gillespie invites the reader to think beyond both contemporary ideologies and historical categories in order to explore other ways of seeing and thinking, when he calls upon us to "hear the questions that our own existence thrusts upon us," then we are led to ask whether such existential questions could ever be adequately understood as theoretical *as opposed to* practical, or as philosophical *as opposed to* moral, political, and religious. And the same kind of question might apply in various forms to each of the other essays. If, as Fuller writes, "liberal learning and the liberal political tradition can be friendly, but they cannot simply identify with each other," then must we not ask what exactly is the basis of that friendship? Is there not more than an accidental or instrumental or, for that matter, unidirectional connection between the good of the "conversation" of liberal learning and the freedom toward which liberal politics (at least at its best) aims? And what of Bloom's reply to the radical notion that all education is deeply political? If political understanding is central to the philosophical and literary tradition of the West, as he says, then is this only contingently the case, so far as the highest ends of education are concerned? Why, exactly, is political passion indispensable to the full pursuit of knowledge? What if we were to take Bloom's advice regarding the application of our theories to ourselves a step further than he seems here to recommend: what if we apply (in the spirit, perhaps, of Nietzschean rigor or probity) the scrutiny of what he calls the "pure love of truth" to itself? Without contesting the beauty or fecundity of this idea or, indeed, its appropriateness in contesting the threatened prostitution of learning to vulgar ends in the contemporary academy, is it not, finally, fair or perhaps necessary to ask: Is this purity really so self-evident, this love so self-contained, this truth so obviously absolved from human attachments to all other goods, as Bloom's rhetoric seems to require? Is it possible, finally, to locate a zone in human existence, in our own experience, in which an interest in "truth" can be so neatly distinguished or thoroughly insulated from all other interests, needs, longings, or aspirations? If not, then can our interest in studying "culture" ever be entirely separate from the problem of "acting on" our "culture"?

To apply the same kind of questioning to Rosen's formulation of the issues: Can we affirm with confidence that "politics is not an end in itself," but is properly, rather, directed toward the formation of "free, just, and cultivated spirits" if we are never sure to have altogether absolved the meaning of a "free, just, and cultivated spirit" from our moral, political, or religious ends and aspirations? Likewise, regarding Nuechterlein's view that the religious university must honor the claims of rational truth-seeking *as distinct from* the demands of faith, it is notable that this truth is described as pursued "for its own, *secular,* sake," and that secular universities are later said to fail to ask the question of the Good or of God (my emphases). This suggests that an a priori determination to separate the pursuit of truth from the love of the Good or of God narrows that pursuit to a realm understood in advance as somehow "secular." But this seems to imply that to resolutely insulate the purpose or the desire to know from the desire for what is good or divine is to risk mingling this purpose uncritically with an orientation toward the "secular."

Like Nuechterlein, Michael Platt highlights the distinction between reason and revelation, between Socrates and Christ, but he also associates them as the parents of the West, the dual source of that "greatness" we recognize especially but not only in the Great Books. If "the soul longs for answers to the greatest questions," this theoretical longing also has a practical dimension: "the soul wants to become great." But this greatness, as understood by Platt, even when conceived more practically than theoretically, would never be separable from knowledge, especially self-knowledge, and therefore from the *question* of greatness. Further, in addition to this ultimately mysterious tension at the heart of what is great, Platt introduces a distinction between what is great and what is good. The relation between the great and the good as envisioned by Platt is rich and complex, as appears in this summary statement:

> The good and the great are distinct; they are even sometimes at odds; but that they are ultimately harmonious is vouchsafed by the fact that those who have the most to say about the good are the greatest, Socrates on the idea of it, and Christ, its redemptive emissary, on its Creative Father and the destiny to which the good calls his best image, man. (p. 111)

Whereas educators in other ages might have been concerned particularly to awaken students to the distinction between the good and the great, Platt believes that the present generation of students presents an unprecedented and profound challenge: "the orphans of the West need, as well as the Great Books, the good." So little acquainted is this generation with ordinary familial, religious, and patriotic goods that they may be said to "have grown up in no cave at all," but "instead . . . in a pit below the Cave." In the place of imperfect opinions about the good, they have only the opinion that there is no good, or that all opinions or tastes are equally groundless. In confronting such a generation of metaphysical orphans, educators face a new danger, or perhaps an old danger on a radically new scale: "Those who seek the true without having enjoyed the good may make the true become the enemy of the good." The soul needs a home of conventional goodness from which to ascend in its quest for the elusive home of its greatest—its most truly natural or eternal—aspirations.

Though Platt is by no means confident of any practical remedy to this moral and thus metaphysical abandonment of the latest offspring of the West, he does invite a consideration of the possibility of the provision of "storm homes" to avert or repair at least some of the damage. In particular, he suggests to educators, "it is well for the orphans of America to learn something about the good of their own country, America. . . . The orphans of America, the generation of the Teenager, may be the first people on earth to need to strengthen their love of their own, themselves and their fellow Americans" (114). Platt thus proposes (among other things) a renewed study and appreciation of the "foundation of America" as a possible "storm home" for today's students.

The suggestion that it might be part of the role of higher education today in any way to provide what might be called moral and intellectual shelter obviously goes directly against the grain of the most respected views on this subject, including both friends and enemies of an emphasis upon the Great Books. Apart from those most concerned with the obvious and inevitable technical and occupational functions of colleges and universities, the idea that learning must be pursued for its own sake, and therefore without the hindrance of any substantive moral (not to mention patriotic) commitments, is only contradicted by those who regard the subversion of any remaining traditional shelters as a positive imperative of contemporary multicultural education. In the contemporary academy, therefore, Platt's suggestion appears as truly radical, not only because it is unusual and unpopular, but because it is based upon a reflection on the root problem of the relation between the great and the good. Whether it is any way a practicable suggestion for most institutions of higher education today I will not attempt to determine. Rather, I offer some thoughts on the American founding in relation to the ideal of liberal education as a concluding effort to explore the possible meaning of Platt's recommended recourse to traditional expressions of goodness in our attempts to access the greatness of the Great Books, or what is highest in higher education.

What can the Founders of the American republic teach us concerning the freedom of the intellectual life pursued for its own sake? Addressing the question of the Founders and liberal education, a frank and reasonable reply might be: "precious little." Consider the following, quite characteristic statements on education by prominent Founders. In his *Notes on the State of Virginia,* Thomas Jefferson appears to propose political and economic ends as the main justification of a proposed system of public education—including higher education. The most complete education would be limited to the superior half of "twenty of the best geniuses, [to be] raked from the rubbish annually" not (or not solely) for their own individual fulfillment, but in order "to avail the

State of those talents which nature has sown as liberally among the poor as the rich."[1] In a somewhat similar spirit, George Washington, in his Farewell Address, urges the "primary importance" of "institutions for the general diffusion of knowledge" not, it appears, for the pure sake of untrammeled learning, but because "virtue or morality is a necessary spring of popular government." And since "reason and experience both forbid us to expect that national morality can prevail in exclusion of religious principle," the education Washington intends to promote must have a religious dimension. Though this does not necessarily imply an explicit role for religion in *higher* education, Washington elsewhere (in his Eighth Annual Message) clearly recommends a moral and political function as among the advantages of a proposed national university. Such a university, which would make education in "the science of government" a "primary object," would encourage "the *assimilation* of the principles, opinions, and manners, of our countrymen" and thus make our citizens "more homogeneous."[2] And in case you are wondering how political science classes might be expected to produce homogeneity, Washington, in a later letter (to Alexander Hamilton, 1 September 1796), specifies that by "enlightening" citizens he has in mind "giving [them] *just* ways of thinking."

To be sure, Washington's idea of "just ways of thinking," however representative in general of the founding generation, cannot be simply identified in every particular with the views of all the Founders. On the religious question, in particular, James Madison, like Jefferson, would be inclined to emphasize that "religion and government will both exist in greater purity, the less they are mixed together." But this in no way allows us to conclude that Madison has in mind anything like our contemporary, open-ended idea of liberal education. For it is in a late letter to Jefferson himself, and commenting on Jefferson's proposed course of study for the University of Virginia, that Madison associates such a curriculum with a "political creed," in which the requirement of standard texts might "*control* or counteract *deviations* of the Professor." But this is merely Madison's fall-back position, for "the most effectual safeguard against *heretical* infusions into the school of politics, will be an able and orthodox Professor."[3]

If these examples of political constraint on free learning are not enough to disqualify the Founders as spokesmen for liberal education, then we might consider the still more unabashed statements of Benjamin Rush. Rush recommends "one general, and uniform system of education, [to] render the mass of the people more homogeneous." Such a system would be based upon the religion of the New Testament, and would make it possible, in Rush's words, "to convert men into republican machines." The "wills of the people," he explains, "must be fitted to each other by means of education before they can be made to produce *regularity* and *unison* in government."[4]

In overview, the thought of the Founders on education, including in some respects higher education, may be summarized in four main inter-related characteristics: (1) It aims at assimilating citizens, or making them in some sense the same. (2) It serves a conservative political purpose. (3) It depends on the inculcation of morality and, in many versions, religion. (4) It looks to the cultivation of a national elite or "national aristocracy." What then has the Founders' view of education—homogeneous, politicized, moralistic, elitist—what has such a view to teach us regarding liberal education in our day, a day of diversity, equality, and openness?

I might take as representative of likely responses that of Alan Kors, professor of history at the University of Pennsylvania, who responds to the question whether the contemporary university ought to act in loco parentis to supervise the morals of students. His answer, in two letters, is "no." But here is a slightly longer version: "What a dreadful model for the mind in search of intellectual integrity: a second-class citizenship for students; a crimping of individualism and independence of spirit and thought; an orgy of indoctrination [and] brainwashing."[5]

To avoid the shame of "indoctrination and brainwashing," I feel almost compelled, in my search for the meaning of liberal education, to abandon any consideration of the American Founders in favor of more contemporary and undogmatic views. Consider, for example, the appealing "invitation to liberal learning" extended or renewed by the British philosopher Michael Oakeshott: "that is, the invitation to disentangle oneself, for a time, from the urgencies of the here and now and to listen to the conversation in which human beings forever seek to understand themselves." For Oakeshott, "learning itself is the engagement and it has its own standards of achievement and excellence." Thus, he writes elsewhere, "a university is not a machine for achieving a particular purpose or producing a particular result; it is a manner of human activity."[6]

Oakeshott's notion of learning as "conversation" is a rich notion, and it is beyond the scope of these remarks to explore it fully. But one can get a sense of Oakeshott's ideal of liberal education from two defining contrasts, two forms of the "urgency of here and now." For there are two main fronts on which the autonomy or integrity of the conversation of liberal learning must be defended from invasions of "extrinsic uses." First, "liberal education" implies that the learner is "liberated from distracting business of satisfying contingent wants." Second, it resists the "impulsive longing to be given a doctrine or to be socialized according to a formula rather than to be initiated into a conversation."[7] In sum, one might say that liberal education is equally opposed to utilitarianism or careerism, and to moralism or ideology.

Oakeshott's observations point us toward what is distinctive in liberal education. My interest is to explore the connections between this conversation and the practical ends to which he opposes it.[8] Such an exploration might begin with a consideration of perhaps the most famous "conversation" in the literature of the West—the conversation recorded in Plato's *Republic*. It is certainly Plato, after all, to whom we are indebted above all other authors—and perhaps to the *Republic* above all books—for the notion that knowledge might be pursued "for its own sake." And yet this very conversation reveals the profoundly problematic character of this notion, or of the aspiration to liberate the mind altogether from moral and political concerns. For example, if Socrates is able to get the better of Thrasymachus in Book I, this is not because of some purely theoretical refutation of Thrasymachus's idea that what we call "justice" is nothing more than the interest of the stronger, or that might makes right. Rather, Socrates takes advantage of the fact that, if this proposition is true, it makes no sense *as a teaching* (and Thrasymachus, of course, is a professional teacher). If it is true that there is no reality to the distinction between right and wrong, no intrinsic binding quality to moral norms, then it would not make sense to announce it. By entering into a rational discussion, Thrasymachus has put himself on Socrates' turf—on the turf, that is, of a serious interest in mutually accessible standards—an interest, ultimately, in the reality of some "justice."

Socrates deconstructs Thrasymachus's argument by exploiting a contradiction, one might say, between its form and its content: Thrasymachus defends unlimited (therefore formless, arbitrary) self-interest, and he also, implicitly, defends rationality—he wants to teach, after all, what is *really* to one's advantage. It is because Thrasymachus implicitly defends rationality that he must refuse the help of Cleitophon, who suggests retreating to the more defensible position that defines justice simply as whatever the ruler says he wants. But Thrasymachus wants to be a man of reason, of knowledge. He wants the ruler to be rational, that is, to be the practitioner of an "art." And this means doing things in some sense "right," according to some rule, according to a rational principle, by some standard "higher than" mere interest.

Thrasymachus's problem is that he is committed after all to showing that injustice is good, but Socrates knows his interlocutor has not thought about what a good or advantageous way of life is. Socrates reduces Thrasymachus to a blushing, grudging silence by showing that the *rule* of reason is inconsistent with the *arbitrariness* of pure injustice. The unjust take advantage of anyone, indiscriminately, but if reason rules, then reason can't take advantage of itself. At bottom, that is, Socrates takes advantage of the fact that Thrasymachus claims at once to do whatever he can get away with and at the same time to live by a rational principle, to live rationally—and to teach others the life of reason. But it seems that the commitment to reason bears some likeness to justice: one's desires or whims are limited by a principle of reality accessible to others. By the very fact of entering a conversation, Thrasymachus must open himself to a certain goodness of justice. There would thus seem to be some intrinsic (and not merely prudential or rhetorical) connection between philosophy and morality, between our interest in truth and our interest in justice. This is not to deny that the connection is elusive at best. Socrates can appear to have revealed it in the *Republic* only because, in refining the notion of justice, he ends up carrying "justice" almost completely beyond its political and moral meaning.

I say, *almost* completely: in Book IX, it has finally dawned on Glaucon that Socrates has long ago left the horizon of conventional, political justice far behind. The truly just man, he now understands, is a philosopher who "won't be willing to mind the political things."⁹ But then, as if to correct the tendency of would-be philosophers to believe they can simply set aside ordinary human concerns, Socrates replies: Yes he will—the philosopher will mind the political things, but in "his own city." The order of the philosopher's soul mirrors the city in speech, not accidentally or merely rhetorically, but because it is formed by attending in speech to the deepest concerns of citizens of an actual city.

A parallel point regarding the relationship between philosophical conversation and the moral concerns of the political community might be developed through a reading of Aristotle's *Nichomachean Ethics*. Because Aristotle appears to take the morality of the gentleman somewhat as an empirical given rather than as a claim urgently to be questioned, his (the philosopher's) relationship to the city might be said to be at once closer and more distant than in Platonic dialogues: in adopting the viewpoint of morality, he may seem to set aside the properly philosophic quest for the ultimate Good, as if it were a separate matter. The intrinsic good of theory is bracketed in order to let the distinct goods of practical life speak for themselves. In order to explore the realm of morality on its own terms, the philosopher Aristotle needs a kind of sleepwalking guide—and so he is careful not to wake him.

Thus, when he turns his attention in Book X to philosophy itself, he seems to have moved on to a separate and distinct concern, to have changed the subject—and even to have changed his mind. For now study or contemplation is held to be "the only activity which is loved for its own sake," and the practical virtues, earlier presented as intrinsically good, are held to be merely instrumental, means to other ends. It is only in disinterested contemplation that man attains his true, self-sufficient, and "divine" end.[10]

But no sooner has Aristotle called forth our longing for transcendence than he brings us abruptly back down to earth. If "intelligence above all else is man," then it is no less true that this "divine element" is never entirely free from its connection with what is simply human. Man's end is divine, but man never quite attains his end; though man at his best is thought, this "at his best" remains ever distinct from the reality of the human condition.

If, therefore, the philosopher must stoop to study politics and morality, this condescension and the ascent that follows appear to be more than a ruse or a contrivance. "The student of politics," Aristotle writes, "must obviously have some knowledge of the workings of the soul, just as the man who is to heal eyes must know something about the whole body" (291). The study of politics is the study of a part, and is thus restrictive. But it is the study of a singularly open and comprehensive part; it is in a sense the eye of philosophy, which studies the whole. Knowledge of politics must begin as, and in a sense ever remain, political knowledge. The highest good, contemplation, never achieves perfect self-sufficiency or autonomy. If philosophers need friends with whom to converse, it would appear that this friendship itself can never be based purely and simply on intellectual goods; the mutuality of interest in knowledge for its own sake can only spring from and can never completely replace a pre-reflective trust and kinship.

Returning to Plato's *Republic*—if Socrates accedes to Glaucon's and Adeimantus's pleas (Book II) that he refute their amplifications of Thrasymachus's argument, it is only because he notices something "divine" in their characters (in their interest in some intrinsic good) that contradicts and provides a germ of a refutation of their nihilistic arguments. He can only elicit what he calls the justice written in "big letters"—the city in speech—because he can see the small letters of justice already inscribed inarticulately in their souls. And when Socrates protests that he is incapable of refuting their nihilistic arguments, we ought to perhaps read more than irony in his protestation. The evidence of the questions, the small letters in the political and moral soul, remain more evident than any large letters of the derivative city of speech. It would seem, then, that knowledge of justice can never be severed entirely from just knowledge.

The classical pursuit of knowledge "for its own sake" thus appears to be necessarily grafted upon moral and political orientations toward the just, the good, the beautiful. If "liberal education" means "free education" or education in and for freedom, then the philosophical or theoretical meaning of this freedom is necessarily tainted by association with the practical ideal expressed in the traditional formula, according to which this liberal education forms the noble freedom of a person (formerly the gentleman, or aristocrat) not enslaved to his bodily appetites, nor bound by his circumstances to confine his learning to that which is useful to material security and comfort.

If modern philosophy overcame this association of theoretical freedom with the practical excellence of the gentleman, it appears this was only possible by contracting a more complete and demanding association with the universal needs of humanity. Machiavelli's rejection of the idealism of the classical tradition of political philosophy with its "imaginary republics" in favor of the "effectual truth" may be taken as emblematic of this turn. Machiavelli vindicates Thrasymachus's notion that justice is power, not by showing theoretically that this *is* so, but precisely by suppressing the theoretical question of the just and the good in order to make virtue work in practice—which is to say, to make it *appear* to work. Machiavelli's so-called "realism" consists in putting aside the question of reality in favor of "the appearance and the result." Thus Machiavelli severs the connection of philosophy with the moral-political horizon of the nonphilosopher by in effect vindicating Thrasymachus's wish to be a teacher of immoralism; he discovers a way to construe "might makes right" as good news for humanity, and therefore as a teachable doctrine. But this can only be at the cost of suppressing all discussion of the question of what a really good life might be. For this reason Leo Strauss, unlike his student, Allan Bloom, denies an essential continuity between classical and modern philosophy.

> Philosophy and its status is obfuscated not only in Machiavelli's teaching, but in his thought as well. . . . As a consequence he is unable to give a clear account of his own doing. What is greatest in him cannot be properly appreciated on the basis of his own narrow view of the nature of man.[11]

Such a suppression would appear to be incompatible with the praise of the love of learning for its own sake—or, for that matter, with the love of anything except of the fame or "recognition" that the philosopher wills for himself by perpetually satisfying the end-less desire of the rest of mankind, while stupefying them in their delusion that they in fact love something for its own sake, or that there is something intrinsically good or holy.

The subtle and pervasive temptation inherent in the rhetoric of learning's autonomy with respect to morality and politics lies in the fact that this rhetoric is not neutral or transcendent with respect to practical concerns but is in fact already part of the strategy of modern liberalism. The transcendence of liberal education with regard to politics is already a part of the politics of liberalism. The root of Stanley Rosen's differences with Michael Platt might be examined in this light. Platt would appear to be one of those "conservatives" whom Rosen urges to recognize the openness of nature to truth. And Platt, indeed, sees a (conventional, traditional) familiarity with the good as a (necessary?) stepping stone to acquaintance with the great. Rosen appears to believe in the possibility of a more direct, unmediated access, at least for the few "aristocrats" of the mind and soul with whom he is primarily concerned. From Platt's point of view, Rosen might be among those who thus risk setting the true at odds with the good. And it is important to note that this is not only a moral-political risk, but a genuinely philosophical and spiritual risk as well—for the true understood as simply apart from the good would be inadequately understood. Such an inadequate understanding would be vulnerable to co-optation by the deepest, ultimately Machiavellian, motives of modern liberalism, in which the question of the intrinsic goodness of the true is suppressed in view of the extrinsic utility of knowledge. If, as Rosen suggests, today "moderation can be made palatable only when it is adorned with the habiliments of extremism," then a first step toward an articulation of the relation of theory to practice adequate to our times might be to remain ever alert to the conventionally modern attractions of an extreme rhetoric of pure theory. Perhaps philosophy can be truly self-knowing and therefore truly radical only by taking seriously the orientation toward something intrinsically good or holy embedded within every practical horizon. If so, then true philosophical radicalism might only recover its savor, and therefore its power to ennoble human existence in the contemporary world, through a certain chaste solicitude for extra-theoretical goods. Perhaps, that is, theoretical extremism has more than an instrumental interest in the habiliments of moderation.

If, however, there is some intrinsic connection between the (premodern) praise of learning "for its own sake" and what might be referred to broadly as a certain classical idealism, according to which the intellectual virtues are understood in some sense as the fulfillment of aspirations at least dimly present in practical virtues, then this connection would appear to count against any hope of renewing the spirit of liberal education at the springs of the American founding. The founding, according to a most searching reading, was (despite residues of classical republicanism and of Christianity) "penetrated and shaped by Lockean language and categories"[12]—a vocabulary that is finally traceable to Machiavelli's modern realism.

Thomas Pangle's reading demands our attention because, of all interpreters, Pangle most clearly distinguishes the search for true or rational *foundations* from the mere survey of the most commonly held opinions.

Mercilessly pointing up the incoherence of prevailing "classical republican" readings of the period, he traces the formulation of what he regards as rational foundations from "the few greatest Founders" back to
Locke, whose sources he has traced back to Machiavelli. On this view,
there would thus appear to be little hope for renewing the disinterested
love of learning (or of anything) at the springs of the Founders' thought.

However, Pangle implicitly invites a rethinking of this Machiavellian-
Lockean view of the American founding (a task he seems to leave to
others) when, at the end of his book, he questions the full rationality
or adequate self-understanding of the Lockean system itself.[13] By this
apparently incidental concession he opens up the possibility of a very
different interpretation. For once the full rationality of the Founders'
founder is questioned, we are free again to consider whether some co-
herence may be recovered, some Lockean blind spots illuminated, by
reference to the more common and apparently less philosophical or rational opinions that shaped the rhetoric of the founding. It is possible,
after all, that the penetration of Lockean and classical-Christian categories did not work only in one direction. Without evidence that the
Founders were fully and self-consciously esoteric Lockeans, there is
reason to expect an exclusively Lockean framework to illuminate their
actual political practice only if one is convinced of the adequacy of this
framework on its own terms. Absent such a conviction, the fact that the
Founders' vocabulary often echoes that of Locke is not enough to establish the decisive ascendancy of Lockean categories over American
thought. Thus, rather than assuming that Locke must in effect have used
America to accomplish his own ends, why not consider that America
might have used Locke? At the risk of appearing to sympathize with a
"postmodernist" relativism, let me suggest that what theory we find
ascendant in the founding must depend upon our contemporary judgment as to what theory is simply most adequate in itself. Since the
authoritative, political speech of the founding reached neither the
heights nor the depths of Plato or Machiavelli (and what political speech
does?), any questions left unanswered or unasked we are thus left to
consider for ourselves, as best we can. The question of a modern versus
a classical interpretation of the American founding cannot be insulated
from the question: who saw the most important things the most clearly,
the ancients or the moderns?

It is not the case, moreover, that the interpreter of the founding has
only silences to build upon in constructing a view friendlier than a
Machiavellian Locke's to the intrinsic goodness of learning. It was
James Wilson who declared in the Philadelphia convention itself that
the "improvement of the mind"[14] is the highest end of constitutional
government. To be sure, the convention as a whole seems to have pre-

ferred the ends embraced under the apparently more modest or realistic term "liberty" as a guiding star. Thus Wilson's high-minded outburst may appear somewhat as the classical exception that proves the modern rule in the discourse of the founding. Still, simply to dismiss Wilson's high-mindedness is to presuppose that there is no positive connection between liberty and intellectual cultivation—which does not at all seem to be the view of the Founders. It was certainly not that of Wilson himself:

> It is only under a good constitution that liberty—the precious gift of heaven—can be enjoyed and be secure. This exalting quality comprehends, among other things, the manly and generous exercise of our powers; and includes, as its most delicious ingredient, the happy consciousness of being free. What energetic, what delightful sensations must this enlivening principle diffuse over the whole man! His mind is roused and elevated: his heart is rectified and enlarged: dignity appears in his countenance, and animation in his every gesture and word.[15]

Wilson is quite aware, moreover, that this praise of liberty is incompatible with Locke's skeptical idealism. Drawing upon Thomas Reid's "philosophy of common sense," Wilson links Locke's modern epistemology, or "principles of the philosophy of the human mind . . . subversive of all truth and knowledge," with "principles of law" that are "destructive of liberty." For Wilson, the authority of law indeed rests upon consent, but consent itself is understood as governed by the laws of nature and nature's God: "Human law must rest its authority, ultimately, upon the authority of that law which is divine."[16]

Though Wilson developed his views on natural law more fully perhaps than any other Founder, he was by no means alone in understanding natural liberty as oriented toward or limited by natural law. Nor was he alone in pointing to the despotic implications of modern skepticism. John Adams, in the vigorous and often insightful and copious notes he made in his retirement in the margins of leading books of the Enlightenment, leaves no doubt as to his view of post-Lockean skepticism. When Bolingbroke denies the theologians' teaching that there is a law of right reason common to God and man, Adams replies: "This is dogmatically, presumptuously, and arrogantly said! If there is not such a law there is an end of all human reasoning on the government of the universe!" And when Rousseau argues that "Reason engenders self-love," and that "it is philosophy that isolates a man from other men," Adams's pithy reply is: "Alias atheism." Rousseau's Lockean reduction of the Golden Rule—"Pursue your happiness with as little harm to others as possible"—Adams pronounces "a maxim of eternal justice to creatures of the same Creator deriving equal right from him. But a maxim of idiocy or lunacy to atheists." Responding to Condorcet, Adams writes further that "there is no right or wrong in the universe without the supposition of a moral government and an intellectual and moral governor." The idea of "equality" derived from the "philosophy of the eighteenth century" is thus "fraudulent," a "swindler" behind the mask of which the "enlightened," adopting the maxims and practicing the arts of ancient priests and modern Machiavellians, have proclaimed their "new heaven." The new high priests of Skeptical Enlightenment have thus, Adams argues, retarded "improvement . . . in the condition of mankind for at least 100 years," and have in fact "cheated millions out of their lives and tens of millions out of their property."[17]

Where are we left, then, in our hope to learn something from the Founders regarding liberal or free education? If Machiavellian skepticism undermines the intrinsic goodness of the life of the mind, would not natural law subordinate the mind's freedom to some morally and politically defined "goods"? Is there no third alternative to dogmatic and reductionist skepticism on the one hand or moralistic dogmatism on the other? My point is precisely that the alternative is far less easy to discern or to articulate than contemporary defenders of academic freedom or liberal learning tend to suppose. Liberal education is in a way necessarily suspended between two forms of dogmatism—as Leo Strauss explains, philosophy shuns traditional sectarianism only at the risk of the somewhat facile ecumenical relativism of that modern substitute for the sect: "the Republic of Letters." The turn from answers to questions always risks becoming just another kind of answer, indeed a particularly closed and complacent kind. It follows that "the danger of succumbing to the attraction of solutions is essential to philosophy, which, without incurring this danger, would degenerate into playing with the problems."[18]

I would suggest further that the Founders were not unacquainted, in their practical way, with this suspension between dogmatisms; their awareness of the dangers of dogmatic skepticism did not simply push them into the camp of the more traditional moral or religious dogmatists. Adams was not at all embarrassed to confess that "man is a riddle to himself. The world is a riddle to him. He puzzles to find a key, and this puzzle is called philosophy." One might also cite on this point Madison's moderating account of the permanent limits of political science in *Federalist* 37: Even the Almighty himself, Madison explains, must address human beings in the only medium of thought available to them; even if divine truths were directly applicable to political life, they would be "rendered dim and doubtful by the cloudy medium" of language.

James Wilson's more developed theorizing on natural law certainly appears more dogmatic, but one should notice that the premise of his reasoning is precisely commonsensical or practical. Indeed, as Jack Riley has argued, "The self-evident proof of the dangers of skepticism is its practical consequences—despotism. The ultimate grounding for Wilson's theoretical contradiction of Locke is political reality."[19] To point to the *political* core of Wilson's teaching is emphatically *not* to imply that this teaching is either unconsciously or esoterically utilitarian or Lockean; for despotism is precisely the political face of moral and epistemological skepticism; one of the opposites of liberty. If freedom and morality are mutually supportive, this would be precisely *because* neither can be reduced to the other. Thus, when Washington insists (as he so frequently does, particularly in the First Inaugural and Farewell Address) upon the connection between virtue and happiness—the ultimate public and private concerns, one might say—he does not attempt theoretically to collapse either one into the other. Indeed, if he is so given to repeating the pairing "public and private," as in his "tendering homage to the great author of every public and private good," the effect is to remind us of the *distinction* while denying the possibility of *separation*. Might this not be understood as a political image of that philosophic suspension between relativism and dogmatism?

The stability of this suspension of the ends of the political community between the private and the public may require the support of a mild and liberal religion: "Can it be," Washington asks in his Farewell Address, "that Providence has not connected the permanent felicity of a Nation with its virtue?" But it would be dogmatic and therefore impossible to ground this liberty, moderately private and moderately public, beholden finally neither to ancient nor to modern dogma—it would be impossible *finally* to ground this liberty on anything but its own nobility: "The experiment," Washington continues—the experiment of connecting happiness with virtue—"*at least,* is recommended by every sentiment which ennobles human nature" (my emphasis). And such an experiment, Washington adds, is not undermined by our ignorance whether vice might render its success—or the experiment itself— "impossible."

In an 1822 letter, Madison asks "what spectacle can be more edifying or more seasonable, than that of *Liberty and Learning,* each leaning upon the other for their mutual and surest support?"[20] It should by now be clear that it would be as wrong to reduce liberty to the service of learning—as with Allan Bloom—as to reduce learning to the service of liberty, following John Locke. In the phrase "liberal education," the integrity of each term can be seen to depend upon the integrity of the other. A striking feature of the Founders'—especially George Washington's—praise of liberal education is a preoccupation with "national honor" and national character. Contemporary advocates of learning "for its own sake" might learn from the Founders that the "liberty" of liberal education would lose all form and meaning without implicit reference to a *shared* and *noble* understanding of political liberty. The Founders provide us no theory of the intrinsic goodness of liberal education, any more than of the nobility of liberty itself. If such a theory were available, then reason could dispense with tradition (or "the veneration which time bestows," *Federalist* 49)—as if honor could be a matter of calculation. If American education is to be something more than what Gouverneur Morris called the instruction of "a number of men without national spirit or sentimental presum[ing] to call themselves a Nation . . . a herd of piddling huckstering individuals, base and insensible except to blows, who in the stroke of a cudgel estimate only the smart and comparing it with the labor and expense of resistance submit resentment to the Rules of Calculation," then it cannot be that "national honor, national dignity, and national glory are wholly forgotten." "The genius and excellence of the arts," Morris continues, "depends upon a greater liberty than that reducible to base calculation"; greatness in the life of the mind must be nourished by "national greatness"—by the "high, haughty, generous and noble spirit which prizes glory more than wealth and holds honor dearer than life."[21]

I offer this rather extreme formulation of Morris's as an alternative to the high indifference of certain contemporary defenders of liberal education to moral and political honor. Morris's lofty rhetoric may not be typical of his generation; many Founders were no doubt more concerned than he to combat dogma and hierarchy. But since today we must attend particularly to the dangers of relativism and of a leveling egalitarianism, Morris's rhetoric might still represent the practical message of the Founders to the most clear-sighted of defenders of liberal education today (which is by no means to recommend that such rhetoric be directly imitated). If respect for the dignity of theory or unconstrained openness to truth saves the citizen from moral fanaticism and from materialistic vulgarity, so the dignity of theory might depend in turn on a certain openness to practical goodness and greatness.

The conversation that is liberal education must indeed transcend moralism and ideology, as Bloom and Oakeshott, with many others, have urged. But I would regard this less as a premise than as a never completed task. Philosophers are human beings, and therefore political and moral beings, and the conditions of their conversation always lie partly beyond that conversation; articulate reflection does not create ex nihilo the trust, the fellowship, and finally the *meaning* on which it depends. The philosopher who sets no limits on his reflection cannot help but be *interested* in the moral-political realm—in both senses of that term: he is curious about, and he has a stake in the meanings he, along with his fellow citizens, inherits and inhabits. Philosophy, Strauss suggests, would dissolve into relativism or ideology without the immediate (and always historically conditioned) experience of "human nobility"— without the "assumption . . . that the well-ordered soul is more akin to the eternal order, than is the chaotic soul."[22]

The moral citizen—especially the moral citizen within the breast of the philosopher—may be a sleepwalking guide, but without this guide's dim, inarticulate notion of where he is going, the philosopher himself would first wander, then slumber. Or, to exploit this metaphor still further: if the practical nobility of the moral citizen provided no bearings to the philosopher, if the citizen could take not a step on his own toward what is good "for its own sake," then the philosopher would be left with no option but to seize his hand and march him resolutely wherever either one of them happens to be facing—or else to abandon the citizen and wander until philosophy itself slumbers. If you listen now in the contemporary academy, you might hear both the marching and the snoring.

Notes

1. Merrill D. Peterson, ed., *Jefferson's Writings* (New York: Library of America, n.d.), 272, 274.

2. William B. Allen, ed., *George Washington: A Collection* (Indianapolis: Liberty Fund, 1988), 509, 649.

3. James Madison to Edward Livingston (10 July 1822), and James Madison to Thomas Jefferson (8 February 1825), in Philip B. Kurland and Ralph Lerner, eds., *The Founders' Constitution*, vol. 1 (Chicago: University of Chicago Press, 1987), 689, 691, 692.

4. Kurland and Lerner, *Founders' Constitution*, 686.

5. *Academic Questions* 4, no. 3 (Summer 1991): 62. Alan Kors's very legitimate apprehensions concern contemporary pressures for "political correctness." I sympathize. But my question is precisely whether appeals to "individualism" and a sort of morally neutral intellectual autonomy are an adequate response to the liberationist antimoral orthodoxy.

6. Timothy Fuller, ed., *The Voice of Liberal Learning: Michael Oakeshott on Education* (New Haven: Yale University Press, 1989), 24, 96.

7. Fuller, *Voice*, 28, 42.

8. Timothy Fuller has called attention to the striking contrast between Oakeshott's "quiet voice of refusal to compromise the idea of education" and Allan Bloom's appeal to the university to stand against the moral and spiritual crisis of Western civilization. For Fuller, Bloom's famous, or infamous, *Closing of the American Mind* seems to represent the dangers of the intrusion of moral

and political concerns into the free conversation of liberal learning. Yet, as I have argued above (in chapter 4), a review of Bloom's own premises reveals anything but a dogmatic moralism or ideology; indeed, in his discussion of the core of liberal education, Bloom seems at least as eager as Oakeshott to insulate the life of the mind from ordinary practical concerns. (See Fuller, *Voices,* 13, 14.)

9. I quote here from Plato, *Republic,* Allan Bloom's translation (New York: Basic Books, 1968), 274.

10. Aristotle, *Nicomachean Ethics,* Martin Ostwald translation (Indianapolis: Bobbs-Merrill, 1962), 289.

11. Leo Strauss, *Thoughts on Machiavelli* (Chicago: University of Chicago Press, 1958), 294.

12. Thomas Pangle, *The Spirit of Modern Republicanism* (Chicago: University of Chicago Press, 1988), 35.

13. Pangle, *Modern Republicanism,* chap. 21: "Locke has mysteriously left out of his account of human action his own action as a philosopher" (269). He is guilty of an "apparent failure to explain his own civic spirit" (270). He has apparently not understood that "the Socratic understanding of political philosophy for more than one reason presupposes reverence and a world suffused with reverence, out of which but also against which political philosophy comes into being" (274).

By here emphasizing what modern philosophy asserts itself by suppressing—the "out of which"—I do not at all mean to deny the "also against which."

14. Max Farrand, *The Records of the Federal Convention,* vol. 1 (New Haven: Yale University Press, 1966), 605. Quoted in Pangle, *Modern Republicanism,* 74.

15. James Wilson, *The Works of James Wilson* (Cambridge: Harvard University Press, 1967), 307.

16. Wilson, *Works,* 221–22, 124; quoted in Jack Riley, "James Wilson, John Locke, and the American Version of Natural Right," draft prepared for the American Political Science Association Meeting, 3 September 1992, 13, 17.

17. In Zoltan Harastzi, *John Adams and the Prophets of Progress* (New York: Grosset & Dunlap, 1952), 71–72, 86, 252, 258, 256, 257.

18. Leo Strauss, *On Tyranny,* rev. and exp. ed. (New York: Free Press, 1963; reprint, 1991), 195.

19. Riley, "American Version," 18.

20. James Madison to W. T. Barry (4 August 1822), in Kurland and Lerner, *Founders' Constitution,* vol. 1, 691.

21. "Gouverneur Morris, National Greatness," in Kurland and Lerner, *Founders' Constitution,* vol. 1, 687–88.

22. Strauss, *On Tyranny,* 201.

Index

173

About the Contributors

Allan Bloom (1930–1992) received his Ph.D. from the Committee on Social Thought at the University of Chicago. At the time of his death he was the John U. Nef Distinguished Service Professor in the Committee on Social Thought and the Co-Director of the University of Chicago's John M. Olin Center for Inquiry into the Theory and Practice of Democracy. He was the author of *Shakespeare's Politics* (with Harry V. Jaffa), *The Closing of the American Mind: How Higher Education Has Failed Democracy and Impoverished the Souls of Today's Students, Giants and Dwarfs: Essays 1960–1990,* and *Love and Friendship.*

Timothy Fuller is Professor of Political Science, Dean of Faculty, and Dean of the College at Colorado College. He has written extensively on Hobbes and has been editor of the *Hobbes Newsletter* since 1983. He is the editor of the papers of Michael Oakeshott and has edited three volumes of Oakeshott's papers for Yale University Press and a new edition of *Oakeshott's Rationalism in Politics* for Liberty Fund. He has just completed a manuscript, On Leading and Leadership, and he is at work on a new book on Hobbes's political philosophy and is preparing an Oakeshott Reader.

Michael Allen Gillespie is Professor of Political Science and Philosophy at Duke University. He is the author of *Hegel, Heidegger, and the Ground of History* and *Nihilism before Nietzsche.* He is co-editor of *Nietzsche's New Seas* and *Ratifying the Constitution.* He is also the author of many articles and chapters on a variety of topics in the history of political philosophy.

Ralph C. Hancock is Professor of Political Science at Brigham Young University. His writings in political philosophy include *Calvin and the*

181

Foundations of Modern Politics and contributions to *The Legacy of the French Revolution,* which he edited with L. Gary Lambert.

James Nuechterlein is Editor of *First Things: A Monthly Journal of Religion and Public Life* and Associate Professor of the Institute on Religion and Public Life in New York City. He served from 1981 through 1988 as Professor of American Studies and Political Thought and Editor of *The Cresset* at Valparaiso University (Indiana). From 1964 to 1981 he taught American history at Queen's University in Kingston, Ontario, Canada. His articles on American history, political thought, and culture have appeared in *American Scholar, Commentary, National Review, Public Interest, Queen's Quarterly, Review of Politics, South Atlantic Quarterly, Virginia Quarterly Review,* and many other journals. He was educated at Valparaiso University and Yale University.

Michael Platt received his Ph.D. from Yale, and studied earlier at Harvard and Oxford. He has taught literature, political science, and philosophy, at Dartmouth and the University of Dallas, where he directed the literature portion of the Philosophic Institute, and at Heidelberg. He has published widely on Shakespeare and Nietzsche. His long consideration of the matters treated in Allan Bloom's *Closing of the American Mind* appeared in *Interpretation* XVIII, 3 (1991). His work has been supported by the Earhart Foundation, the National Endowment for the Humanities, and the Alexander von Humboldt Stiftung (Germany).

Stanley Rosen is Borden Parker Bowne Professor of Philosophy at Boston University and Emeritus Evan Pugh Professor of Philosophy at Pennsylvania State University. He is the author of a dozen books and many articles, and he has lectured throughout the United States and in Europe.